THE
ECONOMIC WAR
AGAINST
THE JEWS

THE ECONOMIC WAR AGAINST THE JEWS

Walter Henry Nelson

AND

Terence C. F. Prittie

RANDOM HOUSE New York

*Copyright © 1977 by Walter Henry Nelson
and Terence C. F. Prittie*

All rights reserved under International and Pan-American
Copyright Conventions. Published in the United States by
Random House, Inc., New York, and simultaneously in
Canada by Random House of Canada Limited, Toronto.

Library of Congress Cataloging in Publication Data
Nelson, Walter Henry.
  The economic war against the Jews.
  Includes bibliographical references and index.
    1. Arab countries—Commercial policy.   2. Boycott—
Arab countries.   3. Boycott—Israel.   4. Jewish-Arab
relations—1973–   I. Prittie, Terence Cornelius
Farmer, Hon., 1913–   joint author.   II. Title.
HF1610.N44   341.5'8   77–6026
ISBN 0–394–40717–2

Designed by Anita Karl

Manufactured in the United States of America
2 4 6 8 9 7 5 3

FIRST EDITION

ACKNOWLEDGMENTS

IT WAS IN THE SUMMER of 1975 that we began research on this book, encouraged in the first instance by Morton Yarmon, the able director of public relations of the American Jewish Committee in New York. He made available the facilities of the Blaustein Library and started us off on a long round of interviews with persons knowledgeable about the Arab Trade Boycott. Those of the American Jewish Committee in New York who helped freely and generously with advice and background material included Marilyn Braveman, Milton Ellerin, Sonya Kaufer, Murray Polner, Samuel Rabinove, Seymour Samet and George Salomon. We are indebted also to the committee's executive vice-president, Bertram H. Gold, for assisting our work, and to the committee's Washington representative, Hyman Bookbinder, and Sue Rubin of his staff, for their support and advice.

There are a great many others to whom we are also impelled to acknowledge a debt. In Washington we met with I. L. ("Si") Kenen, retired executive director of the American Israel Public Affairs Committee (AIPAC); Kenneth Wollack, in charge of legislative liaison for AIPAC; Dr. Jess N. Hordes, director of the Research Project on Energy and Economic Policy; and Larry Rubin, Washington representative of the American Jewish Congress.

No less generously given was the assistance extended in every possible way by the Anti-Defamation League of B'nai

[[vii]]

B'rith. We are especially grateful to its general counsel and associate director, Arnold Forster, for seeing to it that we had complete and unrestricted access to the ADL's extensive files on the boycott; and to Mort Kass, head of the ADL's Library and Archives, and Jerome Bakst, head of Research and Evaluation, who translated that generous directive into action. The ADL's Middle East affairs director, Zev Furst, and its European affairs director, Dr. Lawrence S. Leshnik, have played key roles as well, in assembling information for us and helping our research in sundry ways. The interest shown by ADL's national director, Benjamin R. Epstein, was equally vital. And the key roles in fighting the boycott which have been played in Washington both by David Brody, the ADL's representative there, and by Morris Amitay, executive director of AIPAC, should be acknowledged here as well.

Albert Chernin, executive director of the National Jewish Community Relations Advisory Council in New York, kept us continually informed of the latest U.S. developments and provided us with important briefing papers, as did Jess Hordes, whose memoranda on U.S. legislation have been invaluable. We are happy also to acknowledge a debt to the American Jewish Congress's Philip Baum and Joseph Robison, as well as to Walter P. Stern, Marc Dubroff, Yehuda Hellman and Daniel Rose, among others too numerous to list.

Ze'ev Sher, Economics Minister of the Israeli embassy in the United States, was helpful, as was Joseph Vardi, director of the North American Office of the Government of Israel Investment Authority. At Israel's embassy in London, we are indebted to former Economics Minister Amos Lavee and his staff, and to others for help and advice. Notable among these are the former Israeli Ambassador to Great Britain, Gideon Rafael; the former Information Minister in London, Benad Avital, and his successor, Yosef Ya'akov, as well as to the former Press Counsellor Gaby Padon. In Israel herself, our primary debt is to Dan Halperin and the members of his staff, notably Ami Lurie, for information supplied, for advice on many aspects of the study, as well as for reviewing the manuscript. In London, we are

Acknowledgments

grateful also to the members of the Anti-Boycott Coordinating Committee, notably Justin A. Kornberg, Harry C. Schwab and Fred S. Worms, as well as to the chairman of the Anglo-Israel Chamber of Commerce, Lewis R. Goodman. Eric Moonman, MP, who has been active in the fight against the boycott within the House of Commons, has been a good friend and a staunch supporter throughout. In London also, we were helped by George Garai, director of public relations of the Zionist Federation; by Martin Savitt and Dr. Jacob Gewirtz of the Board of Deputies of British Jews; by Hayim Pinner of B'nai B'rith; by Dr. Stephen Roth of the Institute of Jewish Affairs. To these must be added Abe Karlikow of the American Jewish Committee in Paris; Ruth Hasan in Finland; Alexander Reiter of Association France-Israel, Paris; K. Niedermaier of France's Centre du Documentation; Professor Isi Foighel of Denmark and Egon Lansky of Sweden; Daniel Lacks of the World Jewish Congress in Geneva; R. A. Levisson of Holland; as well as Eliahu Salpeter and Dan Bawly of Israel.

We want to extend very special thanks to Bertha Glenton of London, who devoted much of a year to organizing thousands of documents and press clippings, and without whose help the job of writing this book would have been infinitely more complicated. An equal burden fell on Anita Groves, who typed the several versions of the manuscript with consummate skill as well as good humor and patience. Others who helped in the same way are Rachel Lightman and Leila Cumber. Finally, we are much indebted to our editors at Random House, Robert Loomis and Kathy Matthews, first of all to Bob Loomis for his immediate interest in what he saw as an important subject, and then to both for their skill and support throughout. It goes without saying that no one but ourselves is responsible for whatever errors and shortcomings the book may contain.

CONTENTS

Introduction

I FIRST BECAME involved in the battle against the Arab boycott when I came to the House of Representatives in 1965. At that time—and in 1969 when a mild anti-boycott provision was included in the Export Administration Act—my concern was motivated more by the principles involved than by the effect the boycott was having. Before the October War of 1973, the quadrupling of oil prices, and the world-wide energy crisis, the Arab boycott was more a nuisance than a serious threat to Israel and American Jews.

That all changed in 1973. The massive increase in the volume of U.S. trade with the Arabs meant that more and more companies were coming under pressure to comply with the boycott. In 1974 there were 785 business transactions involving the demand for boycott compliance by American firms; by September of 1975 there were 7,545 such transactions. In the next six months there were almost 25,000 such transactions, and in 90 percent of the cases, the American firms acquiesced. A minor nuisance had become a stink in the nostrils of democracy.

The implications of all this have been frightening. The authors of this volume are not exaggerating when they call the boycott an "economic war against the Jews," for that is, quite precisely, what we are talking about. This volume tells the story of the widespread surrender to the boycott and also of those companies that stayed true to American principles by defying it.

The anti-boycott legislation which I sponsored and which President Carter signed soon after taking office should succeed in ending the most blatant forms of U.S. compliance, but the fight to end the boycott is far from over. The boycott will continue until the Arab world becomes convinced that Israel is here to stay. The boycott is a major weapon in their war against Israel and Jews throughout the world, and it is a weapon the Arabs will not abandon until they abandon their goal of destroying the Jewish state.

Congressman Jonathan B. Bingham
Washington, D.C.

THE
ECONOMIC WAR
AGAINST
THE JEWS

CHAPTER I

Scapegoats and
Oil Spirals

FOUR WARS have been waged in the Middle East since the State of Israel came into being in 1948; another could break out at any time. Each war has been more savagely destructive than the previous one, and each has brought an increased risk of global confrontation. Despite the "interim agreement" between Egypt and Israel, despite all the diplomatic initiatives of the United States, the Middle East dispute continues to smolder, and while it does, no nation can feel snug and safe.

The Middle East war, in fact, appears to be a war-without-end, for the Arab states regard themselves as being in a permanent "state of war" with Israel; already the conflict has become another "Thirty Years' War," waged in fits and starts like that of the seventeenth century, and as devastating. Arms have poured into the Middle East in frightening quantities, and after years of hesitation, blunders and policy-swapping, the USSR now stands squarely behind the most incendiary elements in the area: the ultra-extremist Palestinians and those regimes which hope to gain most from fresh conflict.

Soviet prompting, policies and arms have played a key role; so has the immense oil wealth the Arab world has accumulated since 1973. The dangers to world peace today do not, therefore, stem only from the barrel of the Arab gun, to which the leader of the Palestine Liberation Organization (PLO), Yasir Arafat, referred at the United Nations in November 1974, but also from the barrel of Arab oil, that symbol and source of Arab wealth which has increased fivefold since 1973. This oil wealth has now become the most important factor in the Arab campaign to destroy the State of Israel, a campaign which has been periodically relaxed but never abandoned.

The message of this book is that another war has been declared by the oil-rich Arab world, one fought not in the remote corners of the Middle East, but throughout the length and breadth of the outside world. It has taken the outward, apparently innocuous shape of an economic war, but the ultimate goal is the same as that proclaimed by Arafat: the destruction of the State of Israel, and the expulsion of the bulk of its population. The immediate targets, however, are not only Israelis or Jews the world over, but also *non-Jews* who accept Israel's right to exist.

That right has been challenged four times by the Arabs on the battlefield; four times they have failed. That is why they have resorted to the weapon of economic strangulation and why this new war is being waged from the boardroom, not the front lines. It is a war which knows no boundaries, a war of economic coercion, extortion and blackmail; it involves boycott and blockade, and is waged against the world business community, using wealth derived from Middle East oil as its principal weapon.

Economic warfare is an essential component of total war; anti-Semitism is the ideological concomitant of the Arabs' total war against the Jewish state. Anti-Semitism imbues this economic war with hatreds which have historic roots within the Arab world; it is an endemic feature of the boycott, despite the Arab claim that they have a quarrel only with "Zionists," not with Jews.*

Israel is the ultimate target, but the Arabs have chosen two other countries as battlegrounds in their economic war. The first

---

* Anti-Semitism is here, and throughout this book, used essentially in its *anti-Jewish* sense.

[[4]]

is the United States of America, selected because it is Israel's principal trading partner and staunchest supporter. The second is Britain, for many years Israel's second trading partner; her economic plight and desperate urge to obtain a fair share of Arab trade and Arab oil have made her peculiarly vulnerable to pressure. Other countries are under threat as well; indeed, the threat is global.

THIS ARAB ECONOMIC WAR is not new; it has been waged ever since the State of Israel came into being. Until recently, however, it was never an effective sanction against Israel, nor a danger to the world. That situation changed dramatically at the end of 1973, when the Arabs began amassing immense wealth. Petrodollars—the dollars paid by the oil-purchasing to the oil-producing nations—made the Arabs the world's biggest spenders, and trade with them became enormously alluring.

While the West wanted to repatriate as many petrodollars as possible, the Arabs needed to spend their surplus billions to industrialize and create proper infrastructures. The Soviet Union, without an efficient and sophisticated infrastructure of its own, could not satisfy their needs. Only the West could help them.

Some Western supporters of increased trade with the Arab world insist that it will be socially civilizing and politically moderating—that trade can actually discourage war. Indeed, this was part of the strategic thinking of former U.S. Secretary of State Henry Kissinger, especially with regard to Egypt, but it remains a gamble. The Arabs have shown that one use for their new-found economic muscle is to destroy Israel, and it is in pursuance of that aim that they have stepped up their boycott of Israel. Furthermore, the Arab oil producers use 6 to 8 percent of their oil revenues to support the "confrontation states," those spearheading the Arab world's war with Israel; this amounts to a tax levied on the oil-consuming countries of the world, a tax in which the oil producers play the part of tax collectors.

The "oil weapon" is part of a determined, planned Arab strategy of economic warfare; their new wealth has allowed the Arabs to place great pressure on companies the world over which hope to trade with the Arab Middle East, warning them that they will not be able to do so if they invest in or do business with Israel. These warnings are issued from Damascus, Syria, where the Central Office for the Boycott of Israel is located, and from similar national offices in the desert capitals of the Arab world. They represent foreign interference in world commerce which is entirely new, and on a massive scale.

THE ROLE ARAB OIL is playing is crucial; so, too, the background to Arab hatred of the Jewish state. The latter involves a good many scapegoats the Arabs have found for much that is held to have gone wrong in recent Arab history. The first is Britain's World War I coalition government of Prime Minister David Lloyd George. In 1917 it promised British support for the establishment of a Jewish "National Home" in what was then loosely defined as "Palestine." It did this in an informal "letter of intent" which Foreign Secretary Arthur Balfour addressed to Lord Rothschild of the Anglo-Jewish community. That vaguely worded Balfour Declaration has been the target of Arab denunciation ever since. The Arabs charge it was an act of gross interference in the affairs of the Arab world, violated promises made to Arab patriots who fought with Britain against the Turks in World War I, and lacked any legal basis.

The document and the arguments for and against it became a matter of endless debate. What is certain, however, is that the right of the Jewish people to a home of their own, in their own historic land, did not depend on the whims or maneuvers of a British wartime coalition government, but on other factors altogether.

The Jews of Biblical times founded a state of their own, ruled it for a thousand years, and their descendants have maintained a continuous presence in that land ever since. The first "Zionist," in fact, may be said to have been Moses, for it was he who led the children of Israel to their homeland. Later, in spite of conquest by the Roman Empire, the Jews continued to constitute a majority in their own country until the fifth century of the Christian era. Thereafter they maintained their presence in this land, against all odds—of deprivation, invasion, even

[[6]]

extermination. When nineteenth-century Zionism was born, it was, as the historian James Parkes put it, "no case of Jews returning to a land they had left two thousand years ago. As a people they had never left it, either physically or spiritually . . . All through the centuries Jews had tended to return."[1]

By 1872, Jews actually were a majority of all the inhabitants of Jerusalem, over Moslems, Christians and others combined.[2] By the beginning of the twentieth century, there were 30,000 Jews in Jerusalem, against 10,900 Christians and 7,700 Moslems.

Those Jews who, as Parkes noted, returned continually, did so in spite of poverty, lack of means of transportation, and restrictive Turkish legislation. They returned over vast distances; many covered two thousand miles to reach their destination from central Russia, often on foot. Theirs was an indomitable spirit; they returned in peace, to live thriftily, and if possible, harmoniously, with their Arab neighbors. They returned neither to destroy nor dispossess, but to build.

The land they found was graphically described in 1869 by Mark Twain, no Zionist, in *Innocents Abroad*:

> Of all the lands there are for dismal scenery, I think Palestine must be the prince. It sits in sackcloth and ashes. Over it broods the spell of a curse that has withered its fields and fettered its energies. The hills are barren, they are dull of color, they are unpicturesque in shape. The valleys are unsightly deserts, fringed with feeble vegetation. The Dead Sea and Sea of Galilee sleep in the midst of a vast stretch of hill and plain where the eyes rest upon no pleasant tint, no striking object, no soft picture. One may ride ten miles, and not see ten human beings. A blistering, naked, treeless land.

In 1921 another observer visited Palestine, after a few decades of Jewish enterprise. Like Mark Twain, he was no Jew, nor Zionist propagandist. Winston Churchill wrote:

> Anyone who has seen the work of the Jewish colonies which have been established during the past 20 or 30 years in Palestine will be struck by the enormous productive results which have been achieved. I had the opportunity of visiting

the colony of Rishon-le-Zion about 12 miles from Jaffa, and there, from the most inhospitable soil, surrounded on every side by barrenness and the most miserable form of cultivation. I was driven into a fertile and thriving country estate, where the scanty soil gave place to good crops and good cultivation and then to vineyards and finally to the most beautiful, luxurious orange groves, all created in 20 or 30 years by the Jewish community who live there.[3]

These and other Jewish settlers—there had been nearly 100,000 by 1914—were creating the first integrated community in this part of the Middle East for the better part of fifteen hundred years. Not only had they returned in peace, but they were bringing into that underpopulated and economically neglected corner of the collapsing Turkish Empire a degree of prosperity which enabled the Arab population to double during the years of the British Mandate, 1919–1948. They reclaimed areas uncultivated since the days of Ancient Rome: the swamps of Hadera and the Emek, the sand dunes of Tel Aviv and Ashkelon, the barren and treeless hillsides of Galilee, the deserts of Lachish and the Negev.

The British role in the Middle East expanded after the end of World War I. Great Britain emerged as regional arbiter; in Palestine, Britain was Mandatory Power, responsible to the League of Nations. The Arabs often claim Britain created this position by deceit, but that is an oversimplification.* Obviously, Britain's international interests made control of the Suez Canal desirable, but Britain and France also moved into the Middle East because a vacuum had been created there by the disappearance of Turkish rule. Nor were there then firmly based, cohesive Arab national movements to fill it.

It is true, however, that Britain's mistakes were responsible for much that "went wrong" in the Middle East. In Palestine the British Mandatory Power failed to create a spirit of compromise and to establish working arrangements between the emerging

---

* Recent research indicates the Arabs built sandcastles of hope on British undertakings which were both limited and imprecise. See Elie Kedourie's *In the Anglo-Arab Labyrinth* (London: Cambridge University Press, 1976).

and increasingly self-aware Jewish minority on the one hand, and the socially and economically backward, as well as divided, Arab majority on the other.

In 1922 Britain tried to placate the Arabs by creating the Arab Emirate of Transjordan by means of the informal and stealthy detachment of that area, east of the River Jordan, which constitutes 75 percent of "historic Palestine." Jews were forbidden to settle there. Here was a typically British compromise: it put three quarters of their historic homeland outside the reach of the Jews, but it failed to mollify the Arabs.

Continued failure to find a satisfactory social and political solution in Palestine led to the civil wars of 1920–21, 1928–29, 1933 and 1936–37. Pilot schemes were evolved—for joint administration, for "cantonization," and for outright partition. They were discussed endlessly and earnestly—then dropped. Britain continued fumbling.

Inevitably, she was attacked by both sides: by the Arabs for ever having allowed Jews into the country and for having promised them a "National Home" in the first place; by the Jews for clamping down on Jewish immigration at a time when hundreds of thousands persecuted in Nazi Europe were looking for a refuge.

Apart from political opposition and armed terror, the Jews in Palestine early on faced economic pressure and discrimination. A call went out in 1922 from the Fifth Arab Congress, meeting in Nablus, for all Arabs to boycott Jewish businesses; seven years later, the First Palestine Arab Women's Congress asked "every Arab to buy nothing from the Jews but land, and to sell them everything but land."[4] Other, similar calls went out in 1931 and 1933, and in 1936 a boycott of all Jewish products was proclaimed by Haj Amin al-Husseini, the Grand Mufti and spiritual leader of all Moslems. This was the forerunner of today's Arab Trade Boycott of the State of Israel, as well as of the economic war against the Jews and all non-Jews who support Israel's right to exist.

The Grand Mufti's 1936 boycott of Jewish shops and tradesmen may well have been copied from the Nazi model, then very much in evidence; even before Hitler came to power in 1933, storm troopers picketed Jewish-owned shops in Germany and urged a total boycott of Jews. The Mufti's boycott was not as effective as he would have wished, for the Jewish community in Palestine was already largely self-supporting, but it should help to dispel the myth that the present Arab Trade Boycott is a response to Israeli "territorial aggrandizement," for it actually predated the establishment of a State of Israel by a dozen years.

In 1944 Britain took a step with far-reaching political and economic consequences: she sponsored the formation of the Arab League, creating an embryo of Arab unity which had not existed before, and which has progressed little since, except with respect to the boycott.

The underlying logic of this British initiative was plain: as the Balfour Declaration had been a gesture to the Jews, so sponsorship of the Arab League was to be a gesture in favor of the ideal of Arab unity and in deference to increased Arab restiveness under Anglo-French colonial rule.

The contrast between the two gestures was, however, startling. The Balfour Declaration aimed to help Jews to live peacefully and productively in their own land. That the Arabs had no such pacific intentions became evident immediately. One of the first acts of the Arab League was to plan the reimposition of a boycott of all Jewish businesses and their goods. In May 1945, a year after the Arab League was formed, and three years before the State of Israel was proclaimed, the League's members decided unanimously to establish boycott offices in all their capitals, and to establish a central office as well.

The newly formed Arab League Council issued its first formal boycott declaration on December 2, 1945. It included these words: "Jewish products and manufactured goods shall be considered undesirable to the Arab countries." Arab individuals and institutions were asked to "refuse to deal in, distribute, or consume Zionist products or manufactured goods."[5] The terms "Jews" and "Zionists" were interchangeable in this declaration; so they would remain.

Involvement of the Arab League in the dispute between Palestinian Jews and Palestinian Arabs extended the numbers of those participating in the conflict. Yet only Jordan, Syria,

Lebanon and Egypt were contiguous to Palestine and in a position therefore to assert that they had some interest in the matter; the other Arab League states were not. Unfortunately, Britain had in 1938 provided the opening for interference by even the most distant "outside" Arab states. That year the British convened a Palestine Conference and invited the attendance of Arab states as far distant as Yemen. Thus she tacitly admitted the right of outside Arab intervention in an area still under exclusive British control, and the Arabs were not slow in noting this. An annex to the charter of the Arab League confirmed this right of intervention in 1945. Another British miscalculation thus proved of far-reaching consequence.

In 1946 the Arab League's Boycott Committee resolved to establish its permanent boycott office in Cairo; in 1949 this Central Office was moved to Damascus, where it took some years to establish common procedures and penalties.* Meanwhile, however, the Arabs had taken other steps:

In 1949 they confirmed the closure of their frontiers with Israel and declared themselves in a permanent state of war with that nation. This followed the United Nations decision of November 1947 to partition Palestine, the proclamation of the State of Israel on May 14, 1948, and Israel's victory in her War of Independence.

Secondly, Egypt closed the Suez Canal to Israeli ships and to the ships of other nations carrying goods to or from Israel. And thirdly, in February 1950, Egypt unilaterally decreed that oil was among the strategic goods which should be denied to Israel. In order to prevent Iranian oil from reaching Israel's embryonic Red Sea port of Eilat, Egypt embarked on a second blockade of an international waterway, the Straits of Tiran and the Gulf of Aqaba.

These three steps need to be considered more closely.

Closing Israel's land frontiers had considerable long-term effects, not all detrimental to Israel. Had her borders not been

---

* Iran, though Moslem, is neither Arab, a member of the Arab League nor a participant in the trade boycott of Israel.

sealed by the Arabs, or the country deprived of a natural hinterland and forced by blockade to abandon the potential and natural role of a Middle East *entrepôt*, Israel might well have developed into nothing more than "a second Lebanon," a Levantine state on the Mediterranean littoral, a "warehouse" for goods traveling between industrialized Europe and the Middle East, Asia and Africa. Total blockade of land frontiers forced Israel to build up the most complete social and economic fabric of any small nation in history—indeed, to begin the fulfillment of the Jewish dream, of creating in a Jewish state a totally self-sufficient society.

Blockade forced Israel to overcome enormous difficulties. She has few raw materials and a population less than half that of New York or London, or about the size of Chicago's. She needed to develop every kind of industrial, agricultural and commercial skill; to build manufacturing facilities; to sell her products in far-distant markets; and to do all this with little capital and while absorbing hundreds of thousands of destitute immigrants, many from educationally and economically backward Arab states.

Geopolitically, Israel suffered a total, terrifying isolation. Denied her hinterland, trade had to be sought in Western Europe, 2,500 miles away, and in the United States, more than twice that distance. No small country since Carthage has had so many problems. But these very difficulties, and the determination and ingenuity they engendered, made for Israel's triumph over enforced isolation. The Israelis turned it into a modern "Western" state economically, industrially and agriculturally— as well as sociopolitically. In the end, blockade proved a partial blessing.*

---

* Not until 1967 did Israel loosen the vise fastened to her frontiers. She then launched a policy of "open bridges" across the River Jordan, a policy which King Hussein of Jordan wisely accepted. This led to the exchange of millions of dollars' worth of goods between Israel and Jordan, and provided new freedom of movement for the Arabs of Israel as well as for those of the West Bank. This has continued without hindrance for a decade, despite the fact that Jordan participates in the Arab Trade Boycott of Israel.

[[12]]

The second Arab move, the closure of the Suez Canal to Israeli ships and goods, was not only a violation of international agreements but flouted every United Nations resolution on the subject of the Canal. The 1888 Suez Canal Convention set the policy for the Canal: it was to be free for the passage of all ships under all circumstances, even in time of war, during which it was meant to be "demilitarized," meaning only that troops or munitions could not be unloaded.

Egypt undertook to respect that Convention, including the articles stating that the Canal should never be blockaded nor obstructed in any way. In 1922, when the British Protectorate over Egypt ended, she again agreed to these clauses.

In 1949, however, Egypt unilaterally closed the Canal, ignoring UN protests. On September 1, 1951, and again on October 13, 1956, resolutions were tabled at the UN Security Council instructing Egypt to lift restrictions on shipping in the Canal and to end her state of belligerence with Israel; Egypt's President Nasser ignored all such attempts to restore the Canal's international status. Except for two years, 1957–1959, the Canal stayed closed to Israeli ships.

Closure of the Canal was an initial step in the ensuing economic war. In 1950 Egypt began blacklisting ships of all nations if they carried goods to or from Israel. By 1955 more than one hundred vessels had been blacklisted, including ships of U.S., British, Dutch, Swiss, Greek and Italian registry.

In 1953 Egypt declared foodstuffs to be contraband, as they might sustain Israel's capacity to wage war, and a cargo of meat was seized from a Norwegian ship, the *Rimfrost,* as well as meat and hides from Italy's *Franca Maria.* Clothing and bicycles were confiscated from Norway's *Laritan,* and in May 1956 building materials and Israeli-manufactured automobiles were taken from the Greek *Pannegia.* In this case, the Egyptians ignored the spread of illness among the crew members, forced them to remain aboard for ninety days, and even restricted their drinking water. Similar brutal treatment had been meted out earlier to the crew of an Israeli vessel, the *Bat Golim,* which in September 1954 had tried to run the blockade; it was seized at Suez

[[13]]

ultimately confiscated along with its entire cargo, while its crew members were released (due to UN Security Council efforts) only after fourteen months of Egyptian imprisonment.

On July 26, 1956, President Nasser nationalized the Suez Canal and expropriated $100 million worth of British property in Egypt—in violation of the pledge he had given to respect the 1888 Convention when the British agreed in July 1954 to withdraw their troops from the Canal Zone within twenty months. Three months after nationalization of the Canal there came war —first between Egypt and Israel, and then with France and Britain intervening on Israel's side. Nasser closed the Canal completely then, by sinking fifty blockships in it.

U.S. pressure ended that war quickly, but that led to a further consolidation of Nasser's rule. What the 1956 Suez crisis showed most clearly were the dangers to peace which are inherent in economic warfare and blockade.

Throughout this period Egypt had also maintained her closure of the Gulf of Aqaba, by means of guns covering the only navigable channel in the Straits of Tiran—despite a March 1954 demand by the UN Security Council to lift this blockade. Access to Israel's one Red Sea port of Eilat was denied until the 1956 war, when a victorious Israel made the lifting of that blockade a condition for withdrawal from the Sinai Peninsula.

It has been estimated that the combined Suez and Aqaba blockades may have cost Israel as much as $25 million between 1949 and 1956. This would be a very sizable sum for a small, beleaguered nation, especially during those years, for Israel was at the time absorbing and resettling about 700,000 Jewish refugees, mainly from Arab countries. They actually outnumbered Israel's initial 1948 population.

While these blockades continued, Israel's only outlets consisted of the seaports of Haifa and Tel Aviv, for the land blockade was total, and the port of Ashdod had not yet been built, while that of Ashkelon then consisted only of a single landing jetty. The only other way into the Jewish state, or out of it, was by air. That access route was also threatened by the Arabs. In

1950 they forbade all aircraft bound for Israel from flying over Arab territory. That prohibition, which violates the Chicago Convention and the rules of the International Civil Aviation Organization (ICAO), continues even today. In 1954 the Arab League tried to tighten the air blockade by issuing an ultimatum to all international airlines: if they continued to fly to Israel, they would be banned from Arab states. This, however, sparked such a unanimous, immediate protest by ICAO members that the Arabs backed down.

The Arab blockade of Israel is meant to be as total as possible, the aim, of course, being the strangulation of Israel's economic life. It even affects travelers, for those whose passports are stamped with an Israeli visa are denied entry into Arab states. Some, but not always all, Arab countries permit travelers to present a second, "virgin" passport to their customs officials, but as late as 1977 visitors to Israel who wished to go on to Arab destinations needed to double back on their tracks to Cyprus, and fly on from there.

The 1954 climb-down after ICAO members had resisted Arab blackmail was not the first Arab retreat. In 1952 they had to suffer the same humiliation, but this time in the political arena. That year, they actually tried to threaten the Federal Republic of Germany with a total trade embargo if a treaty giving Israel $822 million worth of West German goods, services and cash over a twelve-year period was ratified. The threat was rebuffed, and the Arabs chose not to retaliate.

DURING THE 1950's the Arabs assessed the difficulties ahead. They were still politically, economically and militarily weak, while the West (mainly Britain) held real power in the Middle East. Britain remained protector of the Kingdom of Jordan, and her forces were stationed in its only port of Aqaba. Britain was the friend and ally of Iraq, which belonged to the Western-sponsored Baghdad Pact, along with Turkey, Iran and Pakistan. Britain was also guardian of the Gulf States, from Kuwait to Oman, and had forces and bases in Aden, the Hadramauth and the islands of Perim, Socotra and the Kuria

Murias. The Canal Zone remained under British control until 1954, and the Sudan until 1956. Extension of the Arab economic war against Israel, in a way which would involve the Western world, was out of the question for the time being.

Yet there are clear signs that the Arabs were making their preparations to extend the economic war and to press it with vigor. Around 1951 the Central Office for the Boycott of Israel began framing and refining the extensive regulations and questionnaires which were to govern and impose the boycott on the world outside the Middle East, and by the mid-1950's most had been formulated. The Arab economic war had already taken on organizational form, with boycott offices established within all the member states of the Arab League. A new aggressiveness became distinctly apparent in the mid-1950's, although it would not be until 1973 that the Arabs had the economic muscle to extort more widespread compliance with the boycott's rules.

The new aggressiveness of the 1950's was rooted in a new self-confidence, and for a good reason. The Arab world had at last found a powerful ally against Israel and her Western supporters, the Soviet Union. The Russians, early backers of Israel, had done a complete *volte face*.

Russia, of course, had always dreamed of a drive south to the warm-water Persian Gulf and the Indian Ocean, but interest in Czarist times had for defensive and religious reasons been concentrated on Istanbul (then Constantinople). Russia's main preoccupation in the farflung provinces of the Ottoman Empire was the exploitation of Arab resentment against Turkish rule.

Towards the end of World War II, Soviet concern over screening its southern flank led to a revived claim to Istanbul and Thrace. Soviet forces occupied Northern Iran, withdrawing only after heavy Western pressure. To the Russians, the Arab world remained an area of accepted Western dominance. They did no more than give intermittent help to Arab Communist parties, which were small, illegal and ineffectual because they were out of touch with Arab nationalism; Communism had little appeal to an Arab world which treasured its Islamic faith, family life and individualism.

[[16]]

Believing they could make little headway with the Arabs, the Russians supported the foundation of the State of Israel; indeed, the USSR became the second great power (after the United States) to recognize Israeli statehood. Support for Zionism made sense to the Russians at the time: the Jews had beaten a British "colonialist regime," and Britain, still the patron of the Arabs, was then refusing to recognize the new state.

By 1954 Soviet policy towards Israel had begun to shift. When Iraq joined the Baghdad Pact, the Soviet leaders became convinced that Nasser's "revolutionary regime" in Egypt was the best horse to back if Western influence was to be undermined. (Egypt was the obvious alternative to Iraq for leadership of the Arab Middle East. Syria was less promising. Like Iraq, she possessed a pseudo-socialist "Baathist" Party, but the two parties quarreled perpetually and the Russians found that they only burned their fingers with both.)

Soviet arms shipments to Egypt began in 1955, the USSR having switched from the Israeli to the Arab side at the United Nations. In September that year, the Russians carried out a major arms deal with Egypt, shipping weapons camouflaged as Czechoslovak in origin. From then on, the Soviet Union became the main arms supplier of all the so-called "revolutionary" Arab regimes—in Egypt, Syria, Yemen, the Sudan, and finally in Iraq, after the fall of the pro-British Nuri al-Said regime in 1958. The main guidelines of Soviet policy in the Middle East had now become clear: uncompromising hostility towards Israel, support of any Arab regime which showed itself to be amenable, and the unceasing quest for dominance in an area of immense military significance, apparently boundless oil wealth, and profitable and expanding markets.

Although traditionalist and theocratic Moslem states such as the Kingdom of Saudi Arabia loathed and feared Communism, the Soviet Union's strong anti-Israeli stance clearly gave the Central Boycott Office, and some of the national offices, a tremendous psychological boost. Embargo and boycott were now pressed, to include everything which might either strengthen Israel's economy or her defense establishment. No holds were barred, and the Arab League began aiming to take action against any firm in any part of the world that violated its *diktats*.

Inevitably, this led to discrimination against Jewish-owned firms and to boycott pressure against the employment of Jews in non-Jewish firms. The most flagrant example in the 1960's was the Norwich Union affair, which involved the resignation of a Jewish peer, Lord Mancroft, from that British insurance company's board of directors, because of direct Arab pressure.* Such discrimination against individuals is the hallmark of an anti-Semitism which remains not far below the surface. As one prominent British Jew, Sir John Cohen of the Tesco foodstore chain, commented: "Deep down I have always had the feeling that something may be stirred up again; that somebody may start screaming and shouting and that we may have to take up our bundle and run . . . I feel that our security in this country is centered round Israel. If Israel goes, it will make it a lot worse for us . . ."[6]

That goal—Israel's destruction—remains the central and ultimate aim of the economic war. That has been intensified immeasurably since 1973, when the Arabs began wielding their "oil weapon" against the world. This weapon now needs to be assessed.

A YEAR BEFORE the 1973 Yom Kippur War was launched, the Arabs weren't thinking of using the price of oil as a means of intensifying their fight with Israel and her supporters. Price rises, and the call for a bigger Arab share in their own natural resources, had been discussed, but as late as 1972 King Faisal of Saudi Arabia warned his fellow-Arabs that "it is dangerous even to think of the idea" of using the oil weapon against the West. The United States, he said, could survive without Arab oil, and cutting production or exports would merely hamper the Arab war effort against Israel.[7]

At the time, Arab rulers agreed. Some were intent on stepping up production, to find money for large-scale industrial expansion, while others were dependent on the West for military

---

* Details in Chapter III.

support, technical advice, and goods and services they wanted to buy. Interest in using the oil weapon as a political instrument was restricted to the two leading "confrontation states," Egypt and Syria, and two of the oil-rich countries, Libya and, to a lesser extent, Algeria. The Arab adage—"You can't drink your own oil"—still held good.

The Yom Kippur War changed this dramatically and suddenly, giving the Arabs a huge injection of self-confidence. In order both to punish the United States for the support given to Israel after she had been attacked, and in order to pressure the United States to compel Israel to sign a cease-fire agreement on terms favorable to the Arabs, Saudi Arabia on October 18, 1973, just twelve days after the war began, announced immediate cuts in oil production and threatened to stop supplying the United States altogether. Abu Dhabi's action followed the next day. It embargoed all oil supplies to America and all other countries that had supported Israel in any way during that war. Holland was placed under total embargo; all other Western European countries and Japan were subjected to a 25 percent cut in supplies. In November the oil producers declared this would continue, that their oil output would be cut still further, and that they would set up a joint Arab committee to categorize states as "friendly," "hostile" and "neutral." This was tough talk. Even more remarkable was the Saudi Arabian threat to cut output by 80 percent if the United States, Europe or Japan took any countermeasures.

Combined with these threats was an astounding increase in the price of crude oil, and this led to such wild leapfrogging that by December, when the Organization of Petroleum Exporting Countries (OPEC) raised the price to $11.65 (it had been $2.59 in January and $5.17 in October), some Iranian crude oil was auctioned at a staggering $17.40 a barrel. The Shah of Iran, clearly delighted, even began to chide the West for its unwillingness to pay, telling it to improve its disorganized labor relations and "get down to work."[8] Some European countries, he predicted, might "go bankrupt and disappear," but he warned that there was no chance whatever of oil prices coming down.

In January 1974 there was a cease-fire and a disengagement

agreement between Egypt and Israel, but the Arab oil embargo against the United States continued. Two months later, at the OPEC meeting in Vienna, most Arab states agreed to resume shipments to America, but Libya and Syria refused to do so, Algeria postponed shipments until after June 1, and Iraq stayed away from the meeting. The oil embargo was maintained in full against Holland, Denmark, Portugal and South Africa.

The Arabs were now wielding the oil weapon against Israel and states friendly to Israel, while at the same time amassing ever greater oil wealth which could be used to promote the economic war against the Jewish state. In June 1974 Saudi Arabia more than doubled its ownership share in the Arabian American Oil Company (ARAMCO), from 25 to 60 percent, and other Arab governments took similar action. The oil-producing nations had, in effect, found a new weapon. Apart from just raising the price of crude oil, they could simply take a bigger slice of each dollar that it earned.

Another shock to a dazed, divided and indecisive outside world came when the Vienna OPEC Conference of September 1975 led to a further 10 percent price increase. This caught the nine-nation European Economic Community (EEC) completely by surprise, and it reacted with frenzied panic. France, predictably, cast around for a scapegoat and found two, the United States and the United Nations. She blamed the United States for joining with the Soviet Union in fixing a cease-fire formula without consulting its Western allies, and the United Nations for its obvious impotence. She then began negotiations with individual Arab states, to secure whatever advantages each could offer. Meanwhile, in Britain the reaction was less calculated but equally deplorable. Car owners panicked for about three weeks, causing shortages with their hoarded gasoline. No European government showed an intelligent interest in American proposals, such as the creation of an "oil-users association," and towards the end of 1974 American patience began to wear thin. By December there was open talk of using armed force to safeguard oil needs. Successive warnings came from Kissinger,[9] the political scientist Robert Tucker[10] and President Ford.

[[20]]

Kissinger admitted no situation existed in which force might *not* have to be used: "It is one thing to use it in the case of a dispute over price, it's another where there's some actual strangulation of the industrialized world." President Ford confirmed that three U.S. divisions could in certain contingencies be used in the Middle East.

Constructive plans were also discussed—for the recycling of surplus oil earnings, the creation of a fund to help nations in difficulties, and for getting international lending institutions like the World Bank to cut off loans to oil-rich countries.[11] For their part, the Arabs were keenly alive to the possibility of a concerted U.S.-led action, and thought it was under way. The Algerian Foreign Minister, Bouteflika, for example, "discovered" what he believed to be a "veritable crusade" by the United States against OPEC.[12] In fact, however, the West remained divided and the "grand strategy" the Arabs feared failed to materialize, contrasting dismally with OPEC's noteworthy, if not total, unity.

THE OIL REVENUES were to be used against Israel, but just as important to the Arabs was that they be used for constructive purposes. One priority might have been to support the non-oil-producing countries of the Third World, for the fivefold increase in the price of oil had caused the poorer Third World states immense problems. As London's *Economist* commented in 1975, the OPEC countries were "now seen as the shadow of a new imperialism that has already dealt hefty blows to the poor of the world."[13]

The impact of these blows was made clear by Kissinger in January 1974 when he revealed that year's oil bill for the developing countries would approach $30 billion—$18 billion more than in 1973. Furthermore, it was sure to grow. An estimate by a leading member of the Organization for Economic Development and Cooperation (OECD) claims it jumped by a further $20 billion in 1975, to a total of $42 billion.[14] The accumulated deficit of developing countries may climb to $200 billion by 1980.

Nor was OPEC financial aid of real assistance. London's

Times showed that about 70 percent of OPEC aid was earmarked for Arab countries taking part in the Arab war of attrition against Israel and 90 percent of OPEC's aid was politically motivated.[15] Furthermore, as Britain's *Financial Times* revealed in late 1975, two-thirds of Arab aid to Third World countries went to "Arab oil importers"—to the poorer brethren of the oil-rich Arab states.[16]

This still leaves vast amounts of petrodollars available for investment, and although estimates vary widely and should be treated with caution, the OPEC states were believed in 1974 to have earned $55 billion in surplus money. (Receipts of $85 billion; imports of $30 billion.)[17] By 1980, OPEC is expected to have an accumulated investable surplus of $300 billion.[18]

Where were these funds going? The United States was believed to be getting over 25 percent of OPEC's surplus, half of it invested in U.S. government securities. American banks became the chief intermediaries for Arab investment; some established investment advisory agencies to channel Arab funds into real estate, transportation and capital-intensive industries. Something over 15 percent was being placed in Europe. Roughly as much Arab money as went to the United States and Europe combined was retained for the use of Arab countries and others of the Third World, as well as put into institutions like the International Monetary Fund (IMF) and World Bank.[19]

Most publicity, of course, went to some of the more spectacular examples of Arab efforts at investing in the U.S. economy. Saudi Arabian interests, for example, bought a million shares (at about $9 each) in Armand Hammer's Occidental Oil Company; a further (but undisclosed) interest in an offshore exploration outfit, Ocean Drilling and Exploration Company; a controlling interest (for about $10 million) in the Bank of the Commonwealth of Detroit; 15 percent of the shares of the Arizona Land and Cattle Company, for about $9.2 million; and controlling interest in two Californian financial institutions, the Security National Bank and the Bank of Contra Costa.

Iran bought options on 13 percent of the stock of Pan

American Airways for $300 million. The Kuwaitis were involved in the successful purchase of Kiaweh Island, off the coast of South Carolina, at a cost of $17.5 million, and of a 50 percent share in the Atlanta (Georgia) City Center, a downtown commercial complex, for $10 million. Arabs tried unsuccessfully to buy two Pennsylvania coal companies, General American and Blue Coal. The fear developed that they might also invest massively in "strategic" areas of the American (and Canadian) economy—the aircraft industry, electric power and nuclear energy.

Arguably, however, Arab oil money will never dominate the American economy, which is huge and innately dynamic. The Arabs need brand-new infrastructures for their own lopsided economies, and must turn to the West; their long-term aim is to live as well as the West, and that means getting help from America. The United States therefore has a tremendous economic role to play in the Middle East—something which President Anwar Sadat of Egypt, for one, has fully recognized, and which the Syrians are also beginning to appreciate.

The Saudi Arabian government stated in February 1977 that its foreign investments between 1972 and 1975 totaled $11 billion, and in 1975 represented 13.8 percent of the country's gross national product. The Saudis would continue investing abroad, but also planned to channel more money into huge domestic industrial development plans and such other needs as roads, harbors and schools. Neither the Saudis, nor Iran, which also has big development plans of its own, have therefore been eager to help Egypt's plan for turning the Suez Canal area into an industrial zone. Kuwait also has ambitious plans, and there are major schemes, too, for the development of Arab petrochemical industries, mining projects, pipeline construction and for the development of tourist facilities in Morocco and Tunisia. Needless to say, all Arab states with oil resources are also interested in strengthening their control over them. Total nationalization is their declared universal objective, and on December 1, 1975, Kuwait was the first Arab oil-producing state on the Persian Gulf to achieve this.

The damage done to Western and Third World economies does not seem to worry the Arab world any more than does the damage done by their boycott. They argue that their main preoccupation has been to spend their oil revenues profitably and not whether others suffer in the process. But this has to be said in answer:

In the first place, they launched an oil strategy at the end of 1973 that was, first and foremost, politically motivated. The aim of it was to force a peace settlement, on their terms, upon Israel, and the method used was coercion of countries deemed friendly to Israel. So, like boycott and blockade, crude oil became a lever the Arabs could use against Israel.

Secondly, the Arabs acted entirely on their own, without reference to any international organization, including the UN, in which they by then had a built-in majority. Finally, they both underestimated and later chose to ignore the inflationary effects their oil warfare would have both on underdeveloped countries and on industrial nations then suffering from recession. If a major world economic crisis develops, the Arab oil-producing states will bear a heavy responsibility for it, and for the famine which would inevitably result in the Third World.

One other aspect of this economic war deserves mention. The astronomic increases in the price of oil have created a dangerous spiral. The Arabs have successfully held the industrialized West *and* the emerging nations to ransom, forcing them to finance the Arab League war against Israel. The money extorted from them by means of oil price rises serves to increase Arab economic "muscle"; this in turn allows the Arab boycotters to pursue ever more energetic and extortionary policies against the world community.

It is, once again, a classic example of the relationship between blackmailer and victim, only here *two* intended victims are involved: the world economic community as a whole, and the State of Israel. The Arabs aim to force an uninvolved world to pay for and promote the economic strangulation and eventual destruction of that state.

[[24]]

CHAPTER II

Blackmail and Blacklists

ECONOMIC BOYCOTTS were nothing new in 1936; they have a long history, although the word itself dates back only a hundred years—from the surname of the rent collector of the Earl of Erne, Captain Charles Cunningham Boycott, of County Mayo, Ireland. Notorious for his severity, he was singled out for punishment in 1879 and became the first target of the action which would forever afterwards bear his name. No one would work for him, speak to him, or supply him with goods or services; ultimately, he was driven out of his home, and out of Ireland. In his case, the technique had worked.

The international boycott, however, is a different matter, and has not been so successful. It appears to have been an American invention, first urged by Thomas Jefferson in 1793. America, he said, would give it as "another precious jewel to the world," bringing nations "to do justice by appeals to their interests as well as by appeals to arms . . ."[1] In 1919 Woodrow Wilson pursued the same theme, suggesting that the League of Nations apply this "economic, peaceful, silent, deadly remedy" instead of war.[2] And in 1952 John Foster Dulles also urged the use of economic sanctions, claiming they can be "very potent," while avoiding "that resort to force which is repugnant to our objective of peace."[3]

Since then, there have been many international boycotts, but few if any seem to have been effective. During the 1930's Britain applied sanctions against the USSR in response to Soviet arrests of British subjects, and through the League of Nations against Italy for its invasion of Ethiopia. Then came the 1936 Arab boycott of Jewish settlers in Palestine, leading to the Arab League Boycott of Israel. After the end of World War II, the Soviet bloc boycotted "Titoist" Yugoslavia and, later, "Maoist" Albania; India boycotted the Portuguese colony of Goa; the Organization of American States, led by the United States, boycotted first Trujillo's Dominican Republic and, later, Castro's Cuba; various African states boycotted the Republic of South Africa and Portugal, the first for its apartheid policies, the second for colonialism; in 1965 Britain and other UN nations began their boycott of Rhodesia. Most of these boycotts failed. They did not hurt the state under boycott nearly as much as expected.[4]

Adam Roberts of the London School of Economics compared economic sanctions with another overrated weapon: strategic bombing. Both are characteristically employed by large and wealthy states; both are meant to produce far-reaching effects "by remote control, and at minimum cost to the sender."[5] The oil-rich Arab nations, whose economic muscle backs the boycott of Israel, have of course put difficulties in Israel's way, some already mentioned. Israel's national development would have been faster without foreign blockade and boycott (foreign investment in Israel dropped sharply after 1973), but the Arab economic sanction has nevertheless failed to cripple the country. Israel's trade has never stopped growing; indeed, Israel claims "the world's record in economic growth." It has doubled national output every four or five years since 1948 (except during 1974–1975); in 1976 its exports were worth $4.4 billion, and of this, $1.9 billion were industrial goods, 20 percent of them the outcome of Israeli research and development.[5]

If boycotts do not achieve their objectives, there must be other reasons why countries resort to them. Roberts suggests they are in fact options employed by countries which feel "the need to do something, but not too much." They "keep the issue alive," he says, and strengthen the idea "that the receiver of sanctions is in some sense an outcast."

Roberts also observed what many fail to note: that economic sanctions can be a direct cause of war. "By 1959, as General Dayan has related, the blockade of Israeli cargoes in the Suez Canal had contributed to Israeli exasperation with Nasser," writes Roberts. "In 1967, the Egyptian closing of the Straits of Tiran, and the economic threat which that represented, had a much stronger and more immediate effect on the Israeli government. Similarly, before the Second World War, American economic pressures on Japan contributed to the Japanese decision to join in the war. *These and other cases suggest that, at least sometimes, economic sanctions are not so much an alternative to war as a prelude or even accompaniment to it* [emphasis added]."[6]

Blockade and boycott are particularly dangerous in the highly explosive Middle East, for it might not be possible to confine a renewed Arab-Israeli war to the area. The Soviet Union continues to watch for every opportunity to keep the Middle East pot on the boil and to exploit all tensions in the region. And if the Soviets were to involve themselves on the Arab side in a new Middle East war, that could, in turn, bring in the United States.

WHILE THE ARAB EFFORT to strangle, first, the Jewish community in Palestine and subsequently the State of Israel has failed, the boycott is no longer the "paper tiger" it was regarded for many years. Prior to 1973, when the Arabs began accumulating vast oil wealth, it was treated almost as a joke and regarded as a "toothless and gutless" propaganda device, as J. Q. Purcell notes in a paper for the Anti-Defamation League of B'nai B'rith (ADL).[7]

Ever since 1973, however, oil wealth has dramatically altered the picture. The drop in investment has hurt Israel, and while the boycott is still unable to strangle Israel economically, it is beginning to hurt. It is also becoming a growing irritant in those other countries outside the Middle East in which it is applied. It has become the focus of a great deal of public discussion, in the U.S. Congress, in the British Parliament, and in newspapers throughout the world. The general public is still

[[27]]

woefully uninformed about it, but leaders in government, business and the financial world are keenly aware that Western industrial nations have come under massive pressure. Those who run the Arab Trade Boycott of Israel mean to use the lure of oil billions "with strings attached," as Purcell put it, to force the West to sever or restrict its commercial links with the Jewish state.[8]

More than one boycott is involved. The first—or "primary" —boycott consists of the refusal by the Arabs to trade with Israel in any way. This is of no direct concern to the Western world, and the choice of trading partners is anyone's right, the Arabs' included. It is an obstacle to peace in the Middle East, but largely a matter for the two sides in the Arab-Israeli conflict.

The other boycotts which the Arabs operate—as part of their economic war against Israel—are an entirely different matter, however. These reach out beyond the Middle East to "third countries" (i.e., those other than Israel and the Arab League states), giving the boycott a global character.

The "secondary" boycott is aimed at companies that invest in or do business with Israel. By violating the extensive, confusing and often contradictory boycott regulations, they are subject to blacklisting, which means exclusion from Arab markets. Even more insidious is the "tertiary" boycott, which also operates in "third countries" and which can threaten firms trading with anyone who does business with Israel—even with companies that have "Zionists" (read "Jews") on their boards or in executive positions.

What emerges is a picture of the world business community, even nation-states, being held to ransom by a small group of countries—all of them, in varying degrees, economically, socially and educationally backward, fundamentally undemocratic, often downright feudal, and demonstrably indifferent to internationally accepted standards of behavior. The global boycott the Arabs are waging today is not, after all, the kind of economic sanction envisaged by Jefferson, Wilson or Dulles; it is directed against totally uninvolved companies, business communities and nations, and by one party in a complex dispute.

[[28]]

Particularly disturbing to the outside world has been the vague, even wayward, manner in which this boycott has been applied. Whether this is partly or wholly deliberate Arab policy is unclear, but the resultant uncertainty has caused much confusion, irritation and dismay. This, of course, has served the boycotters well, although the conflicting ways in which boycott rules are applied has also often blunted the boycott weapon.

A LETTER OF SEPTEMBER, 1964, from the Central Office for the Boycott of Israel casts some light on the method of approach in the secondary boycott applied in countries like the United States and Britain. It was signed by the Office's Commissioner-General, Mohammed Mahmoud Mahgoub—who was still carrying out his duties in 1977—and addressed to the Foreign Trade Exchange of Dallas, Texas. Mahgoub advised them: "We have acquired reliable information to the effect that your company imports women's wear from Israel." The letter went on:

> We believe that it is of mutual interest to both of us to draw your attention to the fact that the Arab countries are still in a state of war with Israel which usurped a dear part of the Arab homeland, dispersed its inhabitants, deprived them of their properties and possessions and failed to comply with any of the resolutions of the United Nations. Therefore, as a measure of self-defense and with the view of safeguarding the rights and the vital interests of the Arabs of Palestine, the Arab countries strictly adhere to a set of boycott rules directed at Israel.
> In brief, these rules prohibit Arabs from entering into any sort of dealings with Israeli natural or artificial persons. They also prohibit dealings with foreign natural or artificial persons who contribute to the promotion of Israel economy or war potential through any of the deeds defined by the Boycott Law and Regulations.

Mahgoub required a declaration, certified by a chamber of commerce and authenticated by an Arab consulate or diplomatic mission. The Texas firm was called upon to answer these questions:

[[29]]

1. Do you have any branch, office or agency in Israel? Please state the nature of its activity.
2. Do you act as general agents of Israeli companies or import Israeli products, particularly women's wear?
3. Have you ever owned shares in Israeli firms or businesses?
4. Is your firm or any of its directors a member of any foreign-Israeli chamber of commerce in Israel or abroad?

Mahgoub explained that if the answer was affirmative, the Foreign Trade Exchange would have to produce three documents or be blacklisted: a copy of any existing agency agreement in Israel or with an Israeli company, documentation to show that such agency or agreement had been terminated, and a promise never again "to represent Israeli companies or import their products."

This economic ultimatum from Damascus concluded by telling the American company:

> You will understand the consideration which render this request which is basicly aimed to the interest of your company and . . . will not consider it, according to misleading zionist propaganda, an attempt to exert pressure on you or intereference in the affairs of your company. On the contrary, the Boycott Apparatus do not absolutely think of that. Our sole aim is to avoid stopping trading with your company without giving it a fair chance to explain . . .

The threat of blacklisting came rather sanctimoniously at the end. If the company was unwilling to mend its ways, Mahgoub warned, then "the Boycott Apparatus upon the expiration of the specified time-limit will be forced, with deep regret, to recommend banning transactions with your company."[9]

This letter, the standard formulation of that time (and one that has hardly changed since), is interesting in that it has nothing to do with goods of strategic military or economic value; it deals with women's wear, and is motivated by the thought that all Israeli exports strengthen Israeli's economy and ought to be stopped. It interferes not only with the Dallas firm's freedom to trade with whomever it chooses, but also with that company's right to keep its affairs confidential.

Another letter, revealing a different facet of boycott rules and regulations, was sent by the national boycott office of the Kingdom of Saudi Arabia to a British firm, The Gramophone Company Limited, of Blyth Road, Hayes, Middlesex. The firm was required to appoint a Mr. Samir Shamma, of Riyadh, Saudi Arabia, as its agent in the "registration of renewal of trademarks, patents or designs." It was also called upon to sign and attest the following document:[10]

> We hereby solemnly declare that the company is *not a Jewish company nor controlled by Jews or Zionists and it has no relations with Israel* [emphasis added] which may contradict the following boycott principles:
>
> 1. Establishment of a branch of the factory in Israel.
> 2. Establishment of assembling factory in Israel or presence of an agent who assembles the products of the company in Israel.
> 3. The availability of general agents or central offices for the Middle East in Israel.
> 4. Granting the right to use the company's name by Israeli companies.
> 5. Participation in Israeli factories or companies.
> 6. Giving advice or experience to Israeli factories.
> 7. In case one of the promoters is an Israeli national.

The British firm also had to state whether it had invested money in Israel, had sold or "circulated" Israeli products, or had manufactured goods which had an "Israeli content." If the company failed to make the necessary declaration, its business with the Arab world would end.

The specification in this document that the company should not be "a Jewish company nor controlled by Jews" was in common use for a great many years and contradicts the repeated assurances of boycott-office spokesmen that their efforts are not directed against Jews, but only "Zionists."* That this distinction is meaningless was clear as early as 1955, when the chairman of

---

* The wording on the Saudi document was altered to eliminate references to both Jews and Zionists, as a result of a 1974 economic cooperation agreement negotiated between the United States and Saudi governments. The new version contains the same seven points of the original, however, and still includes the words "no relations with Israel."

a firm in The Hague, Holland, received a letter from one of the boycott offices which was subsequently reprinted in the *Congressional Record* of July 17, 1959. It included the following five questions:

> 1. Do you have any Jewish employees in your company, if yes, how many and what are the positions held by them?
> 2. Are there any Jews in your board of directors as members?
> 3. Is any of your managers or branch managers a Jew, if yes, please give name of the department headed by such a man.
> 4. Is any of the persons authorized to sign on behalf of your company a Jew?
> 5. What is the number of Jewish laborers in your factories and offices?

Another letter from the Central Office for the Boycott of Israel, this time to Tork Time Controls, Inc., of Mount Vernon, New York, sheds additional light on boycott rules and regulations. In this letter, Commissioner-General Mahgoub began by claiming he had "reliable information" that the company had a subsidiary called Tork Israel Ltd.[11] He then asked seven questions, which called for detailed answers concerning any arrangements the company might have in Israel. The company was to tell him whether it had or had ever had a branch, a factory or an assembly plant in Israel; whether it maintained offices there, or had ever granted Israeli firms or persons the right to use its names, trademarks, inventions or products; whether it participated, or owned shares, in Israeli businesses; whether it rendered or had ever rendered technical help to an Israeli firm and whether it had ever represented an Israeli company either in Israel or elsewhere.

An affirmative answer to any of these questions meant that boycott rules were being violated. "In such case," Mahgoub added, "we should be more than willing to extend every possible assistance to help you put an end to the violation and thus create the appropriate conditions conductive [*sic*] to the promotion of your relations with the Arab world." But this offer of "help" entailed, for the American firm, furnishing no fewer than seven attested documents. These included a statement of the Profit and Loss Account of the Tork subsidiary in Israel, a banker's certificate showing that all funds had been withdrawn from Israel, a document proving that all the company's drawings and plans had been returned to the State of New York, and "an undertaking to the effect that your company will never in the future render any technical knowhow or consultation to the said Israeli factory or any other party or company in Israel."

The Arabs were clearly becoming both more sophisticated and more importunate, for here an American firm was being required by Damascus to give binding assurances about its future operations and a great deal of confidential information about its past ones.

A similar request, but one that included some significant additional points, went from Mahgoub's office to Belvedere Products, Inc., of Belvedere, Illinois. The company had written to Damascus to ask why it had been blacklisted, and Mahgoub replied that this was because it was a subsidiary of Revlon, Inc., "which is banned in all countries of the Arab world." But, as Belvedere had told him it was no longer even partly owned by Revlon, Mahgoub was prepared to "consider" removing it from the blacklist, if and when certain documents were presented to his office. These consisted of proofs that it was no longer affiliated with Revlon, a declaration showing the nature of Belvedere's relations with Israel, and two other items: documentation to show all details of share capital, and the names and nationalities of stockholders, as well as the names and nationalities of board members both before and after the company's relations with Revlon ended. In asking for these, Mahgoub was plainly reserving the right to object if he spotted a "Jewish name" on the list. This is not unusual, and firms with officers who bear suspiciously "Jewish names" have been asked to provide evidence that the persons involved are in fact not Jewish.[12]

All these letters show the basic documents that are required before a company under threat by the Arabs will be allowed to trade with the Arab world.

The first is an affidavit, signed by a company officer, proclaiming that the company is not contravening the general principles or specific rules and regulations of the boycott offices. This must be authenticated by an Arab consulate or diplomatic mission, or by one of the bi-national chambers of commerce the Arabs have set up in countries such as the United States, Britain, Germany and France.

The second is the standard boycott-office questionnaire, which contains detailed questions about the firm's business, as well as the warning that no Arab country or company will be permitted to trade with it if the firm violates boycott provisions. This is sometimes accompanied by another questionnaire which relates specifically to the company in question.

The third basic document required is a "negative certificate of origin," which in most cases must accompany goods shipped to Arab countries. This declares that the goods being shipped "are not of Israeli origin nor do they contain any Israeli material." These certificates are quite different from normal certificates of origin, in that they are discriminatory and don't merely report the origin of goods being exported. Negative certificates have been universally condemned by business groups as completely unacceptable and contrary to all the principles of free trade. The International Chamber of Commerce, in Paris, twice passed resolutions stating that chambers of commerce and industry should "under no circumstances" deliver such negative certificates;[13] in Holland, notaries have refused to notarize them, and in the United States, the State Department has similarly declined to authenticate such documents. (The British Foreign and Commonwealth Office, however, cooperates with the boycotters by "authenticating British notaries' signatures on negative certificates at the insistence of Iraq.

These negative certificates have been the most commonly used weapons of the Arab boycott offices. Demands for them accounted, for example, for 614 of the 836 boycott requests filed with the U.S. Department of Commerce during just one four-week period in 1976* and they are further involved in

---

* October 7 to November 4, the first period in which public disclosure of these requests took place.

pressure on international shipping lines. Certificates attest that cargoes shipped to Arab destinations will not sail on blacklisted vessels—not just Israeli ships, but any which calls or has ever called at Israeli ports, or carries Israeli cargoes.

Early in 1977 it was announced that several Arab countries would no longer require negative certificates of origin from U.S. firms, and this appeared to have been both in response to anti-boycott legislation then being considered by the Congress, and an attempt to discourage such legislation. Saudi Arabia said the move had been made to give America "a chance" and that the negative certificates could be reimposed if anti-boycott legislation to which it objected were passed. One lesson came through quite clearly: where the boycott is confronted by firm legislative action, the Arab states will back down. In Britain, for example, governmental resistance has been *nil*, and it is there that the Arabs feel free to intensify pressures and demand full compliance with boycott rules.*

A COMPANY receiving Arab questionnaires, letters and demands has a number of options, but only one basic decision to make: to comply or not to comply. Willingness to comply amounts to a confession that the company's officers are susceptible to intimidation and commercial pressure, and that they are prepared to endorse discriminatory practices for the sake of profit. This, if publicized, can of course damage a company's reputation and standing, both in the eyes of the public and the business community, where compliance is often seen as craven submission to foreign pressure. Compliance can also lay a company open to all sorts of domestic legal problems. In the United States, compliance could mean the company is actually breaking the law—not just anti-boycott legislation, but laws which treat some boycott practices as conspiracies in restraint of trade.

---

* An end to negative certificates might not hamper the boycotters too much, claimed the Secretary-General of the Arab-British Chamber of Commerce. His organization would issue all documentation needed for goods going to the Arab world, and would be able to impose the boycott rules in any event.

Boycott-inspired anti-Jewish practices are of course also prohibited in the United States, the United Kingdom and elsewhere.

The options the company has are as follows: It can advise the Arabs that it has no prohibited ties with Israel, and it may then be allowed to trade with the Arab world. It may admit having ties with Israel, in which case the boycotters will allow between three and six months (this varies) to sever those ties— and sometimes, as we shall see later, to rid itself of its Jewish (or "Zionist") directors. A company may deny that it is violating the boycott, only to find that the Damascus office won't accept its denial. In this case, the company is given only six weeks in which to comply with boycott rules; if it fails to satisfy the Damascus office during this time, it is automatically blacklisted—although Damascus gives it another six weeks to prove its "innocence," in which case it may be taken off the list. Lastly, a company has the option of throwing the boycott questionnaires and other documents into the wastepaper basket. The principle is that a company which fails to supply the information demanded is automatically banned from trading with the Arab world, even though it may have discarded the questionnaire only because it did no business with either Israel or the Arab states.

A very great many "resisters" have, however, got away scot-free, which is to say without being blacklisted at all, while some blacklisted companies have managed to trade with the Arabs anyway. This is because individual Arab states will treat the boycott "flexibly" or ignore it altogether, if it is in their own economic interest to do so—whenever, that is, they want a particular company's products or services badly enough, or the company is either strong enough or courageous enough to treat the boycott demands with contempt. In general, boycott regulations, laws, procedures and blacklists are applied in, and by, each Arab country in varied ways, and there are enormous discrepancies in what in theory is meant to be a relatively uniform effort by the member states of the Arab League.

SCRUTINIZING the entire world's business affairs (for that is what the Damascus office tries to do) is a big job, and it has been reliably reported that a hundred bureaucrats are employed for the purpose. No one knows how many others are occupied elsewhere, in the various national boycott offices of the individual Arab League states or as agents and "enforcers" throughout the world. These bureaucrats have over the years compiled enormously detailed boycott rules, few of them ever made available in full to the company officers throughout the world who are meant to conform to them.

The Central Boycott Office issues a fifty-seven-page book of instructions entitled *General Principles for Boycott of Israel,* and individual Arab League states produce their own. The 1972 Damascus document (English translation by U.S. State Department), is the general guide for all Arab League states; separate instructions are issued by the individual Arab League nations.

A breakdown of the Damascus instructions gives a partial picture of the nature and scope of boycott regulations. They cover the whole field of Arab exports and imports and deal with all foreign institutions and companies held to be "acting in support of the economy of Israel." Separate sections regulate shipping companies, oil companies, banks, insurance companies and aviation companies. Certain markets for Israeli goods are meted out for special discriminatory treatment; at various times these have included Iran, Romania, Hong Kong, Ceylon and Pakistan. In 1976 even Egypt became an object of suspicion at the Damascus Boycott Office, because it seemed to be ignoring the rules, and there are special provisions for supervising goods which arrive in other Arab League countries via Egypt. In fact, however, all Arab League nations are watched by the boycott officials. Even goods that land at Arab airports on their way to a final Arab destination undergo scrutiny. And there are special provisions for preventing Middle East oil from reaching Israel; it is deeply irritating to the Arab League that Iran, though Moslem, is not a participant in the boycott and continues to supply Israel.

A mass of regulations deal with individuals, whether "Zionists," Jews or just people sympathetic to Israel. Automatically blacklisted are "legal persons" (i.e., corporations) held to be "pro-Zionist," foreign actors and films "biased in favor of

Israel," and foreign journalists deemed guilty of "persistent open partisanship toward Zionism and Israel." With regard to the latter, a revealing corollary states:

"No account is to be taken of objective critical positions or balanced points of view that may have been adopted by persons engaged in information work."[14] It means that journalists with a record for objectivity will be blacklisted, if this balance prompts them sometimes to seem friendly towards Israel and Zionism.

The regulations also deal with "Foreign societies and institutions of a philanthropic character that make donations or gifts to Israel in cash or in kind."[15] They state that charitable donations to Israel do not automatically blacklist an organization or a person unless the donors fail to provide "similar assistance to charitable entities and institutions in the Arab countries." Jewish organizations helping Israel in any way are automatically liable to be blacklisted.

Foreign printed matter is also blacklisted, if it contains "propaganda for Occupied Palestine" (i.e., the State of Israel), or is regarded as "defamatory of the Arabs."[16] Such definitions allow the Arab League states to ban all printed matter they find objectionable, books and maps included. Indeed, maps are a particularly sensitive issue with the Arabs; any that shows Israel is banned and even historical maps are suspect. Those, for example, which show the extent of King Solomon's small "empire" are held to encourage present-day Zionist "annexationism" and "expansionism" and are contraband.*

Boycott offices claim the right to delete anything from foreign publications they find offensive, especially advertisements relating to Israel; this has led to a practice the Israelis understandably find galling—the avoidance by many international corporations of any reference to their Israeli connections in ads and other printed matter which might be seen by

---

* An Arab propaganda myth claims that a map hangs in the Knesset (Israel's Parliament), showing the boundaries of present-day Israel stretching from the Euphrates to the Suez Canal. No such map hangs there, nor has one ever.

the Arabs. When, for example, some airlines and hotel chains list their Middle East facilities, they don't mention, or they play down, those they have in Israel. Intercontinental, for one, lists its hotel in Jerusalem, but avoids any use of the word "Israel." British Airways has similarly offended, and there are plenty of others. Directories of the Middle East world, meant for sale in the Arab nations or to businessmen interested in Arab trade, often omit any mention of Israel, while scrupulously providing details of every Arab nation in the area. In some, there are maps in which Israel cannot be located; her territory is often shown as part of Jordan. Even newspapers of distinction are offenders; London's *Times,* for example, published a supplement on Middle East banking in 1977 in which no reports about, or even mention of, Israel appeared. The reason for this is obvious and rooted in Arab paranoia about the existence of the Jewish state: had Israel been mentioned, the supplement would have been boycotted by those Arab companies, banks and governments whose advertising pays the cost of production.

SAUDI ARABIA'S own *Regulations for the Boycott of Israel,* while following the same general lines of the Central Office instructions, include some additional provisions.[17] It talks about films and books which "smear" the Arab states, and there is an oddly worded ban against Israeli "money-bags."[18] It also bans visitors who present a "clean" passport if it comes to their attention that the visitors have another one which contains an Israeli visa.[19] The Saudis, moreover, have their own ideas about oil: their boycott office insists that all oil destined for Israel should be confiscated, and calls for a close tab on all tankers calling at Israeli ports, by reference to Lloyd's of London.[20]

There are severe, sometimes Draconian punishments levied on Arabs who contravene the boycott laws of their own countries. In Egypt these are specified in a 1955 law (No. 506); in Syria by a 1956 law (No. 285); in Libya by a 1957 law (No. 62), and in Jordan by a law passed in 1958 (No. 10). The penalties are specified in Article 7 of each, except for Jordan, where they are given in Article 8. They include confiscation of goods, imprisonment with forced labor in almost every case, and heavy fines.* There is public humiliation, too; the names of the offenders are published in the press and their offense is posted outside their offices, factories, or warehouses (and at their own expense). Moreover, defacing such public posters is itself a crime punishable by a fine and three months' imprisonment.

The case of Yussouf A'lam, an Egyptian paper merchant, is illustrative. According to the January 9, 1977, issue of *al-Ahram,* the Egyptian daily, he had acquired vast wealth over ten years "of swindles" and illegal dealings. Notorious was the fact that in 1974 he had "agreed to import 10,000 tons of printed paper . . . from an Austrian Jew named Mulner" and had generally "commerced with Jewish firms in the paper markets . . . [all] of bad repute." As punishment, the Egyptian Ministry of Commerce confiscated all his wealth.

BECAUSE WESTERN BUSINESS GROUPS, international lawyers and others have repeatedly found that the boycott has no moral or legal justification, the Arabs have made great efforts to justify their action and to explain the basis of the boycott. One explanation was offered by Abdul Aziz al-Sager, the president of the General Union of Chambers of Commerce, Industry & Agriculture for Arab Countries. Writing from Beirut to the Association of British Chambers of Commerce, in London, he claimed that the Arab Trade Boycott was "defensive," and gave these reasons:

Israel had expelled one million Arabs from their homes in Palestine, had seized their property and had prevented them from returning to their homeland;

Israel had refused to implement United Nations resolutions on the refugee question;

Israel had made, and continued to make, savage raids on frontier Arab villages, and had launched aggressive war against Egypt in 1956.

---

* In Egypt, forced labor up to ten years; in Syria and Jordan, forced labor of no less than three years; in Libya, no forced labor, but imprisonment of between three and ten years.

He went on:

> The Arabs are certain that the aggressive Zionist State of
> Israel is planning to expand further at the expense of Arab
> lands, and to turn more Arabs into refugees. The Arabs are
> determined to frustrate this plan of aggression. They are
> determined to defend themselves, their homes and their
> normal living. They are therefore doing no more than trying
> to deny Israel that economic power which might enable it
> to realise a new step in its attempt for the achievement of
> its distorted dream of domination.[21]

Mr. al-Sager understandably made no mention of the 1948
war launched by the Arabs against Israel; of the fact that UN
resolutions provided for the return of refugees to their homes
only if they were prepared to live in peace there; or that every
Israeli raid on Arab frontier villages was in answer to dozens of
Arab raids into Israel. Further on in his letter, he insisted that
the boycott was directed only against Israel, and not against
Jews—a factual inaccuracy, just as the "defensive" claim he
advanced is an historical inaccuracy. As we have seen, the boycott of Israel began as a boycott of Jewish settlers in British-
ruled Palestine, and even the Arab League boycott dates to
before the establishment of the State of Israel.

The Arabs counter by arguing that the 1949 armistice agreements, which ended Israel's War of Independence, did not end
"acts of war", a "state of war" therefore continues, and justifies
economic boycott and blockade. Furthermore, as boycott was
not mentioned in the armistice agreements, it cannot be held to
violate them.

Despite the ideologically doctrinaire character of the Arab
Trade Boycott, it allows for a number of exceptions and for
ambiguity of regulations which permits the Arab nations to
ignore the boycott when it is in their interest to do so.

They have, for example, found it inconvenient to boycott
foreign department stores which sell Israeli products; doing so
could deny outlets for Arab products. The same holds true for
foreign banks, which are allowed to transact a certain amount
of business in Israel, so long as they also operate in Arab states.

Companies which use Israeli raw materials or manufactured parts in their products are often not blacklisted, only the end products being banned; this allows the Arab world to buy "non-offensive" goods from such companies, if it needs them, while still implementing boycott principles.

There are other exceptions. The regulations permit the import of certain manufactured products of blacklisted companies: for example, spare parts for vehicles; vehicles imported by tourists, pilgrims or foreign experts; industrial spare parts which cannot be produced locally or imported from unblacklisted firms; pharmaceuticals for which there are no substitutes. Shipping companies which deal with Israel are not blacklisted—for that would cripple Arab trade—only individual ships that have called at Israeli ports. International airlines stopping in Israel are not blacklisted, though they are forbidden to have flights on shared routes. Finally, there are several major hotel chains which are active in Israel as well as throughout much of the Arab world, among them Hilton, Sheraton and Inter-Continental.

Selling Israeli women's wear in the United States has been held to be a violation of the boycott; selling non-strategic goods *to* Israel, on the other hand, is not banned, though it occasionally lands a company on the blacklist. It all seems to depend on who does the selling, what is sold, who in Israel is the purchaser, and the zealousness of the boycott office interested in the deal. Yuval Elizur claimed in *Israel Magazine* that no company has ever been boycotted "just for selling its products in Israel," but he admits that if and when a company asks the boycott offices "for a ruling about what is 'kosher' and what is not, the answer is invariably, 'not kosher.' "[22]

Two particular exceptions to the rigid application of the boycott should be noted, because both are signs of a new flexibility. The first is the "open bridges" policy, instituted by Israel and acquiesced in by Jordan, under which a reasonably free flow of goods across the Jordan bridges has been maintained since 1967. Periodically, the Central Boycott Office in Damascus has considered pressing for the closing of the bridges[23] to meet clandestine demands put by the Palestine Liberation Organization (PLO). But the main beneficiaries of the "open bridges" policy have been the Palestinian Arab inhabitants of the Israeli-administered West Bank; neither the PLO nor King Hussein of Jordan wishes to forfeit goodwill by taking punitive action in public. This may be the reason why the bridges still remain open in 1977.

The second exception has been provided by Egypt. As it did between 1957 and 1959, Egypt has since 1973 allowed Israeli cargoes to pass through the Suez Canal, albeit only in the ships of other nations. This has led to a confusing situation. Some reports have it that such ships are not meant to be blacklisted, unless they call at *both* Arab and Israeli ports; according to other reports, the ships have actually been blacklisted.

The Egyptian attitude appears to have been modified in another respect. Behind the scenes Egypt has indicated a new readiness to take an increasing number of American firms off her own blacklist[24] and to remove any ban from foreign firms prepared to contribute substantially to Egypt's economic well-being.[25] Some reports from Cairo claim Egypt will lift ban or boycott if a foreign firm which invests in Israel is willing to invest twice as much in Egypt. It was rumored that four other Arab League countries were prepared to follow Egypt's lead in this respect.[26] Syria, surprisingly, was named as one of these four; the three others were, most likely, Morocco, Tunisia and Jordan.

THE ACTUAL SIZE of the Arab blacklists can only be surmised. A few, notably the Saudi Arabian list, have been published in the West, but it is not certain how accurate or comprehensive these are. That they have grown over the years is without doubt. Back in May 1965, Washington's *Near East Report* stated that 164 U.S. firms were blacklisted; by February 1975, when Senator Frank Church made public the blacklist in his possession, the number of American companies on the Saudi Arabian list alone had leaped to more than 1,500.

In 1970 the Institute for Palestine Studies, an Arab source, had claimed that world-wide, 2,686 firms blacklisted, 1,580 of them parent companies and the rest branches or subsidiaries. Two years later the same source gave an approximate figure of 5,000 firms, including 1,500 in the United States. The Central Office in Damascus scaled this down in November 1972, stating cryptically that whereas 12,000 firms had been listed at one time or another, only 2,000 were still "blacked."

From 1974 onwards, most American and British newspaper reports repeated that approximate 2,000 figure and the *Washington Post* on December 6, 1974, said the figure represented a list approved by the Lebanese government "at a closed cabinet meeting in Beirut." The *Post*'s story, by Jack Anderson, added a touch of color. The list, he wrote, was "curiously haphazard. For example, more than one insignificant pet store and a shoe repair firm are listed. Perhaps some Arab diplomat or petty Sheik didn't like the service when he shopped to buy a canary or get his shoes heeled."[27]

London's *Daily Telegraph* moved away from the 2,000 figure when it suggested there were 1,400 *British* firms on the boycott list.[28] Then followed Senator Church's 1,500 figure of American firms on the Saudi Arabian list, to which reference has already been made, and it was evident that far more than 2,000 in all were on different Arab blacklists. Indeed, Reuters reported from Cairo on December 24, 1975, that the number of American and European companies blacklisted totaled 10,000. The probability, and it is no more than that, is that there were around 3,000 American and British firms alone on these lists during 1976–1977.

In early 1976 an enterprising London agency, Pethot Information, offered for sale a consolidated list of 5,000 companies in eighty-eight countries, including 1,400 in the United States.[29] Pethot charged £95 ($200) for its list, which could not possibly be comprehensive, but its manager, a Mr. M. Petal, maintained that he was selling his product at a reasonable price. He denied he was assisting the boycott. "I am a Jewish boy. Would I do that?" he asked.[30]

Newspapers which reported the Pethot affair—it led to inquiries into the firm's activities by the Special Branch of Scotland Yard—quickly reverted to more conservative estimates. Describing the European scene, Ian Watson of the London *Sunday Telegraph* gave figures of 1,000 blacklisted firms in Britain, 200 in France and 250 in West Germany.[31]

Saudi Arabian blacklists for the U.S. and Britain have circulated freely. An Egyptian list of 700 firms, world-wide, was published in Cairo's *Official Gazette* on December 18, 1976, and some countries have on occasion issued short lists of companies they had just blacklisted. Kuwait, Iraq and Lebanon have done this; an example was an official Kuwaiti list of 35 names released in November 1970.[32]

Most restrained of all has been Egypt, desperately anxious to attract capital from the West. But the countries of the "Maghreb"—Morocco, Tunisia and Algeria, with its "radical-activist" regime—have likewise shown little enthusiasm. Libya, as might be expected, has taken her own line; although eager to damage Israel in every possible way, her ruler, Colonel Muammar al-Quaddafi, has been equally determined not to cooperate with anyone else. Libya's blacklist must certainly be a long one.

Anomalies abound throughout these Arab blacklists. Saudi Arabia's blacklist for Britain, for example, includes Blower Brothers, with a note: "Branch of English company William Cussons, with whom it is forbidden to trade." But Cussons itself is *not* listed.

Some firms appear to have been included on blacklists by error. One chemical company was included because a third of its capital was ostensibly held by another firm "with whom it is forbidden to trade." But that firm is *not* listed; on the other hand, it transpired that the chemical company *was* a subsidiary of a blacklisted firm, a different one. Names are often mystifyingly misspelled—"Rave" for Rayne, "Goodman" for Goodmos. One or two of the companies were listed after they had ceased to exist, and there were some far-fetched inclusions: for example, Owens-Illinois of the Bahamas, which was a subsidiary of a Bahamian subsidiary of the American company,

Owens-Illinois Glass, Inc. Predictably, there were many firms which were blacklisted because they simply refused or didn't bother to answer the boycott questionnaires.

Some inclusions on American lists were frivolous, or even farcical. GI Joe, Romper Room, Moon Drops Moisturizing Bath Oil, Natural Medical Total Skin Lotion. American firms selling war equipment to Israel are missing—McDonnell Douglas, United Aircraft, General Electric, Hughes Aircraft, Textron— because the Arabs want to be able to do business with them.

Kaiser Industries appeared on the Saudi Arabian list, although it had good trading connections with three Arab states, Egypt, Bahrain and Saudi Arabia itself. Also blacklisted were the Republic Steel Corporation and the General Tire and Rubber Company, neither of whom traded with Israel—although the latter once had a trading arrangement with Israel and was assured in 1972, after it had ended, that it would be blacklisted no longer. Ford, Bacon & Davis, Inc., and Air Products & Chemicals, Inc., were both banned by Saudi Arabia while doing substantial business with Algeria.

Elsewhere one finds the French firms of Dassault Aviation and Metra blacklisted, though they still sold aircraft and missiles to Egypt, Libya and Kuwait. Even an Iranian cargo vessel found its way onto the Iraqi blacklist, though it had nothing to do with Israel; its "crime" was having inadvertently violated Iraq's territorial waters.

The blacklisting of ships provides an extreme example of the erratic way in which the Arab boycott operates. If, for example, a non-Israeli shipping company wants to get a cargo ship off the Arab blacklist, it does so by announcing that this ship will no longer call at Israeli ports. The ship may then be removed from the blacklist and be able to call at Arab ports. The shipping company next assigns another ship, which does not call at Arab ports, to the Israeli run. As Yuval Elizur says of such maneuvers, "Everybody's happy. No one gains, no one loses."

Infinitely more bizarre is what happens to ships that have ceased to be Israeli-owned. They remain blacklisted, indefinitely, no matter how often they may be sold or how many different flags they may fly over the years. "This is a rather mystical taboo," wrote Susan Dworkin in *Near East Report*. "It presupposes that all formerly Israeli ships yearn for Zion, that although the captain now speaks French or Serbo-Croat, the engine-room still has a Hebrew heart." The vessel becomes a kind of doomed amalgam of Flying Dutchman and Wandering Jew, branded forever.

A certain amount of nonsense permeates the theory and practice of the boycott, as do contradictions, anomalies, muddles and mistakes. That fact was explained by the Arab financier Adnan Khashoggi when he was asked how the Arabs decide whom to boycott. He answered, "When you are at war, when you are in the middle of a battle, you don't see right, you don't see left. This is a confused period. And how can the boycott office in Damascus really decide who is what?"[33]

Unfortunately, that office sometimes doesn't even have to make the decision: companies in the United States, Britain and elsewhere do the job for it. These companies, acting out of fear, engage in a "voluntary boycott," at least as insidious as the secondary and tertiary boycotts combined. Not even waiting to be pressured by the Arabs, they decline to do business with Israel, in the hope of making themselves acceptable to the newly rich Arab states. They anticipate Arab objections and act without having received letters or questionnaires from Damascus or elsewhere; before they even make contact with potential Arab customers and clients, they make sure they are "clean" by Arab standards. This, as U.S. journalist Earl Raab wrote, can lead them to "discriminate against Jewish personnel in hiring, firing or condition of employment ('Make yourself scarce for a week, Sam, while the investors are here.')."[34]

The anti-Semitic aspects of the boycott, detailed later, have even led to attempts at meddling with the world press. The outstanding example of this occurred in December 1973 when Italy's *La Stampa* published a satirical sketch by two of its staff writers, Carlo Fruttero and Franco Lucentini, concerning "the mad mullah," Libya's President Quaddafi. They called him "a creature of the CIA," and continued:

He doesn't move a finger without asking for their authorization. A religious fanatic? Don't believe it. It seems that when he was Marshal Tito's guest he ate an entire boar alone. And it seems he has an ulcer, it seems that he is a homosexual, that he sleeps on a mattress of tobacco leaves, and that he keeps a harem of 48 wives in Switzerland.[35]

The Turin newspaper's humor didn't amuse Quaddafi, who unfortunately reads Italian (Libya used to be an Italian colony). Enraged, Quaddafi threatened to break off diplomatic relations with Italy unless *La Stampa* dismissed the two authors involved; then he invoked the help of the Central Office for the Boycott of Israel, which in turn demanded the dismissal of the newspaper's editor, Dr. Arrigo Levi, whom it described as a "Zionist working against the Arabs." Not only was Levi responsible for what his paper published, but in 1947 he had fought as a volunteer against the Arabs, during Israel's War of Independence.

The real target for the boycott-office threats turned out to be the Fiat Motor Company, which owns *La Stampa*. If its paper did not dismiss all three journalists, the Arabs warned, Fiat's "status in the Arab countries" would have to be revised. This decision, said the Cairo Boycott Office, had been reached by all Arab ambassadors to Italy, meeting in Rome.[36]

A storm of indignation swept Italy. The *La Stampa* staff rallied to their editor's support and denounced the Arab move as "blackmail"; even *L'Unità*, the newspaper of the pro-Arab Italian Communist Party, condemned the Arab moves as "inadmissible interference" in the internal affairs of another country. Italian Senator Giovanni Spadolini, former editor of *Corriere della Serra,* said the Arabs were "swiftly moving" from "oil blackmail" to "blackmail against free opinion and thinking."

The Italian government rejected the demand for the dismissal of the three journalists, but Mohammed Mahgoub announced that his office was not dealing with the Italian government and would wait for a reply from Fiat itself before deciding on Fiat's fate in the Arab world. The response was not late in coming. Giovanni Agnelli, Fiat's president, had a talk with Dr. Levi and then went to Rome to tell the Libyan ambassador that he rejected Quaddafi's demand. At the Libyan embassy, Signor Agnelli was received by only a junior diplomat, but Fiat's message was delivered, as was the Italian government's. Both stood firm.*

Writing of this incident, William F. Buckley Jr. said the Arabs had developed "a fiendish instrument of blackmail"— "and as with other forms of blackmail there is, of course, no strategically sounder remedy than: to refuse to put up with it."[37]

Not to be deterred, however, a Cairo spokesman for the Arab Boycott Office announced less than two years later that both the Columbia Broadcasting System and the National Broadcasting Company were being blacklisted. The prime target appeared to be CBS. Stories had been circulating in February 1975, a month before the Cairo announcement was made, about increased Arab interest in the American press, possibly with a view to buying a controlling share in a medium-sized paper. Some details were leaked to *Editor and Publisher*.[38] This may have scotched the proposed deal, and that may in turn have triggered the action of the head of the Central Boycott Office in Damascus. Mohammed Mahgoub announced that both CBS and NBC would be allowed to continue to cover news from inside the Arab world, but only on condition "that this activity is beneficial to the Arab cause and under supervision of the Arabs."[39]

Mr. Richard Salant, president of CBS News, quickly made his position plain:

> CBS News has covered news in all major Arab cities but never "under supervision," nor would CBS permit any government, including the U.S. government, to dictate the content of our news coverage. Further, CBS News does not cover events with an eye to which group would benefit. We cover events as carefully and objectively as we can, regardless of who benefits. Leaders in the Arab world as well

---

* Ironically, Libya later bought into Fiat (see Chapter VII).

as elsewhere are recognizing that their interests are best served by honest and complete reporting and that Americans will understand the Arab world only through such reporting.[40]

NBC issued a similar statement.

That was the end of the matter, as far as CBS News was concerned. But some Arab blacklists continued to include companies affiliated with CBS. These included Cinema Center Films, Inc., W. B. Saunders and Co. and CBS Theatrical Films Division in the U.S., as well as CBS/Sony Records, Inc., in Japan. These affiliates had been blacklisted since 1971. In March 1976, when the Central Office for the Boycott of Israel held its semi-annual meeting in Cairo, it announced that CBS and NBC had been dropped from the Arab blacklists—provisionally, as it were, for Mohammed Mahgoub said the two firms would be kept "under supervision," and would be allowed to continue their activities in the Arab world only as long as these served the Arab cause.

What is interesting in the cases of *La Stampa* and CBS/NBC is not only the blatant and, indeed, ill-advised attempts by the Arabs to interfere with the freedom of the world press, but the emergence of new conditions within the boycott regulations. The *La Stampa* case showed that anyone criticizing the Arabs is liable to be blacklisted, blackmailed and pressured; the CBS/NBC affair showed that actions "beneficial to the Arab cause" may be demanded if a company is to keep off the blacklist. In both cases, there was absolutely no Israeli involvement. Israel was not central to the issues. Yet the sanction of blacklisting may be threatened and, in the case of the networks, was carried out.

What had begun as an Arab boycott of Israel had developed into a boycott of the world.

CHAPTER III

Images and Headhunting

ONE OF THE EARLIEST CASES of an American company knuckling under to Arab pressure taught the American Jewish community how best to respond. Arnold Forster, general counsel and associate director of the Anti-Defamation League of B'nai B'rith (ADL), said later that damage to a company's public reputation could be more effective than damage to its purse.[1]

The company was Brown & Williamson, which in the 1950's was refusing to sell its cigarettes to Israel. The ADL made an issue of this, and the company tried to evade it by selling its Lucky Strike brand to its British parent company, British American Tobacco, and then allowing the parent to sell the cigarettes in the Arab Middle East, claiming it had no control over discrimination against Israel.

The American Jewish community responded quickly. Jewish War Veterans' posts throughout the United States published leaflets and advertisements headlined *Don't Help Nasser and His Arab Cohorts!!*, and advising readers:

> If you smoke Viceroy, Raleigh, Kools, Avalon, Wings, Life, Du Maurier and other products of the British American Tobacco Company, YOU ARE SUPPORTING THE ARAB CAUSE. . . . The British American Tobacco Company, owners of Brown & Williamson Tobacco Company,

has knuckled under to Arab pressure. They refuse to do business with the State of Israel, the only dependable ally of our country in the Middle East. *Don't Give Them Your Support!!*

Individual Jews switched to other brands, and Jewish leaders made sure the company's cigarettes were not given out at community dinners and similar functions. After the company's share of U.S. tobacco sales dropped from fifth to tenth place, and after it was publicly pilloried, it changed its mind. Today, it sells to both Israel and the Arab states.[2]

Two other early cases reinforced the lesson learned. The first concerned Coca-Cola.

In 1949 Coca-Cola approved the application of a group of investors to establish a bottling franchise in Israel. Heading the group was Abraham Feinberg, a prominent American Jewish banker. David Ben-Gurion, Israel's Prime Minister, was enthusiastic about the deal, but it eventually fell through because of Israel's shortage of foreign currency. Feinberg, a former chairman of Brandeis University's board of trustees, has been quoted as saying, "I made the decision that it was not fair to use up valuable foreign exchange at a time when people in Israel were living in tents. They needed bread, not Coca-Cola syrup."[3]

Seventeen years later, in 1966, the ADL was puzzled to find that Coca-Cola *still* had no franchise in Israel, though it maintained extensive operations in the Arab world. The suspicion grew that Coke was using all sorts of excuses to avoid granting a franchise to an Israeli bottler—especially as one applicant, the Tempo Soft Drink Co., Ltd., of Israel, had been turned down.

Feinberg, who today is head of the Coca-Cola bottling franchise in Israel, denies that fear of the boycott was the cause. Coca-Cola had been involved in a lawsuit with Tempo in 1963, over alleged infringement of its distinctive bottle shape and trademark. That experience, said James A. Farley, then chairman of Coca-Cola Export, "obviously precludes our entering into a business arrangement with it."[4]

That argument failed to satisfy. It was 1966, eighteen years after the establishment of the State of Israel; the company's continuing failure to appoint (or bother to find) a bottler for Israel was seen by many to smell suspiciously of capitulation to Arab pressure, or participation in Arab blacklisting. The ADL went into action.

Arnold Forster says that he and others at the ADL spent nearly a year looking into the reasons given by Coca-Cola for turning down franchise applications. "They had done feasibility studies of the amount of intake of soft drinks on the part of the Israelis, as against other countries," Forster says. "They said to us that it was one against five. They talked about companies needing to have a million dollars in the bank before they could issue a franchise. We examined every franchise that had been issued by Coca-Cola in the previous ten years, including three in Ireland, two of which were given without money because an officer had personal relations and he was a personal friend."[5]

The charge that Coca-Cola was discriminating against Israel was made public. Forster learned that the Anti-Defamation League was taking on a company whose budget was bigger than the Israeli government's and that the ADL would be "destroyed" within a week. He wasn't disheartened, Forster says, "because every Jew in America" would be able "to participate in the fight."[6]

Jews announced in restaurants, at drugstore counters and in grocery stores that they would not drink Coca-Cola; within five days, Forster says, some countermen refused to sell Coca-Cola because they wouldn't be "Nazi agents." Nathan's Famous, a hot-dog stand in Coney Island, took full-page ads announcing it would no longer serve Coca-Cola.[7] Neighborhood bars, restaurants and shops announced they were switching to a rival cola drink.

Meanwhile, Morris B. Abram, then president of the American Jewish Committee, examined the file of correspondence between Coca-Cola and Feinberg; he said there was no evidence that the company was reluctant to do business in Israel so long as "respected and stable" investors were involved in the franchise application. Feinberg and Abram both cleared Coca-Cola of boycott compliance, but the damage wrought by the counter-boycott had been done. Within less than a week, Coca-Cola had lost about $5 million worth of sales.

"They collapsed," says Forster, "not because of the $5 million, but because they could not stand the heat of a public argument about whether or not they had submitted to Arab blackmail."[8] The counter-boycott, comments Yuval Elizur, "is not the only, or even the most effective weapon to be used by friends of Israel. A display of public protest—hurting the company's reputation and pressing it to prove its integrity—achieves more."[9]

Feinberg renewed his application in 1966, and says he did so before the controversy arose. This time he was granted the franchise and he quoted J. Paul Austin, president of the company, as saying, "We're not going to listen to the Arabs." Warned that Coca-Cola might be thrown out of the entire Arab world (it had six plants in Egypt alone), Austin responded, "We don't care. Nobody is going to tell us where to do business." Austin, says Feinberg, is "an independent guy who would no sooner let the Arabs tell him what to do than let the Jews tell him what to do."[10] Maybe so; in any event, a Coca-Cola plant was finally built outside Tel Aviv, and today Coca-Cola is probably the most popular drink in Israel. (Its example encouraged other soft-drink companies, including Schweppes, to do business there. Schweppes then was blacklisted.)

In neighboring Lebanon, the population switched to "K" Cola, for Coca-Cola was indeed thrown out of the entire Arab world when it granted Feinberg his Israeli franchise. Getting all the Arab states to vote unanimously to ban Coca-Cola on November 20, 1966, at the Arab League Boycott Conference then being held in Kuwait, was something of a victory for the Central Boycott Office. For Mahgoub had to prevail over many powerful economic interest groups in the individual Arab nations and the vote is seen by some in Israel as a "test of strength" in which Mahgoub, in this instance at least, was victorious.

Another reason for the blacklisting of Coca-Cola may be found in the signal lack of support the U.S. government gave to this economically important American company throughout its struggles with the Arabs. Diplomatic pressure, or at least persuasion, might have been attempted, and might well have shored up those interest groups in the Arab countries who were prepared to continue dealing with Coca-Cola, despite its violation of the boycott rules; governmental efforts of this kind have, for example, been made by West Germany on behalf of Volkswagen, and have proved successful. The lack of action by Washington in the Coca-Cola case undoubtedly made Mahgoub's job easier.

In 1975 an additional reason for blacklisting Coke was provided by Amin Hilmy, then the newly arrived Arab League observer at the UN. "We started the boycott," he told an interviewer, "when we found that Coca-Cola wanted to send its syrup to Israel and we probably would be drinking Coca-Cola through Israel." This, however, seemed nonsense, as Coca-Cola itself noted when it replied that "it was highly unlikely that the Tel Aviv firm could sell in Arab lands, even if it wanted to do so."[11] The blockade of Israel would allow "the pause that refreshes" to pass only over the "open bridges" Israel maintained with Jordan after 1967.

That the Arabs were continuing their ban on Coke became evident in 1976 when a Coca-Cola spokesman announced that a proposed development by his company of Egypt's citrus industry had been "frozen" by Cairo. The fact that Egypt was even considering dealing with a blacklisted company was not surprising, for she has been the most flexible of all Arab states with regard to the boycott, especially since the agreement Kissinger negotiated with Egypt after the Yom Kippur War. But the freeze appeared to continue, and according to the company spokesman, it was imposed so that Egypt would not appear to be "buckling under U.S. pressure."[12] By December, however, the company's name no longer appeared on the Cairo blacklist.

Coca-Cola's big rival, Pepsi-Cola, has no problems in the Arab world. It operates in Saudi Arabia, Jordan, Iran and Egypt because it carefully avoids Israel. "There's nothing there for us," Pepsi Chairman Donald M. Kendall has said. In 1976 his company came under attack from American Jewish groups, not only for its avoidance of Israel but also for its substantial deals with the USSR. A New York Jewish newsletter linked the fact that Pepsi had "a soft drink monopoly in the Soviet Union" with the charge that it had campaigned against passage of the Jackson Amendment, which sought to induce the Soviets into allowing the emigration of Soviet Jews. A Chicago Jewish group issued posters making these points by asking, "Do YOU drink Pepsi?," and another group in Southern California urged, "Let us all drink something else!"[13]

Pressure was also needed to induce the American Express Company to do business in the Jewish state. In this case, it was not a matter of opening an operation in Israel, but of reopening one closed apparently because of the Arab boycott.

This had happened in March 1956, and American Express cited business factors for its action in closing its offices in Israel. It claimed that the Middle East conflict had reduced tourism, but in fact more foreigners than ever before visited Israel during 1956. It claimed that restrictions on how much foreign currency Israelis could take abroad had discouraged them from traveling, that the U.S. government in 1955 had stopped its personnel from booking passage home through travel agents, and that the devaluation of the Israeli pound had increased business costs. All these factors, however, had also operated in 1955, and that year American Express had actually *increased* its Israeli operation substantially. As *Near East Report* put it, "The question remained: why in 1956 did the operation suddenly become 'unprofitable'?"[14]

The Israel Government Tourist Corporation stated in April 1956 that it was "convinced beyond doubt" that the company's withdrawal from Israel was due to "threats of the Arab boycott." Indeed, that was confirmed when it was learned that American Express had conferred with the State Department, asking for help in dealing with Arab pressure.

The company now also came under pressure from the representatives of the American Jewish community. Arnold Forster of the ADL recalls a visit with top American Express officials. "What we said to them was that the Jewish community in America is probably the most traveling community of any in our country." If it became publicly known that American Express had closed down its Israeli operation for good, then the ADL "could assure American Express that they were dead so far as the American Jewish community was concerned." Forster admits that this community couldn't do American Express any really heavy damage, but he says that wasn't what finally induced American Express to reopen its Israeli offices despite the Arab threats. The company understood, he says, "that there was another factor at play which was important to them in the American scheme of things: one's reputation in business still counts." Today, the company enjoys good relations with all parties, an indication again that the Arabs won't actually black-list a company which ignores the regulations if they want what it offers.

There are curious ways of getting onto the Arabs' capricious blacklist, and the Bulova Watch Company, which has been banned by the Arabs for the past thirty years, is an example. It has no distribution in Israel at all, except in duty-free airport shops, but it once committed the offense of helping Israel train high school students.

As chronicled by *Newsday*'s Long Island business editor, Daniel Kahn, the story of Bulova's tribulations began in the early 1950's when the Arde Bulova Foundation (named after the company's late chairman) established a trade school in Israel to train students in mechanics and tool making; this became part of Israel's Technion Institute in 1959. Bulova maintained a similar school in New York for handicapped students, including Arabs, but this failed to impress the Arab League.

Whether Bulova's school in Israel actually caused it to be blacklisted is still in question; Bulova has never been told why it is on the Arab boycott list. In fact, the firm was on the list eight full years before it even knew it was.

The first the company heard about blacklisting was in

March 1964, in a letter from its marketing man in Switzerland. He had been approached by an Arab agent, who claimed the Central Boycott Office had written to Bulova back in November 1956, and had shortly followed this up with another letter. "We never received either, to my knowledge," says Sol E. Flick, Bulova's vice-chairman and general counsel.

There followed a tragicomic series of maneuvers meant to get Bulova off the blacklist. First on the scene was Colonel Hisham al-Azim, of the Arab Boycott Office in Damascus, who suggested to Bulova's Swiss representative that the company retain a Syrian lawyer in Damascus, one Mwafak Atassi, to negotiate on its behalf with the boycott office. He also claimed that three of Bulova's top executives had shown "tendencies towards Israel." One of the three was Arde Bulova himself, then still chairman; the other two (both now retired from the company) were John Ballard, president, and Samuel Epstein, sales vice-president. Colonel al-Azim seemed to be suggesting that Bulova would find negotiations easier if it got rid of them.

More Arabs appeared on the scene shortly afterward. Mwafak Atassi's cousin Farhan, a naturalized American citizen, turned up in New York to negotiate; Bulova agreed to pay cousin Mwafak $5,000 to represent the company in the thirteen Arab states supporting the boycott, with another $10,000 if he was successful. Then Atassi started making demands—among them that Bulova state publicly that it would not lend further financial or moral support to Israel, and that it was ready to match past help to Israel with help to an Arab nation, preferably Syria—for Atassi was the nephew of Hashim al-Atassi, once Syria's president.

Bulova ignored these demands and grew increasingly suspicious when Mwafak Atassi said the boycott office, favorably impressed with the documents Bulova had sent it, would probably clear the company soon. What documents? Bulova had sent none and Atassi seemed to be making no sense—or was just trying to string the company along. Then a Kuwaiti newspaper announced that Bulova had just been placed on the Kuwaiti blacklist; this confusing news was followed by an assurance from the Swiss representative, who was in touch with the boycotters, that the news from Kuwait was just "routine" and presumably didn't mean anything at all. Bulova's doubts grew. "Apparently," said Vice-Chairman Flick, "you pay one lawyer and you're off the list; the next day you are on another list."

Atassi made further demands later that year, all of them firmly rejected by the company. Suddenly, all demands ceased. In February 1965 Farhan Atassi was sentenced to death in Syria, along with yet another cousin, both convicted as "American spies." Atassi was hanged publicly later that month; his alleged accomplice, an army major, was shot. The United States denied any involvement; perhaps the two men were simply victims of Syria's chronic cycle of coup and counter-coup.

That was the end of the matter for Bulova, but not for some Arabs. New Arab "negotiators" showed up, also suggesting that they could get the company off the blacklist—for a fee. Flick said it all seemed "to be a fruitful source of business for these people," and he added that as all the company's thirty subsidiaries had by then been blacklisted, "the game could have gone on forever."

Bulova's subsidiaries distribute the company's products in 120 countries; in 1974, it had net sales of almost $214 million. This made it a natural target for the Arab blackmailers and Flick in 1975 saw no way out—"unless the Arabs want our product." The company, he said, was indeed losing business which might have been available in Arab states, but the solution, he felt, lay in tougher action on the part of the U.S. government.

"It is wrong," Flick told reporter Kahn, "for any company to knuckle under or permit itself to be blackmailed. To get off [the boycott lists] you'll be asked to do something. They [the Arabs] want you to pay the price; but how many times, and to how many people?"[15]

THE PRICE ASKED is often a head. "Get that Jew off the board!" has often been the boycotters' cry to companies wishing to do business with the Arab world. One of the most notorious cases occurred in Britain in 1963. Briefly referred to earlier, the details provide a classic example of boycott-inspired anti-Semitism. The victim was Lord Mancroft, a member of the board of directors of Britain's Norwich Union Insurance Company.

Stormont Mancroft, who comes from an old Jewish family from Norwich in East Anglia, and who had been a Conservative Party Cabinet Minister in the 1950's, was forced by Arab League pressure to resign from Norwich Union's board, after four years on it. It was claimed that the Arabs did not object to Lord Mancroft being Jewish (the family name had been Samuel), but to the fact that he was also a director of Great Universal Stores, which was managed by another Jew (and a prominent supporter of Israel), Sir Isaac Wolfson. There were other ties. "Gussies" (as Great Universal Stores is known on the London Stock Exchange) had a subsidiary, Global Tours Ltd., and Global had a controlling interest in a Manchester firm, Charles S. Robinson, which did extensive business with Israel. Finally, Sir Isaac Wolfson contributed hundreds of thousands of pounds to Israeli charities, kept a holiday home in Israel and made no secret of his interest in helping Israel in every way.

Norwich Union itself did little business with the Arab world, far less than with Jewish firms in Britain; at the time of its total surrender to Arab pressure in the "Mancroft Affair," its Arab business was estimated to be a possible £100,000, or $240,000 at the time. But it did do a great deal of marine insurance business, and it was through this that the Arab League was able to apply pressure. The company feared the Arabs might blacklist shipping companies that insured through Norwich Union, and prevent their vessels from using transit and port facilities in Arab states.

Lord Mancroft resigned, obviously under considerable personal pressure to get his company off the hook. He did so with commendable dignity, a fact which did not escape the notice of the British public, which admires dignity. At the same time, the British do *not* like public scandals, particularly when they involve a breach of fair and "decent" behavior. The fact that the directors of a major British company had knuckled under to foreign pressure outraged them. That the pressure had been applied by two tiny Arab states (Kuwait and Bahrein had acted as front runners for the Arab League) was an added insult to national pride.

The storm of protest which broke forced Norwich Union to admit publicly that Lord Mancroft had indeed resigned because of Arab pressure and prompted the British government, then led by Conservative Prime Minister Sir Alec Douglas-Home, to take swift action.

The Foreign Secretary, R. A. Butler, spent an hour conferring with the Israeli ambassador about the Arab Trade Boycott, and then Lord Carrington of the Foreign Office summoned three Arab ambassadors: Sheik Hafiz Wahba of Saudi Arabia, M. Abdul Rahman al-Bazzaz of Iraq and Abdel Salam Busairi of Libya. They were told that the government opposed outside interference in British domestic affairs and in British companies' freedom to trade, that the government "strongly resented pressure on British firms to discriminate on any grounds among their British staff," and that it also "strongly disapproved of action by the Arab embassies in London designed to bring pressure on British firms to comply with the boycott." It hoped "these practices would not continue," a Foreign Office spokesman announced.

It was now the Arab League's turn to be outraged. It announced that British "interference" with the boycott would force Arab countries to reconsider their economic ties with the United Kingdom. Lord Carrington's statement, the Arab League said, "constitutes support of the Zionist viewpoint against a system dictated by the legitimate right of self-defense against Zionist aggression."

The British government wanted to stay out of the Arab-Israeli dispute, but Foreign Secretary Butler saw the Mancroft incident as interference in the domestic affairs of the nation, and made this plain. Government spokesmen in Parliament criticized Arab embassies in London for putting pressure on British firms; this in turn led twelve Arab ambassadors in London to tell the British that the boycott of Israel was none of their business.

In the midst of this storm, Norwich Union got rattled and

proposed to Lord Mancroft that he rejoin its board—then perhaps regretting the gesture immediately afterwards, for the Arab Information Centre in London promptly announced that the boycott office would now have to review Norwich Union's case all over again, and that it "would not be surprised if they are put back on the blacklist."

Lord Mancroft declined to rejoin Norwich Union's board, which got the company off the hook. In Cairo the boycott office issued a statement saying that as it had given Norwich Union "three months notice for the removal of Lord Mancroft" and as the company had now "complied with the boycott regulations," it would ask all Arab countries to extend all facilities to Norwich Union.

This shameful situation was not improved by Norwich Union's president, Sir Robert Bignold, telling the Board of Deputies of British Jews that it had never been the intention of his company to encourage, aid or comfort the Arab boycott of Israel. London's *Guardian* made the point that Norwich Union could have snapped its fingers at the Arab threats, but had chosen to capitulate. "Baldly put, it yielded to blackmail by a group of foreign Powers against a citizen of this country," the paper said. It continued:

> With evident sincerity, the directors of the Norwich Union have stated that they are not anti-Semitic. There is an easy answer to that. Anti-Semitism is not simply a matter of beating Jews to death or of reviling them in the streets; it includes any and every kind of discrimination against them. It is a mere quibble to say that Lord Mancroft was forced to leave the Board, not because he was a Jew, but because he was a director of Great Universal Stores, a Jewish firm. In the moral sense this makes no differences at all; in the material sense it is a mere nuance. . . .
>
> The people of Israel are Jews, and connivance with the boycott is anti-Semitism. The "Mancroft Affair" is shameful —most of all for Britons who have preened themselves that they are "not as the Nazis were." The best that can be hoped for from this disgraceful episode is that it may have salutary consequences.

Unfortunately, it did not. Six months after the affair, Lord Mancroft was induced to withdraw his candidacy for the post of president of the London Chamber of Commerce. He had been invited to stand for office before Christmas 1963, and his appointment should have followed as a matter of course. He was asked to withdraw as a result, again, of Arab pressure—direct or indirect made little difference. It was said that members of the Chamber who traded with Arab states might have been embarrassed by the presence of the Jewish peer.

For Lord Mancroft the entire affair was enormously painful; he took it all, however, with forbearance and grace, and even had an ironic comment to make just after the Chamber rejected him. Noting that he was also president of the West Ham Boys' Club, he said he hoped the lads wouldn't "get wind of this business. It might put something into their heads. Fortunately," he added, "I believe the club has few Arab members."[16]

DISCRIMINATION against Jews would have been an inevitable by-product of the total Arab war against the Jewish state, even without the underlying and historical anti-Semitism of the Arab world.[17] But Arabs are not always consistent people, as their boycotting of Jews and Jewish products has shown. This point was made in trenchant terms in New York's *Jewish Press*, by Rabbi Jacob Hecht.[18]

Arabs who are totally "loyal" to their "cause" are, Hecht explained, meant to avoid all contact with Jewish influence. The Arab League, he therefore suggested, might consider instructing Arabs who have syphilis not to use curative salvarsan —discovered by a Jew, Paul Ehrlich. They must not even seek to find out whether they have syphilis, because the Wassermann test, used for that purpose, is also the discovery of a Jew. The same holds for gonorrhea.

Arabs with heart disease must shun digitalis, evolved by the Jew Ludwig Traube. They must manage without cocaine and pyramidon—both Jewish discoveries—and must submit to a whole host of diseases, from polio and diphtheria, because preventatives or cures are the work of Jews. They must not avail themselves of the work and wisdom of dozens of Nobel Prize-winners. In short, Rabbi Hecht suggested, loyal and totally committed Arabs must be prepared to suffer supinely from syphilis, gonorrhea, heart disease, typhus, diabetes, mental disorders, brain damage, infantile paralysis, convulsions . . . The list is endless if the boycott of Jewish products is to be complete.

Arabs, of course, do not for a moment think of depriving themselves of Jewish medical and scientific research. But the *reductio ad absurdum* sketched out by Rabbi Hecht has almost become a reality in other fields. Dozens of artists and entertainers, for example, and any films in which they appear, have been blacklisted by the Central Boycott Office in Damascus. Several of these performers are not Jewish but are considered to be pro-Israel. They include Harry Belafonte, Theodore Bikel, Eddie Cantor, Jeff Chandler, Sammy Davis Jr., Kirk Douglas, Eddie Fisher, Juliette Greco, Laurence Harvey, Helen Hayes, Jascha Heifetz, George Jessel, Danny Kaye, Eartha Kitt, Jerry Lewis, Sophia Loren, Yehudi Menuhin, Arthur Miller, Sal Mineo, Marilyn Monroe, Paul Newman, Edward G. Robinson, Arthur Rubinstein, Phil Silvers, Frank Sinatra, Isaac Stern, Elizabeth Taylor, Esther Williams, Shelley Winters and Joanne Woodward.

Films showing Elizabeth Taylor, a convert to Judaism, were banned in 1959 because of the friendly feelings the actress had expressed for Israel, and for her purchase of $100,000 worth of Israel Bonds. Sophia Loren was blacklisted for having made the film *Judith* in Israel. Paul Newman and Sal Mineo were blacklisted for their roles in *Exodus*, and all the films of Otto Preminger because he had made that movie. Indeed, when *Exodus* was first released, the Egyptian press called for the banning of any and all United Artists films—and Egypt, along with Lebanon, had the only sizable motion picture audience in the Arab Middle East.

Arab sensitivities seem very acute. A kissing scene in *Funny Girl* between Barbra Streisand, a Jew, and Omar Sharif, an Arab, caused great offense, and Joan Baez, the folk singer, also outraged the Arabs—in this case the Syrian press—by some "Zionist" lyrics she sang. One included a reference to standing at a station, "with a ticket to the Promised Land," and another offended even more, as it referred to "the children Moses led through the desert."[19]

Support for Israel doesn't therefore seem the only reason entertainers, films and even motion picture companies are banned or threatened with blacklisting in the Arab world. *Variety*, the show business journal, reported on April 7, 1954, that four American movie companies (Metro-Goldwyn-Mayer, Columbia, Universal and Paramount) had been scrutinized by Arab boycott agents to establish "the number of Jews employed by the four" and "whether their 'principals' are Christian or Jewish."

"Zionist influences" were even discovered in a cantata composed by the Austrian Gottfried von Einem, to mark United Nations Day in 1975. The cantata was based on the Twelfth Psalm, but the Arabs demanded and obtained the omission of the offensive words, "Behold, He that keepeth Israel shall neither slumber nor sleep."

Israel's chief representative to the UN, General Chaim Herzog, protested, as did the Temple University Choir, which was to take part in the concert. Von Einem first claimed his deletion was not politically motivated, that it was derived from an abridged German version of the Psalm. He even offered to compose a special song for the chorus, called "The Keeper of Israel." Finally, a UN "consensus compromise" was reached, and Herzog rounded off the incident with the dry comment that from what he heard in the UN, he "was not surprised they are trying to rewrite the Bible" there.[20]

Two ludicrous boycott incursions into the arts relate to Walt Disney and to a Soviet spy ring. *Snow White and the Seven Dwarfs* was blacklisted because the Prince's horse was called "Samson" in the film—a clear "Zionistic allusion." The Arab boycotters even suggested that the film could be taken off the blacklist if the horse was given a new name. Damascus suggested "Simpson"!

The Soviet spy ring which fell afoul of the Arabs was the "Red Orchestra," an anti-Nazi organization that operated in Europe during World War II. A leading member of its Polish branch survived the war, and applied for permission to emigrate to Israel. It was eventually granted in 1974. When he left for Israel, the international press recalled his work for the "Red Orchestra," which was promptly put on the Arab blacklist— but as a musical ensemble which was assumed to have performed in Israel! A month or two later, red-faced boycotters announced that the "Red Orchestra" was no longer blacklisted.

Equally absurd in its way was the blacklisting of Giuseppe Verdi's opera, *Nabuco*, held by the Arabs to "present an historic event in a way likely to create sympathy for the Jews and serve Israeli propaganda." The "event" was the demand of the Children of Israel to be released from Babylonian captivity under King Nebuchadnezzar.[21] The Arab League felt that this ancient quest of the Jews to be allowed to return to live in their own land had present-day associations.

Another bizarre occurrence was the blacklisting of a Yale Glee Club recording because the Arabs had discovered Hebrew writing on the Yale University seal. And in 1965, according to *Near East Report*, there was even an Arab threat to "boycott" Prince Philip, the Duke of Edinburgh, because he had attended a Glasgow party sponsored by the Women's International Zionist Organization aboard a ferry being built for the Israel Merchant Marine.

The cosmetics firm of Helena Rubinstein has been placed on a blacklist, along with the couturier Balmain and the "Club Mediterranée," the latter because it had a camp in Israel. The same list also included several French wine firms and vineyards, either because they were Jewish-owned or because Jews were investors in them. Château Mouton-Rothschild and Château Lafite-Rothschild were "naturals" for blacklisting among the vineyards of Bordeaux, and Château Smith Haut-Lafite was probably included by mistake. But the Arabs went further and blacklisted entire winegrowing communes: Saint-Émilion, Graves, Médoc and Sauternes in the Bordeaux region; Montrachet, Volnay and Macon in Burgundy; Châteauneuf-du-Pape on the Rhone; Muscadet and Pouilly on the Loire; and the whole area of Chablis.[22]

According to London's *Financial Times,* the main reason why these districts were included on the blacklist was that Arab attempts to buy into properties had been rebuffed by the French growers and wine merchants; this, one boycott official stated, was an "affront."

The French wine trade will have been singularly unaffected by the whole affair. Historically, it has done little business with the Arab Middle East, though it does import a substantial amount of wine from Arab Algeria and Morocco; as for Israel, it produces most of the wine drunk within its own borders.

Even religions have been blacklisted. In 1974 the Middle East News Agency reported from Damascus that the Arab League Boycott Conference, held in Cairo that February, would deal "with the subject of the Bahais, who have their religious center in Israel, and consider ways of combatting their activity, which supports Zionism and its aggressive objectives." The Bahai faith, which claims two million adherents, was founded in 1862 as an offshoot of the Shiite Moslem sect in Persia, and preaches world peace, the unity of mankind and equal reverence for all the founders of the world's religions. It had already been banned for three years in Morocco, Egypt and Iraq, and ever since 1975 was blacklisted throughout all other Arab League states as well.[23] John Wade, the faith's British secretary-general, said the world-wide religion had probably been banned because its members sent money to Israel for the upkeep of its holy places there, which led John Torode in Britain's *Guardian* to wonder, "Will the boycott office outlaw Roman Catholicism next?" His reply was, "I doubt it. The Pope has more divisions."[24]

Both Jehovah's Witnesses and the Watchtower Bible and Tract Society were banned by the Lebanese Boycott Office (and possibly elsewhere as well). *Al-Gurida* claimed in 1971 that the Witnesses followed the instructions of World Zionism. In outlawing them, the Arabs have followed the example of the Nazis, who persecuted the Witnesses, and the Communists, who do so in the USSR and in other East European states. Oddly, while Reform Judaism in the United States, represented by the Union of American Hebrew Congregations, is on the Saudi Arabian blacklist, Orthodox and Conservative Jewish groups are not. Saudi Arabia has, however, taken an extremely anti-Christian line, as shown in a document issued by its boycott office in February 1975.[25] This "Partial List of Manufacturers Whose Products Are Contraband" contained the following passage: "All religious articles, other than [of] the Moslem religion, such as Bibles and crucifixes, will be destroyed."

EVEN COUNTRIES that are fellow-members with the Arab nations at the UN have come under boycott threat and black-listing. In 1960, when a Ceylonese envoy was accredited in Israel, Syria persuaded the Central Boycott Office to ban the importation of products from Ceylon (now Sri Lanka) into the Arab world. And in March 1975, the Arabs decided to boycott the Maldives Republic, declaring that any vessels which visited the Maldives would be prohibited from calling at Arab ports.

The Maldives consist of seventeen groups of small islands, about four hundred miles southwest of Sri Lanka, and have a population of about 90,000. The inhabitants are Moslems. Their livelihood depends on trading, and their fleet of cargo ships did most of its trade with Arab ports in the Persian Gulf, Southern Arabia and Somalia. The Arabs singled out this small and inoffensive country for three reasons. The Maldives had, in spite of political pressure, maintained diplomatic relations with Israel. They had not attended the 1974 Islamic Summit Conference in Lahore. Finally, they had refused to vote against Israel in the UN during 1974, when there were six key resolutions dealing with the Palestinians.* The Maldives had simply absented themselves from these votes, and this was regarded as a hostile act by the Arabs. The boycott set a dangerous

---

* These resolutions were: the invitation to the PLO to be heard at the UN, the status of the PLO, the situation in the Israel-occupied territories, the future of refugees, the political rights of the Palestinians, and the limitation of Israel's right of answer in the UN.

precedent, for while boycotting an enemy may be held to have justification, the victim here was a state which demonstrably wished merely to preserve its neutrality over a dispute in which it was not involved. The Maldives government, under heavy pressure, acted with more discretion than courage, and "suspended" relations with Israel by mutual agreement, whereupon the Arab threat was dropped.

Quite obviously, the Arabs selected both the Maldives and Sri Lanka for pressure because they were small and economically weak; the Arab League has probably never seriously considered banning dealings with all countries which maintain diplomatic ties with Israel. But if they have not blacklisted the United States and European countries such as the United Kingdom, they have certainly not hesitated to put their governments under Arab boycott pressure. In 1977 they even blacklisted the international Masonic order. In June, during a ten-day conference in Alexandria, Egypt, the Arab League boycott offices ordered the closure of all Masonic lodges in Arab countries, and an end to cooperation with Masonic societies throughout the world. The reason given by Cairo's daily *al-Ahram*: the Arabs discovered that the Masons had participated in the first Zionist conference, held in Basle, Switzerland, in 1897, and that they "still maintain close connections with Israel." The Masons, of course, try to maintain good relations with all countries and to steer clear of politics. It is just this evenhandedness which was their "crime" in Arab eyes.[26]

CHAPTER IV

Buck-passing and Bigotry

SINCE THE 1950's the United States government, in certain of its policies, has been periodically helping the Arabs in their war against the Jews. This was most recently revealed in 1975, during hearings before a U.S. Senate subcommittee, which studied the work the U.S. Army Corps of Engineers performs in the Kingdom of Saudi Arabia.

The construction projects which the Corps runs for the Saudis were worth about $4 billion in 1975, fully paid by Saudi Arabia. These are both civil and military in nature, often involve U.S. civilian subcontractors hired by the Corps and, significantly, are governed by a 1964 agreement which specifies not only that Saudi Arabian law applies in all arrangements involved, but that the Saudis have the right to veto American contractors whom the Corps recommends.*

Corps representatives appeared before a Senate subcommittee in February of 1975 and, under questioning, admitted collusion with Saudi Arabian anti-Jewish exclusion policies. The Corps excluded from projects it managed in Saudi Arabia any Jewish soldiers and civilian Jewish employees of American companies working for the Corps.[1]

---

* No other country makes this demand in its agreements with the Corps of Engineers.

Was the U.S. Army "acquiescing on instructions of the Department of State?" asked a senator. Colonel William L. Durham, deputy director of military construction in the Office of the Chief of Engineers, replied, "As I understand the agreements—yes, sir."[2] Passing the buck, the colonel pleaded that the matter was therefore "beyond the purview of the Corps."

About one hundred military and civilian employees of the U.S. Army and its subcontractors were involved; the numbers were not very large, but the senators were more interested in the principle at stake.

"If the requirement of a project is to go to Saudi Arabia, a Jew cannot go?" another senator asked, and the colonel admitted, "That is correct. . . If you're of the Jewish faith, you don't bother to apply to work there."[3]

Next to appear was Deputy Assistant Secretary of State Harold H. Saunders, who said the State Department took a "low-key approach" to the matter, revealing that it chose to ignore the fact that anti-Semitic Saudi Arabian policies were being abetted by the U.S. government within the United States. He claimed the State Department had helped some individual Jews get visas to enter Saudi Arabia, but when asked to prove this by citing specific cases, he declined. Nevertheless, he insisted "there are people of the Jewish faith that go in and out of Saudi Arabia doing business."

Someone cracked, "Kissinger!," and the room filled with laughter.[4]

SAUDI ARABIA'S exclusion of Jews was neither covert nor anything new. As far back as 1950 the Saudi Finance Ministry wrote that the Kingdom's legations could issue visas to company employees "provided the companies give an undertaking to the effect that those for whom visas are required are not undesirable persons, it being understood that undesirable persons include Jews."[5] In 1956 the Saudis refused to allow the United States to station American Jewish servicemen at the base in Dhahran, and although the Eisenhower Administration tried to get them to modify this position, neither King Saud nor his successor, King Faisal, were willing to budge. When that base agreement ended, the problem was thought to have "resolved itself," but the surrender of the U.S. Corps of Engineers in the 1970's proved it had not.

The American press was quick to react to the congressional disclosures. It condemned the cooperation the government was giving the Saudis in implementing their anti-Jewish policies, and pointed out that it was responsible for enforcing the 1964 Civil Rights Act, which forbids bias based on race, religion, sex, age or national origin. Papers drew attention to Saudi Arabia as being the only country in the world where chattel slavery was still protected and encouraged by law and where children were still legally sold into slavery and prostitution. They also disclosed that King Faisal was notorious for handing racist and anti-Semitic literature to visiting newsmen, and for publicly expressing approval of Hitler's policies.

Prompted by the immediate press reaction, James Schlesinger, then Secretary of Defense, reversed Pentagon policies the day after the hearings. The Defense Department announced it would no longer anticipate Saudi Arabian objections by screening out Jewish personnel in advance, leaving the Saudis to do their own discriminatory screening. On February 26, President Ford was questioned about the Army's actions at a press conference in Hollywood, Florida.

"I want there to be no doubt about the position of the United States," he announced. "Such discrimination is totally contrary to the American tradition and repugnant to American principles. It has no place in the free practice of commerce and in the world. . . ."

Ford ordered the departments of Commerce, Justice and State to investigate charges of discrimination against Americans and promised to take "appropriate action" if the allegations proved true. Fearing that Arab investments in the United States might bring Arab anti-Semitism in their train, the President warned foreign businessmen and investors that they were "welcome in the United States" so long as "they are willing to conform to the principles of our society."[6]

[[72]]

That declaration outraged Commissioner-General Mahgoub of the Central Boycott Office. In Cairo he insisted that "the Arab boycott of Israel is a legitimate means of legitimate self-defense" and "constitutes a force to realize a just peace in the Middle East."[7]

In Washington, there followed government declarations against boycott-connected anti-Jewish discrimination, but there were indications that these might prove mainly rhetorical. "Race, religion, color, creed or national origin can never be the bases for personnel actions, award of contracts or for any of our activities," said Army Secretary Howard H. Callaway in an official memorandum addressed to all top Army officials. "We must also ensure that we do not become the screening agent, or act as a proxy, for any discrimination. Our actions must convey the Army's clear and unreserved commitment to the spirit, goals and intent of Equal Employment Opportunity laws and regulations."

Then came the news that a Pentagon agreement with the Vinnell Corporation of Alhambra, California, to train Saudi Arabian national guardsmen contained a clearly discriminatory clause: "All personnel shall be from countries recognized by the SAG [Saudi Arabian Government] and have no history of personal contact or interest in unrecognized countries."

As Israel is not recognized by Saudi Arabia, and as American Jews may be said to have an interest in and possibly contacts with the Jewish state, or even dual nationality, this clause again showed Defense Department collusion with Saudi anti-Jewish policies. The argument that the Saudis simply wouldn't allow American Jews in, and that therefore the U.S. government and U.S. companies were helpless, failed to impress New York Congresswoman Bella Abzug. "What we are really doing," she said, "is allowing another country to determine what the policies of this country will be."[8]

Yet the argument that the United States was helpless in the face of Saudi demands was not dropped. On April 9, 1975, Colonel Durham of the Corps of Engineers again appeared before Congress, this time before a House subcommittee. The

1964 U.S.–Saudi Arabian agreement, he maintained, recognized "the responsibility of the Corps of Engineers to adhere to the laws and customs of that country in performing its mission"; in addition, that Saudi Arabia "shall issue entry visas according to its laws." Requests for visas to Saudi Arabia, he said, had to be accompanied by either the applicant's "baptismal certificate, birth certificate showing religion, marriage certificate showing church wedding or letter from church showing membership."[9]

Senators were angered by U.S. government collaboration in visa restrictions applying to its citizens, especially in a matter involving U.S. assistance to the Saudis. They instituted moves to block $1.45 billion in U.S. military sales to Saudi Arabia unless that nation stopped discriminating against American Jews—and, for that matter, American women and blacks as well. (Saudi policy forbids women entering the country either as personnel of a company or as unaccompanied individuals; the Saudis, in fact, barred American women from working on U.S. Army projects in their country. And the Army accepted this restriction, in violation of equal employment opportunity legislation. Furthermore, the Saudis had also often denied entrance to American blacks. This had been kept quiet "for fear of angering the Saudis," as a source within Senator Church's subcommittee told the press. "They are afraid of Black Muslims getting into the country," he said. "They consider them schismatics—a threat to their faith. After all, they are white Muslims."[10])

Months later it became evident that the U.S. government was still not ready to take a strong stand on the matter beyond refusing to "pre-screen" Jews for the convenience of the Saudis, and inserting a federally mandated anti-discrimination clause into the Pentagon's contract with Vinnell, after the American Jewish Committee had protested to the Defense Secretary. In the matter of Saudi visa policies, however, the Defense Department continued to plead it was defenseless.

"We have been advised by the Department of State that a sovereign state has the right to determine to whom it will issue visas," protested John F. Ahearne, a Deputy Assistant Secretary of Defense. He added that if discrimination against American Jews occurred, Defense would refer the matter to the State Department, which in turn would take it up with the foreign government involved.[11] This was again bureaucratic buck-passing. As the ADL pointed out, Defense was continuing its "cooperation with Arab boycotters" and failing to insist "that a halt be called to anti-Jewish discrimination" as its price for such cooperation.[12]

More evidence of recent U.S. Army discrimination piled up. In the summer of 1975 a report released by a General Officers Steering Committee on Equal Opportunity did more than merely confirm that the Army didn't send Jews to Saudi Arabia. It revealed that the Army also didn't send Greek-Americans to Turkey, for fear of offending the Turks, or Turkish-Americans to Greece, for fear of offending the Greeks; that it assigned a disproportionate number of soldiers with Spanish surnames to Latin American countries, presumably to please the Latin Americans, and nominated women to high-level positions on the basis of looks and personalities, presumably to please the males.[13]

A picture was emerging of the most powerful military establishment in the world pandering to everyone's prejudices everywhere, and while a sorry one, it was neither new nor surprising. In 1975, there had been a similar surrender in a non-Jewish matter, indicating that a tendency to capitulate, rather than any anti-Jewish bias, had probably motivated the Army's action in the Saudi case. That year a black colonel, Travis M. Gafford, was withdrawn from consideration as Chief, Army Section, U.S. Military Group Chile, because Pentagon officers had again engaged in a little familiar "pre-screening," fearing a black officer might be offensive to the Chileans. After this became public knowledge, Defense Secretary Schlesinger admitted the action had been an "error" which "should not be tolerated."[14]

The same might be said to apply to Pentagon collusion with Saudi Arabia's racist policies. In the 1950's, for example, Saudi Arabia required the Arabian American Oil Company (ARAM-

CO) not to employ Jews *anywhere,* and the State Department at that time had been so fearful of offending the Kingdom that it actually intervened on behalf of ARAMCO when the company was charged with violating New York State's laws against discrimination in employment. (The company—and the State Department—lost in the N.Y. State Supreme Court.*)

By late 1975 the Pentagon had begun to learn the obvious lesson and started to take public opinion into account. Calling for bids for the manufacture in the United States of Saudi army uniforms, it stated that discrimination would not be tolerated "in the solicitation, the award or the performance of these or any other Department of Defense procurements."[15]

OVERT U.S. GOVERNMENT collaboration with Saudi Arabia's racist policies may have stopped, but the policies themselves have not been dropped by the Saudi government. In 1976 and 1977 there were intermittent reports that Jewish businessmen were occasionally being allowed into Saudi Arabia, and had actually transacted a deal or two there; other reports said a hospital in Saudi Arabia contained medical equipment of Israeli manufacture and that some markets in the country sold Israeli citrus fruit. The businessmen were distinct exceptions, however, to the continuing Saudi demand that all visa applications provide proof that the applicant was a Christian, if not Moslem;† the fruit and equipment presumably had been re-exported to Saudi Arabia from Jordan, after having crossed the "open bridges" from Israel.

Boycott-related cases of anti-Semitism continue to occur in

---

* Said the Court: "If the enforcement of the public policy of New York State would embarrass the State Department in the Near East, then it should be said that the honor of American citizenship—if it remains for New York State to uphold it—will survive ARAMCO's fall from Arab grace."

† "Non-Muslims should produce a Certificate of Religion, e.g. Original Marriage Certificate if married in the Church, or Baptismal Certificate, or Letter from Church on Church Headed Paper and bearing the Church Seal." (As given in *Visa Regulations and Application,* Royal Consulate General of Saudi Arabia, London.)

the United States and elsewhere. Their total may never be
known, because the people involved seldom want publicity and
also because it is hard to establish with certainty that someone
was fired from a job, or failed to obtain one, because of anti-
Jewish boycott pressures. As has already been mentioned, a "voluntary boycott" has developed in the wake of the Arabs' own
primary, secondary and tertiary boycotts, and this operates without any Arab pressure being applied. Companies which neither
trade with Israel nor the Arab world, but which hope to do
business with the oil-rich Middle East states in the future, often
anticipate boycott pressures voluntarily, and take actions which
they think will make them more acceptable candidates for
Arab trade. They sometimes do this by not seeking Israeli business, or refusing to take it up when it is offered to them (even
business permitted by Arab boycott rules); worse, they often
"launder" themselves of Jewish connections, associations and
employees without ever having been asked to do so by the Arabs.

The cases of voluntary boycott are hard to establish for the
simple reason that it is difficult to prove that a company's
often polite and friendly refusal to trade with Israel is motivated
by fear of the boycotters' possible reprisals. Nevertheless, it is
generally believed by government officials and business circles
in the United States, Britain and other countries, such as West
Germany, that this voluntary boycott is very prevalent, and, as
one Bonn official told us, "the biggest problem of all."

Boycott-related cases of anti-Semitism, however, are just as
big a problem, and these are generally believed to be legion.
While we will take up non-American cases separately, here are
a few "case histories" from the United States alone:

• On July 21, 1975, the U.S. State Department admitted,
in a letter to the U.S. Department of Commerce, that Jordan
had requested an American exporter to certify that none of the
members of his company's board of directors belonged to the
Jewish faith. The State Department was able in this case to
report some success. The U.S. ambassador in Amman, Jordan,
had taken the matter up and had been assured the request had

not come from "responsible" officials.[16] Once again, government support caused the boycotters to back down in double-quick time; in fact, they had here been nailed outright, to the embarrassment of the Jordanian government, for the anti-Jewish nature of the boycott is not always meant to be so explicit.

• In 1975 it was revealed that Bendix-Siyanco of Columbia, Maryland, screened out Jewish job applicants, again to satisfy the Saudis, for whose Army Ordnance Corps it recruited management personnel. The method the company used was simple: it involved a company job-application questionnaire which, in violation of the Civil Rights Act and Presidential Order 11246, asked the applicant's religion. Bendix-Siyanco is a subsidiary of Bendix Field Engineering Corporation, itself a division of a major U.S. defense contractor, Bendix Corporation of Michigan. The U.S. Army Corps of Engineers was involved in this case, for it supervised the Bendix-Siyanco contracts with Saudi Arabia. After these revelations, the company chairman stated that the offending employment application form had been withdrawn (earlier, a company spokesman had claimed it never existed), but he conceded to a reporter that this "withdrawal" would not affect the composition of the work force in Saudi Arabia.[17]

• More cases of anti-Jewish discrimination came to light when ABS Worldwide Technical Services was charged with refusing two engineers permission to apply for jobs in Bahrein, on the Persian Gulf. "ABS" stands for American Bureau of Shipping, consultants to the international maritime industry.

One engineer, Erica Wagner, was flatly told she couldn't enter Bahrein because she was Jewish; the other, Leonard Messer, had a more complicated story to tell. A New Jersey employment agency had sent Messer for an interview with the company, which needed a supervisor of welding operations for Bahrein offshore oil pipelines. The interview, said Besser, went well—until the interviewer asked if he was a Jew. "I was tempted to tell him to go screw himself," Messer reports, "but I was interested in what he really had to offer." He told the interviewer that he was not Jewish, but that didn't satisfy the man completely, for he then asked whether any member of Messer's family was Jewish. Again, Messer replied in the negative, but after he left he had second thoughts, and telephoned to admit that his wife was indeed Jewish. Did that mean, he asked, that he was no longer qualified for the job? "That's right," the interviewer replied.

This interviewer later told the press he couldn't recall ever having met Mr. Messer, and that there was no company policy against hiring Jews for work in Arab countries. Later still, he mentioned visa requirements, and finally resorted to the shopworn Eichmann excuse: "All I do is just follow instructions."[18] A reporter subsequently asked a Bahrein official about visa requirements, and he claimed his country did not exclude Jews, which made either the job interviewer or the diplomat a liar. The fact is, of course, that Arab anti-Jewish exclusionary provisions are not in every case enshrined in writing and in law.

• Another example of anti-Semitic restrictions was brought to light by the American Jewish Committee. Bertram H. Gold, its executive vice-president, revealed that the Advest Company, a leading U.S. investment corporation, was inviting clients to a tour of the Middle East, asking them in advance to supply "a signed statement by a clergyman [preferably on church stationery] attesting that the participant is a Christian." Jewish businessmen, he said, were encouraged to join by "passing" as non-Jews. After the American Jewish Committee protested to Advest, and to the U.S. State Department (which had given its blessing to the company's efforts), the company apologized, disclaiming discriminatory intent, and promised that future trips would be open to all.[19]

• Eleanor Holmes Norton, New York City Human Rights Commissioner, warned employers in late 1975 that they might face legal action if they discriminated against Jews in employment because of Arab or other foreign pressures. She was prompted to do so because a receptionist-typist for the American Independent Oil Company, Inc., whose job required greeting Arab visitors had allegedly been fired because she was Jewish.[20]

• Companies that have face-to-face dealings with Arabs

are the most vulnerable to anti-Semitic pressures, and architectural and building firms working on Middle East projects are prime targets. One American company, for example, with one hundred architects on its staff, began negotiations with the Arab world and, hoping to make itself more acceptable, reprinted its stationery to eliminate twelve Jewish names on its letterhead.[21] This is not a unique case. Hard-pressed American (as well as other) architects have in recent years been finding business in the oil-rich Arab world. "Overseas work for United States architecture and engineering firms is climbing at a rate of 10 to 15 percent annually," reported *Progressive Architecture*, and in Saudi Arabia and the Persian Gulf states architects were "finding eager clients anxious to catch up with the West." The magazine referred to the "ban by Arab bloc countries against anyone judged partisan towards Israel—including American professionals who are Jewish" and reported further that "any architect traveling in one of these nations has to obtain from a clergyman a letter stating his religious views." It revealed that one firm's leading specialist on hospitals had been excluded from trips to his own firm's Middle East projects, while some architects were afraid these Arab anti-Jewish prejudices would determine who gets hired or promoted in America itself.[22]

Some sample cases:

• A Cambridge, Massachusetts, architectural firm rejected the application for employment by an Israeli-American who had superior qualifications on the grounds that sixty percent of the firm's business was with three Arab countries.[23]

• A Watertown, Massachusetts, architectural firm turned down an American Jewish applicant because an Arab country with whom it wished to deal declared that Jews "could neither be placed in charge of a project nor be employed on a project."[24]

• A prominent building contractor in Charlotte, North Carolina, who won a multimillion-dollar contract with Saudi Arabia and opened a Cairo office, was instructed that no Jewish employees were to be brought into Saudi Arabia and that specified blacklisted products should not be used in construction work there.[25]

[[80]]

• A Chicago firm of architects and consulting engineers negotiating with the Saudis was asked to supply a list of firms for which it had worked in the past. When the Saudis asked whether one or two of these firms were Jewish-owned and the architectural company said it didn't know, the Saudis broke off negotiations. The architects have since removed the names of the "questionable" former clients from the firm's published list.[26]

• In an article on how U.S. architectural firms are selling out to the Arab boycott (headlined, "No Jews Need Apply"), Ellen Perry Berkeley revealed in the *Village Voice* that American firms wishing to be included in contracts in the Arab Middle East need to answer seven questions to the Arabs' satisfaction. She paraphrased them as follows:

1. We have not, in the past, done any work for the state of Israel that increased its military strength or Gross National Product.
2. We are not now working for Israel.
3. We have no prospects for working for Israel in the future.
4. We will not assign any Israelis to the project.
5. We will not assign any Jews to the project in any position of authority.
6. We will not assign any Jews at all to the project.
7. We will not have any Jews at all in the office.

The author quoted three typical statements that firms were required to sign.

From the Kuwait Planning Board: "In order that your offer may be considered, it is necessary that you furnish us with a certificate declaring that you have no dealings whatever with Israel . . ."

From the Egyptian Ministry of Housing and Reconstruction: "In submitting a proposal, the consultant declares that he does not possess any plant, firm or branch in Israel, and that he does not participate in any firm or company established in Israel, and he has not any supply, manufacturing, assembling, license, or technical assistance agreement with any firm, company or person established or resident in Israel. The consultant

[[81]]

further undertakes not to have, either by himself or through an intermediary, any such activity in Israel and not to contribute in any way to consolidate the economy or military effects of Israel."

From a Saudi Arabian government ministry: "Enclose a copy of the letter issued by the Royal Saudi Arabian Embassy/ Consulate in your country stating that your firm [and principals and associates] is not on the Arab boycott list."

Because the building industry, architects included, regards Jewish names as an embarrassment whenever Arabs are around, the "voluntary boycott" pervades this field. Some firms "launder" themselves of Jewish connections before even seeking business in the Arab world, and some carefully segregate their Jewish workers to projects where they are unlikely to meet Arab clients.

Restrictions against Jews, according to the president of one chapter of the American Institute of Architects, are fewer whenever the Arabs need Western help. Still, it is believed that anti-Jewish pressure will continue unless firmly resisted. While the Arabs may need Western help, Western firms also need the Arabs. "The bitter truth is that the Arabs are keeping a lot of firms alive," one architect told the *Village Voice*, "and the Jews go along with it, glad to have *any* job when the economy is so rotten."[27]

• In November 1975, Governor Jerry Brown of California ordered his Department of Transportation to "cease any further negotiations" with Saudi Arabia unless "effective assurances" were given to protect California workers against discrimination in the Middle East. Saudi Arabia had wanted to hire five hundred highway engineers, about to be laid off in California, to build roads in that country. It then became known that the Saudis would not accept Jewish—or black or female—workers. The Saudi government denounced as false reports that blacks and women would not be recruited for the $25 million project, but affirmed it wouldn't give any entry visas to "Zionists." J. Anthony Kline, Governor Brown's legal secretary, commented on the Saudi definition of "Zionist": "It is hard to tell exactly what they mean by Zionists even after a week of talks with the U.S. State Department and Saudi representatives. . . In the end I think that, realistically speaking, the Saudi government defines Zionists as all Jews." The contract was canceled by California.[28]

• Also in California, a suit charging religious discrimination was filed against World Airways, Inc., the largest charter airline in the world, on the grounds that the company had threatened to dismiss employees who refused to undertake assignments in the Middle East. It had asked them for "a letter from a church showing membership or proof of baptism, or marriage in a church" and obligingly provided the names of three churches which would supply certificates to anyone needing them in a hurry.[29]

• McGraw Associates, a Florida firm with contracts for construction work in Saudi Arabia, placed a newspaper help-wanted advertisement for skilled workers, stating explicitly: *"We trust you are aware of the discrimination policies of the Arab World before replying to this ad."* The Ormond Beach firm was being charged formally with discrimination by the ADL's Florida regional board chairman, George Bernstein, and complaints were to be filed with the U.S. Equal Employment Opportunity Commission.[30]

• The Lockheed Aircraft Corporation refused to allow a Jewish U.S. Air Force sergeant, Richard Cohen, to apply for a job it was offering in Saudi Arabia. He was stationed at McGuire Air Force Base, New Jersey, when he saw a Lockheed advertisement in June 1975, offering positions "in the sunny Middle East that will match your military training and your expectations." Cohen, who has since completed his military service, said he told Lockheed he'd like a job as an air traffic controller. When the interviewer heard the sergeant's name, he said, "I hope I don't offend you by the next question I'm going to ask . . . Are you Jewish?" As a result of Cohen's affirmative answer, the Lockheed man refused to let him apply. "He wouldn't even send me an application," the former sergeant stated. (Lockheed later that year was reported to have paid more than $106 million in commissions, including straight bribes, to the Saudi Arabian financier Adnan Khashoggi to procure Lockheed orders in his country.)[31]

• The Hospital Corporation of America, of Nashville, Tennessee, which in 1974 began advertising for pharmacists to work in a hospital it managed in Saudi Arabia, was charged by the ADL with discrimination. An applicant had been told he'd have to produce a baptismal certificate or a statement of religion signed by a minister, if he wanted the job.

"They [HCA employees] told me that this was necessary in order to show that I was not Jewish," he said. In point of fact, he was not; his name was Lyman Chan, and he was of Chinese descent.[32] Although HCA President John C. Neff denied that his firm's contract with the Saudis involved discrimination, the ADL cited an interview which had appeared in *Modern Healthcare* magazine in June 1974. In it, Dr. Thomas Frist, vice-president of the firm, explained how HCA got its Saudi Arabian contract. "To be mighty frank about it," he's quoted as saying, "most of the other companies are heavily Jewish-run, and that eliminated those other companies that were capable of doing it."[33]* The $100 million King Faisal Specialist Hospital in Riyadh reportedly pays HCA a $70 million management fee, and about a third of the hospital employees are American.

• A letter on the stationery of the Illinois Office of Education, in Springfield, Illinois, and signed by E. Darrell Elder, assistant director for teacher placement, provided a particularly serious example of anti-Jewish pressure. The letter, dated January 31, 1975, was addressed to placement directors and told them that International Schools Services of New Jersey had reported three job vacancies in Dubai, on the Persian Gulf. They were in an elementary school for 350 students, mostly American, children of oil-company employees.

"Because of some of the problems in the Middle East presently," the letter said, "ISS cannot employ for these positions any teacher who has a Jewish surname, or is an American

---

* Neff claimed Frist had been "misquoted," but the magazine's editor-in-chief, Marvin Rowlands, stood by the remarks as published.[34]

Jew, or has Jewish ancestors. Pleace check on this before you refer anyone."

A week later, Illinois' State Superintendent of Education Joseph M. Cronin warned the ISS that its association with his office would be "immediately terminated" if discriminatory qualifications in violation of Illinois and federal statutes were fastened on applicants.

The case drew the particular ire of the Anti-Defamation League. "No Jews, no people with Jewish names and no people with Jewish ancestry," noted Arnold Forster, "is going as far as you can to reach back to Hitler, which is one of the reasons that we went after the ISS." The upshot, said Forster, is that ISS "really collapsed." "We signed a stipulation of settlement in which they agreed that they would send Jews on every job application that was made," Forster reported; "that they would give us a monthly head count; that they would indulge in an affirmative action program to see to it that Jews come into the program. They would advertise in Jewish publications for teachers, and they would make a joint release with the Anti-Defamation League announcing these four things." Forster called it "a total victory."[35]

Unfortunately, not many such cases can be chronicled in the battle against anti-Semitism. The lure of "Arab money" is very strong. It can commend anti-Jewish policies to businessmen who ordinarily would never discriminate, and it engenders that insidious "voluntary boycott" which is perhaps the most corrupting feature of the Arab economic war against the Jews.

CHAPTER V

Boardroom Compliance and *Baksheesh*

I N 1957 AN INCIDENT involving a tanker, the *National Peace,* led the U.S. government to cooperate in the economic war the Arabs were waging at sea against the State of Israel. The U.S. Navy's Military Sea Transportation Service (MSTS) had chartered this vessel to carry fuel oil from Ras Tanura, Saudi Arabia, to Manila, in the Philippines. When Saudi officials learned that the *National Peace* was a ship which, under another name, S. S. *Memory*, had previously carried on trade with Israel, they refused it permission to load. The MSTS had to charter another vessel, whereupon the owners of the *National Peace* sued MSTS for $160,000 in damages.

After that incident, the U.S. Navy and the tanker industry decided they both needed protection from entering into contracts which could not be fulfilled because of Arab restrictions on freedom of commerce and freedom of the seas. A so-called "Haifa Clause," named after the port of Haifa in Israel, was inserted into all invitations and tenders the MSTS issued for tankers calling in the Persian Gulf. This singled out for special treatment vessels which had previously traded with Israel.

When it became known that the U.S. Navy and the tanker industry were taking official recognition of the restrictions imposed by the Arab Trade Boycott of Israel, and actively abetting its practices, the Congress, the press and the U.S. maritime unions were so angered that the Haifa Clause was dropped in

1960. Not so, however, the Arab boycott of ships, nor the boycotters' pressures on shipowners.

On January 29, 1966, S.S. *President Roosevelt,* a ship of
the American President Lines, sailed from San Francisco on a
world cruise. According to the published schedule, the ship was
to go through the Suez Canal, calling at Alexandria, then Beirut,
and afterwards at Haifa, where it was meant to land on March
14 and leave the next day. It never arrived in Israel, however.
Under pressure from the Arabs, American President Lines had
changed the published sailing schedule and sent the ship to
Greece instead.

Nine years later, the President of the United States, Gerald
Ford, was informed that there appeared to be "a concerted campaign among American shipping companies . . . to comply with
Arab boycott regulations against the State of Israel." The accu-
sation, made in March 1975, came from ADL National Chairman Seymour Graubard, who sent the White House fourteen
certifications of boycott compliance, prepared by different international steamship lines. "Each," he wrote, "indicates unlawful
participation in Arab boycott efforts" and "constitutes proof of a
practice clearly in restraint of trade." The letter also pointed out
that this widespread practice "daily violates U.S. maritime and
other Federal laws," such as the U.S. Shipping Act of 1916 and
the U.S. Export Administration Act.[1]

The latter declares it to be the "policy of the United States to
oppose restrictive trade practices or boycotts fostered or imposed by foreign countries" against friendly nations, and requires
that the Department of Commerce be notified each time a
request for such discriminatory compliance is received. A spot
check of four of the fourteen shipping lines showed that *none*
had complied with the reporting requirement of the Commerce
Department. An investigation showed further that boycott-
compliance forms for the steamship lines are produced and
presigned in mass numbers in advance of shipment. These
certify that the ships are not carrying blacklisted goods, do not
belong to Israel or to "an Israeli subject," and will not stop at
an Israeli port.

Of the companies named, three were American flag lines:

Waterman Steamship Corporation, Lykes Brothers Steamship Company, Inc., and American Export Isbrandtsen Lines, Inc.* Furthermore, these lines were charged with engaging in a tertiary boycott by refusing to do business with a Miami-based steamship and stevedoring company, Eagle, Inc., which had been blacklisted by the Arabs.[3]

Reaction to the charges was swift. William Ballin, senior vice-president of American Export Lines, Inc., told the *New York Times* that his company had about thirty different forms relating to different countries. "We comply with the rules and regulations established by the country to which we ship goods," Ballin said. "Conditions change depending on the hostilities in a given area. We are a common carrier and we comply with the rules to carry the goods."[4]

That compliance, on the part of American Export Isbrandtsen Lines, was embodied in a declaration typed on the company letterhead, and addressed "to whom it may concern." The sample letter, as sent to the White House, was signed by J. Reyes-Montblanc, Manager, Outward Documentation & Rates, and read as follows:

> Shipment was not effected by an Israeli means of transportation.
>
> This vessel is not to call at any Israeli port and will not pass through the territorial waters of Israeli [*sic*], prior to unloading in Lebanon, unless the ship is in distress or subject to force Majeure. No transshipment is allowed unless the vessel is unable to proceed to destination because it is in distress or subject to force majeure.
>
> We hereby certify that to the best of our knowledge the vessel carrying the above mentioned goods is not included on the *ARAB BOYCOTT BLACKIST*.†

---

* The others named were Boise-Griffin Steamship Co., Inc.; Cross-ocean Shipping Co., Inc.; F. W. Hartmann & Co., Inc.; Kerr Steamship Co., Inc.: States Marine-Isthmian Agency, Inc.; Central Gulf Steamship Corporation; Constellation Navigation, Inc.; Bedlloyd Lines, Inc.; Barber Steamship Lines, Inc.; Peralta Shipping Corporation, and Hellenic Lines, Ltd.[2]

† Style, including capitalization, as in original letter.

The form issued by Lykes Bros. Steamship Co., Inc., was similar:

> TO WHOM IT MAY CONCERN:
> We hereby certify that above named vessel is not of Israeli origin and will not call at any Israeli ports of call and nor is it to the best of our knowledge black listed by the ARAB Boycott Bureau of Isracli.*

An officer and board member of another of the named companies, Constellation Navigation, Inc., denied everything. "We're not participating in any boycott," he told the *New York Post*, and then made clear that his company was in fact doing just that. "We're only making a statement of fact, that we're not calling on an Isracli port," he stated. "Because if we did we couldn't be in business. Our ships couldn't call at Arab ports." He said that the practice of honoring client requests on ports of call was "a very common thing in the trade" and had been going on since 1947 or 1948—in fact, since the State of Israel was established and began to be boycotted by the Arab League. Most such requests, he told the *Post*, had come to his company from Libya, one of the most rabidly anti-Israeli states in the Arab world.[5]

The charges against the shipping lines were linked to others made against American banks. These were withholding payment for merchandise sent to the Arab world, until exporters produced proof that the goods did not violate boycott regulations and would not be shipped on vessels blacklisted by the Arabs. That practice effectively made the banks into U.S. agents of Arab boycott offices.†

Testifying in Washington before Senate and House subcommittees three days after writing the President, Graubard warned that "Arab economic power is now being used to accomplish political and discriminatory ends in violation of

---

* Again, spelling and errors as in original letter.
† See Chapter VI for more details on how banks comply with the boycott.

U.S. policy and law." Arab tactics, he said further, "extend to gross discrimination against American citizens who are of Jewish faith or even of Jewish ancestry. They seek to pervert the Constitutional doctrine of equal treatment for all citizens into an Orwellian status that all Americans are equal but non-Jews are more equal." Pointing to the growing power and wealth of the oil-producing regimes, he urged the United States not to permit "considerations of financial expediency or economic leverage to overcome its fundamental policies."

President Ford instructed the departments of State, Commerce and Justice to investigate, but it was noted that neither the Federal Maritime Commission nor the Maritime Administration had then been formally advised of the President's concern.[6] The FMC was aware of the issue because a copy of Graubard's letter to Ford had been sent to the Commission's chairwoman, Helen D. Bentley, as well as to Robert Blackwell, Assistant Secretary of Commerce for Maritime Affairs and head of the MA. What action the FMC was taking remained unclear, although it was expressly charged with administering the 1916 Shipping Act which made discrimination unlawful.

Efforts to secure government action in cases of discrimination by shippers had been necessary long before 1975. Back in 1959 and 1960, two American crews had been held by the Egyptians because their vessel had called at Israeli ports; the Seafarers' International Union retaliated by picketing an Egyptian ship in New York; the International Longshoremen's union honored the picket line, and the vessel's cargo was never unloaded. The AFL–CIO then asked the Eisenhower Administration to protect shipping and seamen against "Arab boycott and blacklisting policy," and after three weeks of public protest the State Department finally agreed it would do all it could, through "appropriate diplomatic action." The boycott at sea continued, however, despite whatever efforts the department did—or did not—make.[7]

In 1975, some days after President Ford had issued his instructions, the Maritime Administration took action to deal with the boycott. It sent a letter to all U.S.-flag operators, federally subsidized or not, to "reapprise" them of the fact that U.S. export regulations require all U.S. exporters who receive a boycott request to report it to the Department of Commerce. The Administration also reminded shipping companies that if they themselves received a boycott request in connection with an exporter's shipment, they were responsible for advising the exporter so that he in turn could report it to the Commerce Department.[8]

U.S. government subsidies to American shipping lines, including several cited by the ADL, made the issue politically much more sensitive. The Maritime Administration, said New York's *Journal of Commerce,* had some "explaining" to do, and the merchant marine subcommittee of the House of Representatives, it noted, wanted some answers.[9]

One answer to the charges came from W. J. Amoss, president of Lykes Bros. Steamship Co. of New Orleans, the second largest U.S.-flag line and one of the three accused by the ADL. Lykes, a subsidiary of Lykes-Youngstown Corporation, denied supporting the Arab boycott of Israel and stated that its vessels regularly stopped at Israeli ports. He acknowledged that some Lykes vessels were certified as not being of Israeli origin, as not calling on Israeli ports during a given voyage, and as not being on the Arab blacklist, but his company issued such declarations "only when requested to do so by the shippers."

"We can live with half of our ships being blacklisted by the Arabs," he added, "but we couldn't live with the whole company on the boycott list. We're happy it hasn't come to that."[10]

Towards the end of March 1975 it was announced that the Maritime Administration had given U.S.-subsidized shipping lines "a clean bill of health" regarding their conduct in the face of Arab pressures. The MA advised the House merchant marine subcommittee that the Federal Maritime Commission had not uncovered violations of U.S. laws and that the lines had fulfilled their legal obligations with regard to the reporting requirement. There was therefore no reason for ending U.S. subsidies of these lines—as had been threatened during a House hearing. However, the MA said, "owing to the nature of this situation and the continuing dictates of United States policies," it would "maintain its surveillance of the pertinent activites of U.S.-flag operators . . ."[11]

It appeared that as long as the shipping lines fulfilled their reporting obligations under the law, they could accept the conditions imposed upon them by all Arab boycott offices. The U.S. government, it seemed clear, would continue to allow foreign states to dictate the policies of U.S. companies, to set conditions limiting the freedom of action of American citizens, and to interfere in freedom of commerce and the seas. Most serious was the fact that nothing was being done to stop both the banks and the shipping lines from engaging in a tertiary boycott—i.e., from refusing to ship (or finance shipments) of goods whose U.S. exporters were on Arab boycott blacklists, or which were banned by Arab states.

This insidious tertiary boycott was of long standing and one company after another, both in the United States and elsewhere, has been compelled by Arab pressure to act as agents—even "enforcers"—of the Arab boycott offices. An early and notorious case was that of Tecumseh Products of Michigan, which in 1962 came under tremendous pressure to break its ties with Israel. As reported by *Near East Report*, Tecumseh was blacklisted by the Arabs after signing a license agreement with an Israeli firm, Amcor, furnishing that company with the know-how to build refrigeration compressors according to a Tecumseh design.

Blacklisting at first didn't bother Tecumseh, as its Israeli business was very profitable, but the Arabs were not satisfied with merely banning Tecumseh from doing business in Arab countries. They wanted to break Tecumseh's ties with Israel, so they harassed large U.S. companies which traded in the Arab markets and which also used Tecumseh products. Fearful of losing Arab business, these firms put unbearable pressure on Tecumseh to pull out of Israel—and Tecumseh, which couldn't afford to lose its big domestic customers, finally gave in. In late

December 1962 it canceled its contract with Amcor and came off the boycott blacklist in 1963.*

A spokesman for one of the large corporations which had been directed by the Arabs to pressure Tecumseh told *Near East Report*: "All the boycott does is to take the honest person and kick him in the teeth and take the guy who can wheel and deal around the boycott and reward him."

One of the most notorious recent examples of how the tertiary boycott can work even on a multinational level is the saga of Britain's Metal Box Company, which came under heavy U.S. and British pressure during 1976 and 1977 to break its ties with Israel.† But the tertiary boycott doesn't only affect large companies; it can damage—and corrupt—even small firms which do limited business in the Arab world. An example is provided in correspondence inserted into the *Congressional Record* in 1975. This consisted of a letter from Peabody's, Inc., of Virginia, to Kleerpak-Coneco Manufacturing Company of North Hollywood, California, asking it for a written proposal to supply 300,000 meters of plastic film for wrapping soft cheese. Peabody's was acting in this matter as "Agent for the Government of Iraq" and the specification of the tender included the following paragraph:

> The Tenderer shall not incorporate in this Tender any equipment or material that have been manufactured in Israel or by companies sharing Israeli capital or boycotted

---

* The company, says *Near East Report* in its Boycott Supplement of May, 1965, had even gone to Damascus to plead with the boycott authorities. Compressors, it said, constituted only 8 percent of a refrigerator, and boycott regulations allegedly apply to components constituting at least 35 percent of the finished product. But the boycott office, encouraged by the cowardice of Tecumseh's U.S. customers, remained adamant.

† Metal Box claimed that pressure had been brought to bear on the company, to sell its interest in the Israel Can Company, by its own American and British clients. The implication was that these clients had been threatened by the Arabs. Since they used Metal Box-manufactured cans, they were in a position to influence that company, which sold out its stake in Israel. (More in Chapter VII.)

officially by the Iraqi Government or any plant or materials of which any component parts have been manufactured in Israel or by companies boycotted officially, as the import into Iraq of any such equipment or materials or components is officially banned.[12]

The interesting thing about this demand is that, besides its obvious restrictions, it calls quite blatantly for Kleerpak-Coneco to refuse to deal in America with other American companies which have been blacklisted by the Arabs. And this was a demand made by one American company to another.

The landmark case concerning this kind of tertiary boycott involved the Bechtel Corporation of San Francisco, a construction company that did about $3.5 billion worth of business during 1973 and 1974, and which clearly can wield considerable economic power. Its foreign contracts were worth $634 million in 1973 and $450 million in 1974, and it was in connection with some of these that Bechtel got into trouble. In January 1976 it was charged by the U.S. Justice Department with having excluded companies and persons on the Arab blacklist from participating as subcontractors in contracts it had received from the Arabs. The company, the suit also charged, had suppressed competition by asking its own subcontractors not to deal with blacklisted firms or persons.

Bechtel called the charges "totally unwarranted" and insisted that compliance with the laws of foreign governments, such as boycott laws, was *not* illegal in the United States. The case aroused considerable controversy, even within the Ford Administration. The Department of Justice actually postponed filing its suit, to allow the State Department to present its views on possible foreign policy implications. Dr. Henry Kissinger was so worried that he personally cabled Attorney General Levi from China, during President Ford's trip there in November 1975. Writing in the *New Republic*, Sol Stern quoted "a highly placed State Department source" as saying that Kissinger feared this anti-trust action "could be seen by the Arabs as a deliberate U.S. government decision to act against their policy. Thus it could have had an adverse effect on their peace-making process."

A *Washington Post* editorial pointed to these State Department fears of alienating Saudi Arabia, a country vital to the United States not only for foreign policy reasons but also for oil supplies. In both the Treasury and Commerce departments, as well as "in the business constituencies they represent, fear was and is rampant that the suit will cost American companies billions of dollars worth of potential business throughout the Arab world," it said. Justice should nevertheless go ahead with its suit, the *Post* urged. "Nothing in the anti-trust law reserves its application to situations that don't make foreign waves," it wrote, and added, "American participation in the boycott is a standing reproof to the values of the United States."[13]

Levi filed the Justice Department suit on January 16, 1976. A year later, Bechtel signed a consent agreement which neither admitted nor denied that it had violated U.S. law in the past, but in which the company vowed it would not perform or enforce any provision providing for the boycott of a U.S. person or firm; would not require any other person or firm to boycott any U.S. blacklisted person; would not sign any agreement within the United States which provides for a boycott; and would not exclude from lists of possible suppliers any U.S. blacklisted firm.[14]

While the agreement seemed to be a victory against boycott operations in the United States, it contained loopholes. It said that if an Arab client "specifically and unilaterally" chooses a subcontractor who has complied with the terms of the boycott, then Bechtel would not be breaking the law if it worked with that subcontractor. Also, the company remains free to choose *foreign* subcontractors who have complied with the boycott, so long as it at no point ever considers even one American company for the same job. Justice Department lawyers conceded to London's *Financial Times* that "it is possible that any American company might conspire with any Arab client and secretly provide it with the name of a preferred American subcontractor who has complied with the boycott. The Arab client might then go through the motions of 'specifically and unilaterally' approaching the contractor." In such a case, the lawyers admitted, the Justice Department would be powerless to act.[15]

PREDICTABLY, a number of oil companies have been involved in the Arab boycott, abetting it in various ways. Royal Dutch Shell sold its Shell Oil Company of Palestine in 1958, and later that year it and British Petroleum divested themselves of a Haifa refinery they jointly owned. Getty Oil of Los Angeles complied in order to sell oil-field equipment in Kuwait by signing a document stating, "We certify that the goods listed are not of Israeli origin nor do they contain any Israeli materials." It then failed to report this negative certificate request to the Department of Commerce, whereupon it was fined $1,000 in 1975. That fine was the maximum under the law and is imposed only after a company has *repeatedly* violated the requirement that it report all requests to participate in the Arab boycott of Israel. Getty became the fifth American company to be fined the maximum.[16]

ARAMCO has always been the oil company with the sorriest and shabbiest record. "For years," wrote the *Miami Herald* in 1975, "it has been common knowledge that when ARAMCO advertises for American technicians to work in the Persian Gulf sheikdoms the ads might just as well say 'No Jews Allowed.' . . . The restrictions never offended the executives of the major American companies that make up the ARAMCO organization."[17]

Exxon Corporation had been another boycott-complier and, it would seem, a rather unabashed one. Responding on November 12, 1975, to a letter from the American Jewish Committee, an Exxon company representative named D. L. Snook said:

> We certainly regret the conditions which have given rise to boycotts wherever they have been imposed. Boycotts limit international commerce and the freedom of activity of private enterprises, and we would prefer that they did not exist anywhere. However, when they do, compliance with the laws and regulations of the sovereign nations involved is unavoidable if the company or its affiliates are to continue to do business in or with such nations.

[[96]]

That reply of course evaded the question of Exxon's responsibility to support U.S. government policy, which is against boycotts.

In 1975, it was learned that Gulf Oil Corporation had contributed $50,000 to an anti-Zionist Arab propaganda campaign in the United States to help, among other things, subsidize a publication dealing with alleged violations of human rights in Israeli-administered territories. After Gulf on May 16, 1975, voluntarily revealed this contribution before the Senate Foreign Relations Committee's subcommittee on multinational corporations, a boycott of Gulf was approved by a Conference of Presidents of Major American Jewish Organizations, but this was later called off. Gulf executives managed to convince the ADL that they considered such gifts "totally improper" and that they were "deeply concerned." In fact, they couldn't discover who had authorized the $50,000 payment, and even an ADL investigation failed to bring this to light. In the end, Gulf apologized publicly for the support it had given anti-Israel propaganda.[18]

Some light on the mysterious contribution was shed by London's *Jewish Observer and Middle East Review.* The $50,000 was paid in response to pressure from the government of Kuwait, according to the paper's Washington correspondent. Gulf at the time had been a partner, along with British Petroleum, in the Kuwait International Oil Company, though subsequently Kuwait nationalized both BP's and Gulf's assets. The article said:

> The money was also carefully "laundered" through the Middle East, both to conceal its origins and, perhaps, to enable Kuwaiti and other Arab interests to ensure it was really being paid.
>
> It came originally from a secret fund in the Bahamas, was sent through a Swiss bank account to the First National City Bank office in Beirut and was paid from there to a U.S. firm called International Affairs Consultants, Inc.
>
> This company was set up by a number of prominent anti-Zionists in the U.S., including Rabbi Elmer Berger, John Davis, head of the American Near-East Refugee Association (which also received a legal, charitable contribution of $2.2

million from Gulf in 1973 for its work with Palestinian refugees) and two other American lawers.[19]*

The financing of propaganda activities would appear to be nothing unusual for Gulf. In 1976 the former Gulf Italian chairman, Nicolo Pignatelli, revealed that between 1969 and 1972 Gulf had paid more than 400 million lire (about $500,000) to help finance the newspapers and the propaganda campaigns of Italy's Socialist and Christian Democratic parties.

Demands for payments, such as were apparently made to Gulf by Kuwait, are part of a large web of dubious financial dealings that result from boycott and oil-wealth pressures. Some are extortionary demands; others are *baksheesh*, given in the hope that a company may be able to get itself off a blacklist, if it greases the right palms.

The *New Republic* chronicled the efforts of one firm that was prepared to pay plenty to get off the blacklist. This was General Tire and Rubber Company of Akron, Ohio, blacklisted by the Arabs because it held a one-third share in an Israeli tire company and kept on the list even after it had disposed of this holding in 1963, because it still honored a technical services agreement with the Israeli firm.

Sometime around 1970, General Tire & Rubber's top executives were approached by a man named Louis Lauler, who said he represented Triad Financial Establishment, a Lebanese-run conglomerate headed by the multimillionaire Saudi Arabian "fixer," Adnan Khashoggi. Triad knew all the ins and outs of the boycott, Lauler indicated, and could get a company off the blacklist. It had done so for others, and he even produced a brochure which listed the names of companies Triad had helped. In its eagerness to get into the Arab markets, General Tire and

---

* Rabbi Elmer Berger is not new to the anti-Israel propaganda scene. On April 6, 1965, *Near East Report* reported that an anti-Zionist article by Berger was published in the March 5 issue of the West German neo-Nazi organ, the *Deutsche National-Zeitung und Soldaten-Zeitung*. Berger at the time was executive vice-president of the American Council for Judaism, an anti-Zionist group that over the past thirty years never lost an opportunity to attack Israel.

Rubber signed a contract and paid Triad $50,000 in advance, agreeing to pay another $100,000 when Triad delivered the goods. The company got off the blacklist in 1973, although perhaps not because of Triad's intervention; General Tire & Rubber by then had a clean slate because it ended its know-how agreement with Israel. Still, officials of the company thought it best to pay Triad the remaining $100,000, the full fee being allowed by the Internal Revenue Service as a normal business expense, deductible from corporate tax.

The company's vice-president and general counsel, Tress Pittenger, was asked by Sol Stern what Triad had actually done to earn its fee; he replied that it had helped General Tire and Rubber in drawing up the documents that were submitted to the Central Office for the Boycott of Israel, in Damascus. "Khashoggi and Triad," writes Stern, "have been characterized in recent news reports . . . as major conduits for millions of dollars of questionable payments made in bribes paid by American companies to secure contracts in the Arab world. What is revealed here for the first time is that American companies were also paying to get off a boycott list that the Arabs claim is a principled part of their war against Israel."[20]

The boycott regulations contain a specific anti-bribery clause, but this may only be evidence that the boycott-office officials are aware of the part *baksheesh* has always played in the Arab world. Recently, Business International, a private American publishing, research and advisory organization, confirmed that a company can have its name removed from Arab boycott blacklists, provided its contacts with Israel are not too obvious and it is willing to pay between $25,000 and $40,000.

London's *Sunday Times* provided a specific case. While British Leyland, the United Kingdom's biggest automobile manufacturer, was blacklisted (see Chapter IX), Iraq wanted to buy 150 of its bus/engines, but needed the approval of Mahgoub's office. "Leyland," wrote the paper, "influenced the decision of the boycott committee in Damascus by bribing three men." Approximately £20,000 was involved. Some bribes, however, are disguised, according to the Business International study. In Kuwait, companies wishing to do business are required to hire local representatives, who actually perform no work.[21]

The reference to a company's contacts with Israel not being "too obvious" is a reminder that many companies successfully trade with both the Arab world and Israel, by managing to disguise their Israeli business. Doing so can be a pretty convoluted exercise, sometimes involving the use of dummy names, "front" companies and secret dealings through a variety of agents. Israel asserts that hundreds of companies get away with defying the boycott in this way, and make good profits in both the Arab world and Israel,[22] although their names obviously cannot be revealed. A comment on such dealings was made by an official of General Aniline, now GAF Corporation. "The sharp businessman will say the hell with you and lie about his Israeli business," he said. "This boycott was revolting from the beginning and the businessman dealing with it is likely to respond in kind."[23]

Bribery, then, is not the only evil result which the boycott has spawned; the replacement of open, frank, aboveboard business transactions with secret deals is another. Often this is abetted by the Arabs themselves, so that they can get the products and services they want from a company, even if it is on the blacklist.

A telling example was provided by Red Fox Products Company, an American firm which had been partners in a plant in Israel since 1951. Ten years later, a Saudi Arabian company ordered one of its products and a letter of credit was opened with a New York broker. Reporting the story, *Near East Report* said, "It looked like business as usual [until] in May 1961, after ten years of unremarked Israel investment, Red Fox received a letter from Damascus." For the first time since it began working with Israel, Red Fox received the entire barrage of boycott demands: that it terminate its relationship with Israel, liquidate its shareholdings in the Israeli firm and furnish Damascus with the proof.

"The first reaction of Red Fox's president," according to the report, "was to get hopping mad and determine to cancel the Saudi order. Then he read an article in *Fortune* magazine assuring businessmen that Arabs who wanted their goods would buy them, boycott or no. He went ahead with the deal. His judgment proved correct. Arab businessmen were even more cooperative than *Fortune* had prophesied."

The broker wrote to the company that he had talked to Beirut, Lebanon, about the letter of credit with Saudi Arabia, and Beirut had advised him that the shipment should be taken to Bahrein because that "is under English control and the Saudi Consulate is not involved."

Beirut had pointed out that all shipments to Arab countries had to have their invoices presented to the consulates. "There they go over the list of blacklisted ships and companies," Beirut had warned, and if the Red Fox name appeared on the list "it will be picked up in every consulate" and no further company shipments to Arab states would be allowed. The broker told Red Fox that Beirut had made the following suggestions: "We start with a new label . . . You could use any name but yours on the label . . . They would never detect this and you could ship through our firm . . . The shipping cartons would be either just plain cartons or you could use any old ones that don't have your name on it even if the brand name isn't the same."

The order from Saudi Arabia was fulfilled. Subsequent Saudi orders arrived and were also fulfilled, as were subsequent orders from Qatar and Lebanon. "The firm still does business in the Arab world," *Near East Report* wrote in 1965, "business it would have readily forgone if it had not been for the Arab facility at getting around the boycott."[24]

Some companies have refused to deal underhandedly, despite wishing to expand their business into the Arab Middle East. One example was provided by Monsanto, which was blacklisted by the Arabs because it has been connected with the production of acrylic fibers and styrene polymers in Israel. In early 1975, Monsanto announced it was studying its potential in the Arab markets and hoped eventually to be able to do business with *both* Israel and the Arab states.

"We believe that the hope for the Middle East is in everyone working together," a Monsanto spokesman said, "and this includes normal trade relations between countries." He added that "an end to these discriminatory barriers" would help U.S. policy in the Middle East and further "the new climate of diplomatic accommodation in the region."

Whether Monsanto succeeds in getting off the blacklist remains uncertain. Boycotted since 1966, it has been approached by the usual Arab agents. "There have been no end of agents coming to us and offering to get us off the list for a fee," a Monsanto spokesman said. "We decided we just weren't going to pay *baksheesh*."

CHAPTER VI

The Big Banking
Scandal

I T WAS INEVITABLE that the Arabs would enter the world of
international finance as soon as they were rich enough, and
that when they did, the economic war against the Jews would
be carried on in the corridors of the world's great investment
houses.

These investment houses—or merchant banks, as they're
called outside America—are among the wealthiest and most
highly regarded of international financial institutions. Western
economies depend heavily on their ability to provide the vast
sums of money industries and governments periodically need to
borrow. It is the merchant bank that arranges international
bond issues, usually working together with banks of other
countries as well as of its own.* Such huge deals are put
together very quietly, for merchant bankers are publicity-shy and
operate in a dignified low-profile world of private conversations
and gentlemen's agreements. No wonder that when the great
banking scandal of 1975 broke, the resultant fracas proved

---

* Those who organize these syndicates are called the "lead managers,"
while those who are invited in act as underwriters and "selling group
members." Merchant bankers may invest on their own behalf or sell
the bonds to their private and governmental clients; the small commission they receive in return snowballs when the total loan being negotiated
runs into tens of millions.

unbearably painful to the entire merchant-banking fraternity. It revealed an element of cutthroat competition among merchant banks that had always been concealed from the public, and showed some of their executives to be less high-minded than they like to seem.

For years the Arabs had been discriminating against Jewish banks they regarded as "Zionist," while at the same time working quietly with others. The big Wall Street investment houses of Salomon Brothers, Goldman, Sachs & Co., Lehman Brothers and Kuhn Loeb & Co., Incorporated, had had little difficulty in dealing with the Arab world. It was not until after the boycott was greatly intensified, following the 1973 rise in oil prices, that the Arabs began to make more blatantly aggressive moves. Jewish banks which normally would have been invited into any large international bond issue suddenly found themselves excluded, especially when Arab money was involved. And because the Arabs had enormous supplies of money, they became involved more and more often, intensifying the threat of exclusion for Jewish banks. This began to hurt, not so much because the investment houses stood to lose their commissions, but because they would be unable to sell bonds to their private clients, and this might lead those clients interested in "hot" issues to begin using banks the Arabs favored.

In the past, Jewish banks had simply suffered such discrimination with as much good grace and as little publicity as possible, but in February 1975 one Jewish-owned bank kicked. Lazard Frères & Cie., of Paris, complained to the French Finance Ministry that it had been cut out of two international bond issues floated for French state-run enterprises: a $25 million Air France loan raised by a consortium led by the state-owned Crédit Lyonnais, and a $20 million issue for the Compagnie Nationale du Rhône, raised by the Banque de Paris et des Pays-Bas.

"Some Arab banks participating as co-managers have asked that Lazard not figure in these syndicates," a spokesman for the bank explained. "We don't deny the right of the Arabs to make loans where they want, but we don't understand how or why they can take such a position outside their own country."[1]

Lazard Frères's exclusion sent reporters scrambling around to find out which other Jewish banks might be on Arab black-lists; they discovered that S. G. Warburg of London, Lazard of New York and various branches of the Rothschild empire were similarly blacklisted. (Significantly, Lazard Brothers of London wasn't blacklisted—because it was no longer controlled by Jews.)

Other disturbing developments followed. The first was the reaction of the French Finance Ministry, which in earlier years tried to protect French banks from foreign interference, but in 1975 took a less courageous line for fear of offending the oil-rich Arabs. Jean-Pierre Fourcade, the Finance Minister, first refused to comment on Lazard's complaint, and later had a Ministry spokesman say it wasn't a governmental matter, but one for the banks to unravel themselves.[2]

The second disturbing development was the attitude of Kuwait, heavily involved in both deals from which Lazard's had been excluded. This small sheikdom has led the Arab world in investment policy and has for years been regarded in the West as financially sophisticated, pragmatic and flexible. Yet it had been behind both exclusions; either it had joined the Arab "hard-liners" voluntarily, or under pressure.

Lazard's complaint led to further revelations. Rothschild's had been excluded from a City of Marseilles issue, also due to Arab pressure, and both it and Warburg's had been left out of a £25 million issue for the Japanese Marubeni group, because Marubeni demanded that Arab banks participate, and these in turn insisted no Jewish banks could. Kuwaiti banks had also acted as co-managers of the Marubeni underwriting, but significantly they were joined in the Marseilles loan by the Libyans, among the most fanatically anti-Jewish of all Arabs. These would allow two non-Jewish British merchant banks to participate (Kleinwort, Benson Ltd., and J. Henry Schroder Wagg & Co., Ltd.), but no Jewish ones.

This really began to worry London banking circles. If the Arabs were not stopped, they might extend their blackballing to Jewish stockbroking houses, even to insurance companies, discounters, bullion brokers and foreign-exchange dealers with

Jewish connections. Bankers, said the *Sunday Telegraph* of London, are not "anxious to over-react" but "now that the Arab strong-arm tactics have come out into the open" the scandal was "likely to blow up as a vital, and controversial, matter in London and other European banking circles."[3]

"We do not think it does any good to stir things up," a Rothschild spokesman said, the day after the Paris scandal broke. "We are anxious to present a very low profile on this. In fact, we know it has been in the background for the past three or four months . . ."

Rothschild's didn't blame Kleinwort, Benson for excluding it from the Marubeni issue, he said. "Kleinwort's have very good relations with the Arabs and if they can get the money from them, fair enough. It is entirely up to every manager of a loan who he has on his list. There's nothing anybody can do about that. If we wanted to leave Kleinwort's off one of our lists, we could certainly do so. We find the situation distasteful more than anything else, but we don't think it will last. Eventually we will all have to learn to live together."[4]

Rothschild's did not distinguish between an exclusion based on commercial considerations and one based on religious or racial factors. If Rothschild's left Kleinwort's off a list, it would not be because Kleinwort's was owned by Christians, but for other reasons. This was pointed out by London's *Evening Standard*, which called for internationally coordinated action against the boycott; there was no doubt, said the paper, that the Arab ban of Rothschild's had been directed "against Jewish interests as such."[5]

Disquiet grew in the following days as banking circles spoke of at least a dozen other banks besides Lazard, Rothschild and Warburg whom the Arabs were trying to squeeze out.

"It's entirely political," said the director of one London institution.[6] And an American banker commented, "It is the most illogical thing that I've ever heard of and it is impossible that it will continue to exist. The Jewish relationships and connections are so interwoven with the fabric of life that either you do business with nobody or everybody. The fact that some are on the blacklist and some are off is almost amusing, and it certainly shows a certain naiveté. Obviously this list was put together haphazardly sometime ago by someone reading gossip columns or something like that. It's senseless."[7]

A statement by Robert Henderson, deputy chairman of Kleinwort, Benson, followed. He claimed Kleinwort's had no choice but to exclude the Jewish banks, since the Arabs had insisted on it. Sir Cyril Kleinwort backed him up. He said it would "be 'suicidal' for London to stand up on a matter of principle against the Arabs boycotting banks and other companies with Israeli interests.

"We simply cannot afford," Sir Cyril continued, "to stand up on our hind legs and say we are the best financial centre in the world, and you come here on our terms or not at all. All the Arab business will simply go to Zurich or elsewhere. We must maintain an open-door attitude."[8]

That implied slamming doors on Jews, as quickly became evident. London's Jewish bankers had believed that the Arabs' strong-arm tactics could only be stopped by the united opposition of "the City," London's financial center. This could be crystallized under the powerful Accepting Houses Committee, which acts as chief joint spokesman for London's merchant banking fraternity. But members of the Committee showed little interest. Charles Villiers said he didn't think it was "a matter for the committee"; Lord Aldington, another member with a keen interest in Arab trade, had "no knowledge of the matter"; the committee chairman, Michael Verey, wasn't available for comment.[9] It was rumored that instead of committee action, a "gentleman's agreement" would be worked out in private.

That this does not always result in Jews being treated in a gentlemanly manner again became evident when another leading London banker admitted that there was nothing new in Arab-instigated anti-Semitic discrimination within the City. "We have always tried to keep Jewish names off the tombstones," he said, referring to the "tombstone ads" listing the banks which participate in an issue. He explained this was done by the use of "nominee names" or by having a participating Jewish bank remain unpublicized, and by working through a non-Jewish bank, when Arab money was being sought.[10] "This is the first time I've known the City not to handle a deal like this delicately," he complained.[11]

It became evident that the City was less troubled by Arab strong-arm tactics than by people trying to resist them, less troubled by anti-Semitism than by those exposing it, and less troubled by the exclusion of highly respected financial institutions than by the attendant publicity. In fact, the City was worried because the scandal had revealed a lot of undignified competition. Some London banks were extremely successful in the Arab world and seemed happy to try and dethrone giants like the Jewish banks of Rothschild's and Warburg's.[12] *The Times* was moved to warn sternly that "accepting racial or national discrimination as a competitive weapon would be disastrous for the standing of the City of London as a major financial centre."[13] And the *Evening Standard* went so far as to ask whether Kleinwort, Benson had been "too easily persuaded by the Arabs . . ."[14]

Resistance, it was pointed out, seemed possible, for the Arabs were showing signs of backing down. When Merrill Lynch, Pierce, Fenner and Smith acted together with Kuwait as lead manager of a $25 million Volvo underwriting, it announced that Kuwait had no objection to the participation of Lazard's, Rothschild's and Warburg's in the deal.[15] And Kuwait was also allowing those three banks into two other bond issues it was co-managing, a $50 million Mexican loan, and another for Australia.[16]

This embarrassed Kleinwort's, implying again that it need not have acted so cravenly, and that it might have done so deliberately, both to cut out the Jewish banks and to secure additional Arab goodwill. But, embarrassed or not, Kleinwort's chairman, Gerald Thompson, freely admitted to the *New York Times* that his bank "would continue to respond to Arab pressures to prevent Jewish banks from taking part in loan syndications with Arab participants."[17] Briefly, this seemed to put Kleinwort's in "a fairly isolated position," as the paper remarked.[18] For Kuwait now seemed prepared to ignore boycott regulations, especially if the extremist Libyans weren't in on a deal, and even the French government seemed to have rediscovered its backbone, when it postponed floating a £20 million loan for its electric power company because of new Arab pressure to exclude Lazard's. A government official claimed the postponement was due only to "market conditions,"[19] but it may have been indicative of a brief resolve to stand up more firmly to Arab pressures.* That it wouldn't last was made glaringly evident in 1977 when France released the PLO terrorist Abu Daoud, for fear of offending the Arab world.

All the publicity was, however, having an important effect on the U.S. Congress, for it helped to arouse the anti-boycott forces and invest their deliberations with a sense of greater urgency. It was also during 1975, and partly because of this scandal, that the Israeli government and Jewish communal groups in the United States, Britain and elsewhere began taking steps to fight the boycott in a coordinated manner, and to press more energetically for laws making compliance illegal.

The Arab reaction to the publicity was mixed. In Paris and London it led two Arab bankers to liberalize their attitudes. The Paris spokesman said Arab banks wouldn't object if a lead manager "insists on keeping the Jewish banks in the syndicate." He explained that "allowing a Zionist bank to buy one hundred bonds entails no active cooperation" with it. The Arab banker in London thought that appearing on a tombstone ad with Jewish banks wasn't objectionable; it amounted to "traveling in the same bus innocently without shaking hands or kissing."[?1] But the full glare of the world's press attention was also making other Arabs uncomfortable. From Kuwait, Richard Johns of the *Financial Times*, London, reported that Arab vigilance was

---

* Another example of this occurred when Jacques Medecin, mayor of Nice, on February 11 rebuffed the Arabs when they threatened to boycott his book fair because Israel was represented. "I will not accept any conditions laid down by exhibitors," he announced. "Israel has never set terms for taking part in the fair. So I will not accept them from the Arabs."[20]

being sharpened to avoid "knowing or unwitting cooperation with institutions having Zionist affiliations."[22]

The three Kuwaiti concerns most often involved in international bond issues conferred and withdrew from the co-managership of both the Volvo and the Mexican issues, because Jewish banks were involved and this had put Kuwait in "a straightforward breach of the Arab Boycott of Israel regulations."[23]

That withdrawal caused endless speculation. London bankers wondered whether Kuwait had dropped out because it was overcommitted, or had surrendered to powerful pressure. Kuwaiti circles felt impelled to deny that Mohammed Mahgoub was behind their new hard line. This immediately had its effect on the French government. Premier Jacques Chirac announced that Lazard's exclusion was "a matter of relations among banks and between banks and their clients," and no business of the government,[24] ignoring the fact that the "clients" were two state-run enterprises, that the banks were partly state-owned and that even private banks presumably deserve protection by government.

Kuwait's turnaround and the subsequent surrender of the French government in the face of Arab pressure was, of course, gratifying to Mahgoub. On February 16, 1975, he issued a "clarification" of the matter. "All activities between Arab banks and banks on the boycott list are prohibited," he announced from Damascus, "and not just participation in international loans managed by Jewish institutions." He explained it meant that "it is not permitted to deal directly or indirectly with any bank banned in the Arab countries." In fact, he claimed, no Arab banks or investment houses violated boycott rules and said he did "not believe that Arab banks dealt with S. G. Warburg or N. M. Rothschild." He also issued a list of the "most important" banks he had banned:

> S. G. Warburg of the U.K. and all its subsidiaries; Banque Belge Centrale of Belgium; Bank Max Fischer of Belgium; National Provincial, and Rothschild (London) Ltd. of the U.K.; London and Colonial Bank of the U.K.; La Société Bancaire et Financière d'Orient of France; Union

Francière de Paris of France; Bank für Gemeinwirtschaft of West Germany; Kreditbank Hagen of West Germany; International Credit Bank of Switzerland; Discount Bank (Overseas) of Switzerland; Lazard Frères of the U.S.; American Bank and Trust of the U.S.; and all Rothschild's banks in the U.K., France, Switzerland, the U.S.[25]

The list, as so often happens, turned out to be inaccurate. The Kreditbank Hagen, for example, had gone out of business in 1961.

No anti-Jewish considerations were involved, Mahgoub insisted. The boycott affected only "whoever supports Israel militarily or economically." Jewish-owned banks were boycotted, he explained, "because their owners have a confirmed position towards Israel and Zionism. Many of these banks helped establish the state of Israel and were supporting it economically and militarily. Do you really imagine that the Arabs could possibly invest their money in cooperation with these banks? This would mean the Arab money would end up in Israel one way or another, so that Israel would buy more rockets and planes to kill the Arabs."[26]

This argument appears to enshrine a new criterion of the Central Boycott Office: that helping to establish the State of Israel in the first instance is a crime punishable by boycott blacklisting. If this were adhered to rigidly, the Arabs would have to boycott the United States, the Soviet Union and the United Nations itself, for all played a part.

Mahgoub now announced that the American Chemical Bank and the First National City Bank of Chicago would be removed from the blacklist, but that "new companies will be added . . ."[27] A bizarre note was added by a Kuwaiti newspaper, *al-Watan*, which called on Kuwait to "support the French banks which are the target of a Zionist plot that could smash the French economy." The sheikdom needed to "prevent France getting into difficulty," it continued, and its money "must support France against this plot."[28]

CONCERTED RESISTANCE to the boycott by the merchant banks seemed remote in the aftermath of the scandal. One

American banker in 1975 said there were already people "going around Wall Street asking if such and such a firm has any Jewish partners."[29] In the heat of the moment, another American financier hinted at dire reprisals. "One real casualty," he said, "will be Kleinwort, Benson. They'll get screwed one day. Those people at Lazard's and Rothschild's don't forget, and they play for keeps."[30]

In West Germany three important banks, the Deutsche Bank, the Dresdner Bank and the Westdeutsche Landesbank, stood firm, successfully refusing to bar any banks under pressure. But in Britain, a Treasury spokesman said the banking boycott wasn't his concern. "We leave that sort of thing to the Bank of England. We don't really know anything about the problem."

The British response to the boycott, according to one financier, was contemptible: "Let me tell you something. If the Arabs told Sir Gordon Richardson to stand on his head for half an hour each day, that's exactly what he would do."[31] Sir Gordon is head of the Bank of England.

In the United States, attitudes were tougher. Merrill Lynch refused to give in to boycott pressure in the Mexican loan affair, even when the Kuwaitis dropped out. Then, the U.S. Senate took an interest and two senators wrote Treasury Secretary William E. Simon of their "grave concern" that Arab discrimination against Jewish banks "seems to be spreading to the United States."[32] The American Bankers Association urged "in the strongest possible terms" that all its members "resist any such pressures, were they to be applied."[33]

The alarm died down surprisingly quickly. The international bankers, preferring to avoid publicity, withdrew from the stage. It had in any event become obvious that the Arabs' blacklist of international banks was erratic, irrational, outdated and uncoordinated. One Wall Streeter who travels much in the Middle East claimed, "I've had Arabs tell me that the list is considered a running joke; sometimes even *they* don't know why a company is on it."[34] Perhaps Mahgoub knows this as well as anyone. He must realize, as *Fortune* put it in July 1975, that "to try to pick Zionist threads from the fabric of banking could lead the Arabs to ludicrous extremes."

"Were they to persist," wrote *Fortune*, "they might be left with no investment bankers at all. They might have to boycott Goldman, Sachs, which has had historically close connections with Kuwait—but whose senior partner, Gustave Levy, has been an active fund raiser for the United Jewish Appeal. They also might find themselves tried by some tribal associations: the Banque de Bruxelles is associated with the Banque Lambert, whose principal owner, Léon Lambert, is a distant cousin of the Rothschilds. Similar difficulties would present themselves if the Arabs were to extend their principles to commercial banks, which hold on deposit about half of OPEC's $55 billion in surplus. Chase Manhattan handles billions in petrodollars, for example, but it is also fiscal agent for State of Israel Bonds."

The Arabs of course have no interest in persisting to ludicrous extremes and even built a fail-safe clause into the boycott regulations. This exempts foreign banks that violate boycott rules *if* "the benefit that accrues to the Arab economy is greater than that accruing to Israel as a result of such banks' collaboration with it," and if "advantages obtained by the said banks from their dealings with the Arab countries are less than the advantages derived by the Arab countries as a result of dealing with them."

A compromise of sorts was struck shortly after the publicity died down. The way European syndications were organized was to be subtly changed, it was reported. Each individual co-manager in an international bond deal would maintain his own group of underwriters, separate from those maintained by others. This would allow "offensively Jewish banks" to belong to one group, and Arab banks to the other. In 1976 and 1977 the Arab bankers seemed to have retreated still further from their more doctrinaire boycott principles, for full-page tombstone ads were being published by the *Financial Times* of London which listed Rothschild's, Warburg's and Lazard's, as well as other Jewish banks, alongside Kuwaiti and other Arab institutions.

ONE TROUBLING REVELATION of 1975 was that the U.S. government was itself a partner in an Arab investment company which boycotted Jewish banks. This was revealed in Beirut, Lebanon, late that February and admitted by the State Department.

The United States held 6.5 percent, or $11 million, worth of shares in the Intra Investment Company, which in 1975 played a major role in boycotting Jewish banks. The remaining shares were held by the governments of Kuwait, Qatar and Lebanon. The U.S. share was in the hands of the Department of Agriculture's Commodity Credit Corporation, which organizes the export of American farm products, and which had loaned Intra's predecessor $22 million. That company had subsequently failed, and the CCC was paid off not in cash but in equity, although it later reduced its share in Intra Investment by half.

A senior U.S. diplomat in Beirut called U.S. government participation in Intra, while it was boycotting Jewish banks, "awkward" and said, "we never should have taken an active interest" in the company. When reporters asked whether the anti-Jewish boycott had been discussed at meetings of the Intra board in which the United States participated, the agricultural attaché of the U.S. embassy in Beirut, Shackford Pitcher, who occupied that board seat, declined to answer. The State Department, however, seemed to admit that the boycott had been discussed while the American diplomat was present, for a spokesman emphasized, "the United States did not concur in the chairman's decision, had no say in it, and does not endorse it." It was then announced that the clearly embarrassed U.S. government would arrange to sell its Intra Investment shares to Lebanon, and in a hurry.[35]

The Arabs weren't confining themselves to the international arena; they have consistently applied pressure on U.S. and other commercial banks as well. Chase Manhattan is a case in point, and it has been in trouble with both the Arabs and the Jews. As already mentioned, it handles Israel's debt financing in the United States, acting as chief fiscal agent for State of Israel Bonds. This put Chase on the Arab blacklist in July 1964, but it got off in January of the following year because it also handles vast quantities of Arab wealth and has even intervened politically on behalf of the Arabs, as Sol Stern reported in the *New Republic*.

"In 1968, David Rockefeller [Chase Manhattan's chairman] and John J. McCloy, along with several prominent oilmen, met with President-elect Nixon to urge on him a Mideast policy more friendly to the Arabs," Stern wrote. "During the 1973 war, McCloy urged the Nixon Administration not to ship arms to Israel. Last year [1975], shortly after the breakdown of the negotiations for an interim agreement between Israel and Egypt, David Rockefeller was part of a delegation of Establishment 'wise men' who met with Henry Kissinger and offered support for Kissinger's criticism of Israeli 'intransigence.' "

Chase therefore seemed to be straddling the Arab-Israeli fence successfully: being of financial service to Israel while being both financially and politically useful to the Arabs. Yet it would soon find itself in the bad books of both.

The issue was Chase's continuing failure to establish a branch office in Israel, while maintaining one in Beirut and planning five more in Arab countries. Questioned about this, a spokesman said Chase had simply "never been asked" to do so.[36] Unfortunately, Chase Chairman Rockefeller had made a very different statement to a Harvard Business School audience on March 18, 1975. If Chase opened a branch in Israel, he said, "all our business with the Arab world would be boycotted and come to an end."[37]

Nine days after Rockefeller made this public admission of surrender to the boycott, a three-man ADL delegation met with him and four of his aides. They failed to reach any kind of agreement.[38] Four days later, Chase again claimed it had never received a request to open an Israeli branch. This time it stated it wouldn't do so because it "could not run a profitable operation that would serve the needs of Israel's people."[39]

Israeli officials confirmed, however, that Rockefeller, during a visit to Israel in January 1975, had refused to open an office there. They also revealed he had declined to join a proposed U.S.-Israel Business Council, while agreeing to join a U.S.-Egyptian Business Council.[40] Some Israeli officials now spoke openly of finding a new bank for State of Israel Bonds, but others argued that Israel Bonds needed a respected bank like Chase Manhattan more than Chase needed Israeli business.[41]

Then suddenly, Chase came under renewed Arab pressure. In Kuwait individuals and companies dealing with the bank were asked to explain their dealings to the Kuwaiti Boycott Office. Indeed, "boycott proceedings had begun" against Chase, according to Peter M. Pirnie, assistant general manager of the Commercial Bank of Kuwait, which Chase manages under contract.[42] This was happening *not* because Chase managed State of Israel Bonds, but for more capricious reasons.

It turned out that a Beirut newspaper owned by the Kuwaitis had complained that Rockefeller, on his January 1975 visit to Israel, said Chase would continue to assist Israel's economic development. He had also praised Israeli renovation of several holy sites in Jerusalem. Finally, he had apparently offended the Kuwaitis in yet another way. During his Middle East trip, he had sought a Friday meeting with Sheik Jabir al-Ahmad, the Kuwaiti Prime Minister and Crown Prince. When Sheik Jabir had asked that the meeting be held another day, as Friday is the Moslem holy day, Rockefeller had reportedly refused and the Sheik regarded this as a snub.[43]

Banking circles felt that the Arabs had too much money invested through Chase to blacklist it. Chase's huge petro-dollar holdings included one billion U.S. dollars from the Saudi Arabian Monetary Agency alone, plus a $200 million Kuwaiti real estate portfolio. It seemed doubtful the Arabs would find it in their interest to boycott one of their biggest bankers. But Chase was now "walking an Arab-Israeli tightrope," as the *New York Post* put it. If it continued supporting Israel, it might lose its Arab billions; if it surrendered to the Arabs completely, then it could "just about write-off the Jewish community in the States."[44]

Rockefeller claimed the bank had never taken sides in the Arab-Israeli dispute, but Chase's political lobbying on behalf of the Arabs made this neutrality a little suspect. What finally happened showed how powerful a major bank can be. Chase dispatched a vice-president to Kuwait, and the Kuwaiti threat to the bank was at once withdrawn.

IT REMAINS A FACT, however, that commercial banks in the United States and elsewhere, Chase Manhattan included, have consistently and repeatedly complied with the rules and regulations of the Arab boycott, even to the extent of serving the boycott offices as agents and "enforcers." In March 1976, twenty-five U.S. banks were charged by the ADL with waging "economic war against Israel in collaboration with the Arabs [and in] violation of U.S. anti-boycott policy."[45] Before the banks were prepared to pay exporters' letters of credit, they demanded proof of boycott compliance from them. Among the banks were such major ones as Bankers Trust, Chemical Bank, First National City and Morgan Guaranty Trust, all of New York, as well as the Bank of America, the Bank of San Francisco and local banks scattered throughout the country.[46] Several were active in Arab-American chambers of commerce and these groups were often suspected of working on behalf of the boycott offices.

Banks, by honoring these boycott-tainted letters of credit, became involved in questions that are clearly of a discriminatory nature, for they require companies to show that they are not in violation of the Arab Trade Boycott of Israel. The banks' position was defended by the president of Irving Trust Company, Joseph A. Rice, in a letter which denied that his bank had in any way "capitulated" to the boycott. He explained:

> As regards letters of credit, the function which an international bank has is *simply to receive instructions* from a foreign correspondent bank or firm to make payments against certain documents, and *its duties are limited to making such payments when the documents called for are presented.* The bank does not suggest that any particular document or any particular provision be part of the export agreement—*it merely receives instructions* regarding payments *and carries them out.* This practice is, I believe, followed by every bank in the United States involved in the international letter of credit business . . . [emphasis added].[47]

This is again the classic I-only-carry-out-orders excuse, but there seems little doubt that Rice was right when he said U.S. banks routinely follow the practice described. They ought, said Arnold Forster of the ADL, to support American "public policy" and refuse to certify documents that show boycott compliance. The Arabs cannot pay for their purchases except by means of the international banks and if they refuse to co-operate with the boycott, it would end, he said.[48] The ADL, however, has made little headway with that argument. The banks tell it to go to Washington and demand laws to defend them; the ADL in turn tells the banks they should press Washington for laws making boycott compliance illegal.

The banks consistently flinched from fighting the boycott. When, for example, the representatives of Chase, Chemical, Bankers Trust and First National City were subpoenaed in early 1975 to testify on this matter before a New York State Assembly subcommittee, they claimed the boycott wasn't intended "in its governing principles" to bring about discrimination against U.S. firms and citizens. They declared that they would therefore "continue to process letters of credit originating from Arab countries even when they contained boycott provisions and requirements."[49]

One bank at least took a stronger stand. Robert L. McNamara, president of the International Bank for Reconstruction and Development, said in October, 1975, that the World Bank didn't recognize the boycott. "The Bank's rules do not permit bidders for a contract financed under a Bank loan to be excluded because they trade with Israel or are located in a country that trades with Israel," he said. "A contract awarded in violation of this rule would not be eligible for finance under a Bank loan."

How much this contrasted with the attitudes of others was shown again when Federal Reserve Board Chairman Arthur Burns sent U.S. commercial banks a letter in December 1975, warning strongly against the issuance of boycott-tainted letters of credit. This was greeted with such consternation that Burns was persuaded in January 1976 to "clarify" the letter. The earlier message, he said, hadn't been "intended to create a new legal obligation for banks," and he assured them that prime responsibility for U.S. policy on the boycott rested with the Commerce Department. The banks, wrote Sol Stern, "uttered a collective sigh of relief and went back to issuing their letters of credit."[50]

Just how many they were issuing became clear in mid-1976, when a House of Representatives panel was told that 119 banks had complied with 4,071 boycott requests during just one four-month period, ending in March.[51] Morgan Guaranty had dealt with discriminatory Arab letters of credit worth more than $40 million during this period.[52] And in October, Chemical Bank and its parent, Chemical New York Corporation, were charged with having processed, since October 1973, 2,500 letters of credit which required boycott compliance.[53]

More revelations emerged from a House committee. In September 1976, Republican Congressman Benjamin Rosenthal reported that fourteen U.S. banks had acceded to 18,000 requests to participate in boycott restrictions against U.S. companies, and these involved letters of credit for more than one billion dollars worth of business. And in the same year, the National Association of Securities Dealers (NASD) had to reprimand two leading securities houses (Blyth, Eastman, Dillon & Co. and Dillon, Read & Co.) for excluding "Zionist" banks from underwriting syndicates. Its investigation, prompted by the Securities and Exchange Commission, led the NASD to conclude that such activities are "inconsistent with high standards of commercial honor and just and equitable principles of trade."[54] That just might qualify as the understatement of the year.

CHAPTER VII

The Willing
Victims

IN DECEMBER 1974 the Arab boycott spokesman in London,
Kamel Georzes, dealt something of a blow to British pride.
Arab boycott offices, he said, didn't need to tighten their regulations.[1] British businessmen were ready to conform voluntarily
with the Arab boycott, in spontaneous surrender.

The Arabs, in fact, seemed to be enjoying treating Britain
with lordly contempt, while buying it up "with all the fervour
and daring of a champion Monopoly player," as London's
Guardian put it in 1976.

In 1974 the Kuwaitis had paid £107 million in cash for the
St. Martins Property Corporation, which has extensive commercial holdings throughout Britain and elsewhere. In the same year
Abu Dhabi bought a multimillion-pound share in the Commercial Union insurance group and many more deals followed.

Individual Arabs also were "spending millions of pounds"
on London properties, said the *Sunday Telegraph,* and the
Evening Standard's view was that "the Arab fraternity is moving
into London in a big way." In 1976 the Arabs even acquired
the fashionable Dorchester Hotel on London's Park Lane for
$15.9 million, putting in jeopardy the hotel's lucrative Jewish

business, which included many elegant weddings and bar mitzvahs and visits from Israeli President Katzir.[2] The Royal Kensington and the Park Tower were also bought by Arabs, the latter for £8 million. By mid-1976, Arab property investments, private purchases included, topped $445 million, according to a *Time* magazine article which described this "Arab invasion" on August 2, 1976. The purchases of one Arab, Mohammed Mahdi al-Tajir, who boasts he is the world's richest man, have been spectacular. While serving as ambassador to London from the United Arab Emirates, he spent nearly £30 million on property in Britain. This included Mereworth Castle, Kent, which he had picked up for $1.2 million, scandalizing London's staid *Times* on May 25, 1975, by having caused "the devastation of a fine garden" on the property; he had wanted this castle, which had once been used as a setting in the James Bond film *Casino Royale* as a place merely "to hang my pictures," he said, as he already owned a $4.5 million estate in Scotland, a town house overlooking London's Hyde Park, and a suburban home on Kingston Hill.

London, wrote *Time*, looked almost "like Cairo" that summer, for the number of Arab visitors had gone up 77 percent over the previous year; by year's end, 230,000 Arabs and 140,000 Iranians had visited the city. Their tourist spending totaled $500 million. Saudi Arabia demonstrated in 1976 just how much cash it had when it hired Britain's Jimmy Hill to build them a top soccer team, with a budget of £25 million ($44 million).[3]

The $6.2 million mosque completed in 1977 near fashionable—and Jewish-populated—St. Johns Wood is another sign that the Arabs had come to stay. The British reaction proved a mixed one, for the British are largely insular at heart and not usually enchanted by exotic ways and forms of dress. And the visiting Arabs, as *Time* put it, are not only "everywhere," but their "tarbooshes and burnooses [are] as ubiquitous as brollies in the rush-hour crowds." Most were vacationers from Saudi Arabia and the Gulf states, who earlier would have sought relief from the summer heat by going to Lebanon; the war there sent them to London instead, and many rich Lebanese fled to Britain for the same reason. Others came for medical treatment.

Bound to excite attention in London, they also aroused suspicion and resentment. That note could be detected in the *Daily Mirror* headline of April 8, 1975—"It's the Cheek of Araby"; the article reported that an Arab League boycott agent, Ahmed Midjali, patrolled outside London stores which were Jewish-owned, demanding the names and addresses of Arabs who went inside. The snoop ran into trouble when he accosted two girls and their mothers at the door of Marks and Spencer in London's Oxford Street:

> After a minute . . . one of the Arab women—they spoke Arabic with distinct Kuwaiti accents—suddenly brought her umbrella down on the hapless Midjali's head. The two teenage girls promptly pulled out hairpins and stabbed his bottom with them. And, more personally, the other woman assaulted him in an area sensitive to males. The sleuthing diplomat has now left London, sensing that his mission had been both painful and useless.

The *Daily Express*, next to chronicle the visitors' foibles, published the following tale on July 20 that year:

> On a visit to London, Mrs. Annissa Abul Hassan from Kuwait, and the wife of a millionaire, nicked 14 night-dresses, 17 pairs of pants, six pairs of pyjamas, four dresses, seven jumpers, two coats, and a few other little odds and ends.
>
> In fact she was thieving on such a scale that she had two of her young children helping her stuff the loot into four large carrier bags.
>
> On the same day two Saudi Arabian princesses were caught at the same shoplifting racket. One of them even bit the store detective.

Another London paper, the *Financial Times*, in a survey on July 9, 1977, reported there had been 3,000 arrests for shoplifting in London during the first six months of 1977, and that half were Arabs, many of whom were carrying thousands of pounds in cash.

There were other bizarre stories. On July 31, 1975, the *Daily Mirror* said that one of London's "chic" casinos was visited by a sheik with his manservant, the latter lugging two shopping bags stuffed with £10 and £5 notes. The sheik left a few hours later; he had lost a trifling £40,000 ($80,000), but the grateful management filled the shopping bags with souvenir ashtrays, fancy boxes of matches and playing cards. Some months later, Saudi Arabia's Minister of Oil, Sheik Yamani, was in the news. The Associated Press reported on December 11 that he spent £35,000 ($70,000) in a single afternoon's shopping spree at Harrods, London's most elegant department store, and then ran into difficulties over transporting the loot. Eventually, he had to have it carried to London Airport in a hastily hired coal truck. At about the same time, individual Arab shoppers in London were reported to have bought an elephant harness for £250,000, a single consignment of £2,000 worth of chocolates and 750 pairs of cotton underpants for a single Arab's wardrobe.

Major Arab interest, however, continued to concentrate on real estate. More than £2.7 million ($4.5 million) was spent to buy "Clive of India's House," 45 Berkeley Square, where Lord Clive, the conqueror of India in the mid-eighteenth century, had committed suicide in 1774. The Consort Lodge apartment house on Prince Albert Road went to the Iraqi government for £2.5 million ($4.2 million) and the pace in the countryside was just as hot. One London real estate agent said in early 1977 that apartments were being rented by Arabs for as much as £3,000 (about $5,300) *a week*, if they met the Arabs' standards of luxury.

But the Arabs were also using this money in a dangerous, manipulative game which they played with the fragile British pound sterling. Britain is particularly dependent on a substantial inflow of foreign funds, for she suffers from endemically adverse trade balances, never earning enough abroad to pay for her imports. Just how susceptible the economy is to the withdrawal of foreign funds was demonstrated in the sensational fall in the value of the pound during 1976. A near-panic gripped London's

City when sterling dropped to below $2 in value, and when it plummeted to barely $1.50, there was real despair. Eventually, it settled at slightly above $1.70.

This slide was partly caused by Arab withdrawals of vast short-term deposits in British banks, as a Bank of England report made plain in mid-1976. These deposits had been considerable, and Britain's reserves of gold and foreign currencies rose to $7 billion in 1974, alongside rumors that the Arabs held 63 percent of these. Then, in early 1976, OPEC countries reduced their holdings in Britain by $400 million, and at the same time allowed only 5.7 percent of OPEC oil to be paid for in sterling. As fewer countries used the British pound to pay for oil, its value diminished further.[4]

Britain also found it more difficult than other European countries to shake off the effects of the recession and inflation caused by the Arab oil price rises from 1973 onwards. Bad labor relations, gross over-manning in some industries, resultant low productivity and low working morale, all plagued the country, as did low industrial investment, antiquated plants, punitive taxation and other hindrances to expansion. Added to these was a general loss of confidence and aggressiveness in management, and the result has been a chronically sick economy. Yet Britain has still to shoulder the responsibilities of a country of continuing importance—the center of the British Commonwealth of Nations, a leading member of the EEC, and the financial capital of Europe.

This combination of a weak economy and continuing influence in world affairs made it a logical, and almost irresistible, target for the Arab boycott offices. British companies, and the British government, are desperate to share in the bonanza they see in the oil-rich Arab states, and this soon began to tell in Britain's trade figures. Up to 1974 Britain sold more goods to Israel than to all the Middle East "confrontation states"— Egypt, Jordan, Syria, Iraq and Lebanon—combined. But by 1976 these five countries took twice as much from Britain as Israel did. The figures for the entire Arab world were even more startling. In the early 1970's Britain was selling £3 worth of goods to the Arab world for every £1 worth sold to Israel. By 1975 this ratio had changed to 6 to 1 and by 1976 to almost 10 to 1. Early in 1977 the British government reported that 1976 exports to the Arabs had been worth £2 billion, compared with £249 million in Israel. Those figures, the government said, had to be balanced against "any emotional view of the rights and wrongs of the Arab boycott."[5]

BRITISH FEAR of the boycott was dramatically demonstrated in 1975 when the Israel Ports Authority approached eighteen British firms, inviting them to build tugboats for Israel worth £3.5 million (then about $7 million). Although tenders were received from thirty-five non-British shipbuilding yards, just two British yards even bothered to reply to the Israeli offer, and these only to turn it down. The tugboats were eventually built in Norway.

Much the same thing happened the following year when four leading construction companies turned down an opportunity to participate in part of a £150 million project to extend Haifa Port. The Israelis had invited seven British companies to tender. Three didn't answer; the others stated that they couldn't take on any more work at the moment, or that they were "not operating in the territory." The (U.K.) Export Group for the Construction Industry was asked to suggest other companies which might be interested; it didn't even bother to reply.

The editor of *Building Magazine* said he found it "astonishing" to hear British firms were "too busy," since the industry "is continually drawing attention to the lack of work in this country and . . . is exhorted to make up its workload by exporting."[6] The inference was drawn that the companies had been frightened off by the Arabs.[7]

There have been many other instances of British unwillingness to do business with Israel, which go far beyond current British lethargy. Some examples:

Plessey, a huge electronics manufacturer that is well-represented in the Middle East, was approached by an Israeli military mission interested in some of its equipment. Plessey advised the Israelis it didn't want to have any direct contact with the Jewish state.[7] Much the same reaction greeted an inquiry from Koor Industries, Israel's largest industrial complex, when it approached two other British firms, hoping to enter into know-how agreements with them. The aim was to set up a ceramics factory in Israel, and the proposition at first interested both companies until one bowed out, saying it would be "most inadvisable" for it "to become involved with Israel in any way whatsoever." The other then withdrew, being reluctant "to go it alone."

Any number of companies have either "found it impossible to appoint an Israeli representative" or to "send supplies to Israel." The files of the Anglo-Israel Chamber of Commerce, in London, are replete with correspondence of this kind. There have even been published advertisements which reflect the impact of the boycott, such as an ad placed by Midline International, a company with agencies throughout the Arab Middle East, which offered to deliver shipments from Britain to "anywhere in the world, excluding Israel." Publishers of trade journals, catalogs and directories sometimes steer clear of Israel. *Middle East Construction*, in reviewing the market potential in the region, not only failed to mention Israel, but omitted it from the map accompanying the article. The entire area covered by Israel *and* Jordan was labeled "Jordan."[8] Similarly, a London directory of Middle East news media omitted mention of the Israeli press.[9] Such examples are minor, but they show a general fear of incurring Arab displeasure.

One request for tender included a particularly blatant tertiary boycott proviso. Qatar required tenderers to notify Kennedy & Donkin, of Woking, Surrey, consulting engineers, that they could meet the following requirements:

> The Tenderer must not be residing in Israel, or hold its nationality or be one of its agents or working for its benefit. He must not possess any branch or assembly factory in Israel. Neither he nor his agents must be involved in any dealings with Israel's products. The Tenderer must not have granted Israeli firms the right or privelage [*sic*] to

use his name, and not be a partner in Israeli companies, factories or establishments.

The Tenderer must declare that he will abstain from any action contrary to the terms laid down in the preceding paragraph. He must also declare that he will abstain from dealing with foreign companies which are proved to have been marketing Israel's products, that he will not distribute the same and that he will not contribute in any manner intended to consolidate Israel's economy or supply Israel with anything which may serve its military efforts.

. . . The Tender must be accompanied by a certificate from the Tenderer and his associates stating:

a) that neither he nor his associates, nor their staff, will indulge in any political activities in Qatar.
b) that neither he nor his associates, nor their staff, will contravene the Boycott of Israel Law nor will they, during the course of the Contract, do anything to cause them to be placed on the Boycott List.

. . . The Contractor and his associates and his or their Subcontractors and staff shall in all ways observe the Boycott of Israel Law and no materials shall be supplied which have been manufactured by any firm which is on the Boycott List nor shall any materials be shipped in any vessel which is on the list.

Each delivery of materials must be accompanied by a certificate of origin countersigned by the Chamber of Commerce in the country of origin, and by a manufacturer's certificate stating that his goods do not include any material manufactured or made in Israel.

What is most noteworthy here is not only the tertiary boycott demand, but its extension into an area of activity which the official boycott regulations actually permit, "marketing Israel's products." Furthermore, the tertiary boycott is here extended not only to companies with which the contracting British company may deal, but also to their employees.[10]

The most flagrant case of tertiary boycott to have emerged in Britain in recent years is that of the Metal Box Company, a major British firm which manufactures cans, tubes and other containers for companies in the consumer goods business, among them some American corporations and their U.K. subsidiaries.

Metal Box has for a long time had a 27 percent investment in the Israel Can Company and a know-how agreement with it; the relationship was profitable and cordial. Metal Box's Israeli investment had of course put it on the Arab blacklist, and in late 1976 and early 1977 the Arabs discovered a way in which they might be able to force Metal Box into severing its ties with Israel.

It appears that Metal Box had put the idea into the Arabs' heads. One of its advertisements showed ten well-known consumer products, seven of which were packed in its containers. The Arabs, led by Saudi Arabia and Kuwait, reportedly attacked Metal Box through these customers, which included such well-known names as Heinz, Campbell's and Pepsi-Cola. Those among them who did business in the Arab world wouldn't be allowed to continue to do so unless they persuaded Metal Box to give up these Israeli investments. The company, which does business worth £500 million a year (about $850 million) feared losing its big-name customers. And so, in early 1977, it announced regretfully it was ending its ties with Israel. Its customers for the most part firmly denied being involved. Jack Heinz called the affair "outrageous" and denied his company had applied any pressure; Campbell's said the same, adding that it sold its products to both Israel and Arab countries. But Metal Box Chairman Sir Alexander Page stuck to his story, and a company spokesman told Britain's *Export Times* that Arab countries had given instructions "that no product packed in Metal Box packaging would be allowed to be imported" into the Arab world. In June 1977 Sir Alexander announced the sale of the 27 percent investment (for about £800,000, or $1.4 million) to the Israeli directors of Israel Can Company, and said the company would then apply to get off the Arab boycott blacklist.[11]

ANTI-SEMITISM is never far beneath the surface of even a society as traditionally tolerant as Britain's, and the racist connotations of the Arab boycott have become apparent in the United Kingdom, as elsewhere. The notorious case of Norwich Union has already been mentioned; another blatantly anti-Semitic case concerned Gulf Oil Company, which, bowing to Arab pressure, withdrew a promotion promised to a non-Jewish British secretary after she had married a Jew, a Mr. Saul Friedlander. Action by Britain's Race Relations Board secured Mrs. Friedlander cash compensation, reportedly £23,000, but she didn't get the job.

Another case concerned a young Israeli architect working for a leading British firm. When his firm in 1975 took on a major design project for Arab customers, the Israeli, Uri, was moved out to a suburban office where his presence wouldn't offend the Arab clients or embarrass his British bosses.[12] Other British firms have refused to hire Jews, and one bank was even accused of having removed Jews from its board.

A number of British businessmen have complained they were unable to visit the Arab world because they were Jewish, and in April 1977 a British parson, Reverend D. A. Jackson, told *The Times* he had just "for the second time issued a baptism certificate to a man who wanted it to prove he was not a Jew," in order to get an Arab visa.[13] A telephone inquiry to the Kuwaiti embassy in London was revealing in this respect:

QUESTIONER: I am phoning on behalf of a client who, although Jewish, is not a Zionist, has never visited Israel, or contributed money to any Zionist cause. He is in the metal manufacturing business and would like to do business with Kuwait. He received a visa application which enquired as to his religion. In order to avoid embarrassment he would like to know in advance whether his application would be accepted.

EMBASSY: He is Jewish?

QUESTIONER: Yes.

EMBASSY: It is out of the question.

QUESTIONER: Even if he is not a Zionist, but happens only to be Jewish?

EMBASSY: That is his problem.

QUESTIONER: What would be the case if my client sent a person who is not Jewish to represent the firm in Kuwait? Could that person get a visa, even if the owner of the firm is Jewish?

EMBASSY: That would be all right. So long as a person is not Jewish he can get a visa.[14]

Many instances of anti-Semitism have been less obvious. There have been newspaper advertisements for employees "acceptable in the Arab world"—meaning "No Jews need apply." There have been "gentlemen's agreements" under which Jewish members of a firm have been kept out of sight when Arab clients visit Britain, and there have been hints of connivance at discrimination against Jews in exchange agreements between British universities and Arab institutions.

In November 1975 there occurred a particularly disgraceful surrender to the boycott's specifically anti-Jewish provisions. The managing director of Mindacre Limited, a British company 30 percent owned by the Cosalt fisheries group, wrote a letter to a company in Philadelphia, offering to sell its products in Europe and the Middle East. The letter asked the company "to kindly confirm that your business is not owned by Jews or controlled by Jewish interests." As it happened, the U.S. company *was* owned by Jews, and its management sent copies of Mindacre's letter to both the ADL and the U.S. Department of Justice. Cosalt later apologized for its subsidiary's action.

International travel companies operating in Britain have shied away from publicizing Israel. American Express International omitted Israel from its Middle East travel brochures in the spring and summer of 1975; it even left Israel off its maps, as though it didn't exist. Advertisements which in 1975 listed eight Inter-Continental Hotels in six Middle East countries omitted the one in Jerusalem, and in 1975 Thomas Cook Ltd. was issuing travelers checks endorsed "negotiable in all countries of the world except Israel."

British Airways seemed to be discriminating in the same way, by omitting Israel from lists and ads in which it ought to have been included, although one of BA's most profitable runs is its service to Israel. Inquiries by the Anglo-Israel Chamber of Commerce to the national airline produced assurances that none of this was company policy, merely "mistakes" by lower-echelon personnel. The airline promptly made amends, advertised its Israeli service and even joined the Anglo-Israel Chamber of Commerce.

Such cases are instructive, for they demonstrate the insidious workings of the boycott, in matters great and small, and also show that if a company is reminded of the discriminatory nature of its actions, it will often quickly abandon them.

Not always, to be sure. When Britain's P & O line (the Peninsular & Oriental Steam Navigation Co.) was questioned by the Anglo-Israel Chamber of Commerce about the negative certificates which it, like U.S. lines, issues, it loftily advised the Chamber to complain to "those organizations demanding [them]"—in other words, go complain to the Arabs!

The case of Richard Costain Ltd., British civil engineering contractors, is instructive, showing to what lengths fear of the Arabs can drive a solidly based company with an annual turnover of about £100 million ($171 million). It does most of its business outside Britain, but not much of it in the Arab world, yet is extraordinarily sensitive to Arab pressure.[15]

In mid-1971, its U.K. subsidiary, Costain Property Investments Ltd., agreed to develop a large office complex in Watford, outside London, with a company whose chairman is a Jewish businessman, Moss Spiro. When Spiro received Costain's draft agreement, he was amazed to find it demanded compliance with the Arab boycott regulations.

"You undertake with us," Paragraph 13 stated, "that at no stage shall we be obligated to do anything that will cause us to contravene the Arab boycott . . . and that you will in relation to the scheme at all times take such steps (if any) as shall be necessary to enable us to avoid any contravention of such boycott."

What was the Arab boycott doing in Watford, a London suburb? No one could find out. When asked, Costain refused to answer or budge. Moss Spiro refused to sign, and backed out of any involvement with Costain. London's *Jewish Observer* offered an explanation. The affair, it said, was "a symptom of the degree to which British civil engineering firms have been conditioned by the Arab boycott of Israel."[16] It remains a disturbing case, for here we see the tertiary boycott being imposed in purely domestic transactions in which the Arabs are in no way involved.

A further demonstration of how the boycott can disrupt normal business was provided when Inchcape, the giant British shipping and general trading conglomerate, compelled a Hong Kong subsidiary, the Gilman Reinsurance Company, to sever its relations with an Israeli firm, Sahar Insurance (of which General Chaim Herzog, later Israel's ambassador to the UN, was a director). Inchcape would not permit Gilman to continue working with Sahar, even if the Israeli company could find some non-Israeli firm to "front" for it. Inchcape's deputy chairman, Sir Hugh Mackay-Tallock, told a shareholders' meeting his company had done business with the Arab world for over a hundred years, and London's *Times* said it was his company's policy to impose a strict embargo on firms even loosely connected with Israel.[17] A "voluntary" boycott was involved here. Inchcape, in London, had for years been completely unaware of the ties its subsidiary maintained with Israel; so had the Arab boycott offices. When the ties came to Inchcape's attention, it ordered its Hong Kong branch to sever them without even waiting for the boycott offices to find out about them and take action.

There were similarities in the transactions of the Fairey Aviation Group. An Israeli company, Kanaf Arkia, had for some years been buying the Fairey "Islander," a light airplane. Sixteen of these were obtained through Britten-Norman, a company with an agency in Israel called MTI Engineering Limited.

Britten-Norman came under Arab boycott pressure. Although its contract with MTI was terminated, it was still prepared to sell the Israelis three more airplanes through its American agents. This meant that the British airplanes would have to be shipped to the United States, and then back across the Atlantic to Israel, a procedure that would add the transport cost, plus 3.5 percent commission, to the purchase price.

Peter Shore, then British Minister for Trade, asked Fairey at the end of 1974 whether this worthwhile order could not be straightforwardly accepted. At first Fairey said it would help, but in 1975 the company lost courage and stipulated that supply must be through the U.S. agents, in the laborious and expensive manner described.

The Fairey group was soon plunged into further controversy. Towards the end of 1974, the Israeli Minister of Labor placed an order for three of its "Plotterscope" mapping devices.[18] On February 18, 1975, Fairey Surveys of Maidenhead replied as follows: "Due to the Arab boycott regulations we have felt unable to deal directly with your office. In consequence we spoke with the Israeli embassy in London seeking their advice, and found them most unhelpful."

The reason the Israeli embassy had been "unhelpful" was that Fairey wanted this time to deal in a roundabout manner through a Swiss agent in order to carry out what should have been a perfectly straightforward transaction. The Israeli government canceled its order for the Plotterscopes. The terms suggested were demeaning, entailed unnecessary costs, and another supplier could be found in another country.

Two other British firms, of diametrically different character, which simultaneously came under pressure from the Arab boycotters were Barclays Bank, the biggest of Britain's "big four" commercial banks, and the giant mining, mercantile and manufacturing conglomerate of Lonrho.

In 1972 Barclays had joined in a 50–50 partnership with Discount Bank of Israel to create Barclays Discount Bank of Israel, an action which angered the Arabs. On September 1, 1975, Barclays was given four months' notice to sever its connections with Israel, or go on the blacklist.[19]

Barclays had opened a new branch in Abu Dhabi, planned further branches in Dubai and Sharjah and had just arranged an equal partnership with the Banque de Caire, to set up Cairo Barclays International, an enterprise not missed by the Boycott Commission, then meeting in Cairo.

Barclays was blacklisted by Mahgoub in October 1976 —and, as so often happens, heard about it only in the press.

This was the boldest Arab boycott move so far in Britain, and represented a major threat to the world financial community. Barclays responded courageously. Its Chairman, Anthony Tuke, said "an international bank cannot submit to pressure of this sort and must work to support tolerance against intolerance." Nine Arab states blacklisted Barclays. But, when the Boycott Commission met again, in June 1977, Mahgoub announced he was taking Barclays off the blacklist. It had submitted "satisfactory" documents. This, however, seemed a face-saving statement. All Barclays had told the boycott office was that it shouldn't be blacklisted, because its banking activities in Israel dated from the time of British-mandated Palestine; it was *not* withdrawing from Israel to get off Mahgoub's list.

Lonrho, which appears on the Damascus blacklist, provides a peculiar story. Together with Volkswagen, Lonrho jointly licensed an Israeli firm to produce the Wankel rotary engine, contravening boycott rules. Kuwait, oddly, holds 28 percent of Lonrho's equity, despite Lonrho's having been blacklisted. In 1976 Lonrho bought a stake in British Combined Food Stores, whose managing director, Murray Gordon, was Jewish, as were other members of the board. When this took place, a leading London merchant banking house sent a coded cable to one of Lonrho's major shareholders, the Kuwaiti Sheik Nasir, advising him that this purchase, "in the light of Arab policies toward Israel . . . gave rise to serious future implications." The implied threat or warning was ignored, both by the Sheik and by Lonrho. This example of a leading British merchant bank acting as "running dog" for the Arab boycotters is particularly odious.[20]

Kuwait was in the picture earlier, in mid-1975, when a Kuwaiti company warned a British firm, Enfield Winding Wires, that it would no longer be able to deal with them unless Enfield adhered to boycott regulations. An Enfield subsidiary, Delta Metal, held a share in an Israeli company, HHM Limited. Enfield accordingly ordered the sale of this shareholding.

THE ARAB BOYCOTTERS, obviously impressed by British readiness to surrender, set out in 1976 to net a very big British fish. Already in September 1975, Mohammed Mahgoub himself had warned the country's biggest electrical company, General Electric (GEC), that it had only three months in which to stop exporting electronic equipment to Israel, or be blacklisted. Victor Gillibrand, a commercial director in GEC's overseas operations, found the threat "puzzling," as GEC's "substantial" trade with the Arab world dated back to the 1920's and GEC's exports to Israel were "very small in relation to [the company's] overall exports."[21]

Even though GEC was bidding for a $15 billion Saudi Arabian program for power stations and desalinization plants, it fought a delaying action, regarding it wrong to cut off profitable and legal trade with any customer. Kuwait froze all business with GEC, pending her own investigation into the firm's business. Jordan asked for detailed information if she was to go on trading with GEC, and got it. In June 1977, GEC was removed from the blacklist, but its trade had suffered and the firm may, as it claimed, have lost £20 million worth of business in 1975 alone as a result of Arab strong-arm tactics.

A sign that the boycott in Britain may be intensifying came in 1976, when a joint Arab-British Chamber of Commerce was established in London as a potential U.K. agent of the boycott offices. The Chamber's secretary-general was Abdul Karim al-Mudaris, formerly the head of the Arab League office in London, and the boycott office's chief agent in Britain.

The Chamber was helped by British chambers of commerce in publicizing its activities. A letter the Croydon Chamber of Commerce and Industry sent to its members advised business-men in the South London and Surrey area that the new Chamber would be "the sole issuing authority in the U.K. for origin declarations for consignments to the Arab states."

"It is the Arab view," the letter advised, "that this is the only system compatible with the terms of the resolution passed by the Economic Council of the Arab League. . . . It is likely that the Arab-British Chamber of Commerce will arrange for documents to be presented to, and collected from the Embassies after legalisation and returned to exporters. . . ."

[[135]]

A Cairo weekly, *Ach'ar Sa'ah,* carried an interview with Secretary-General al-Mudaris on September 8, 1976. It showed clearly how he saw his job.

> We have one reservation concerning the expansion of trade between Britain, through her companies, and the Arab world. We must settle one important matter, namely that the companies concerned should not trade with the Arab nations' principal enemy, Israel. . . . It is unthinkable that Egypt or Algeria, for example, should trade with a company which conducts commerce with Israeli companies. I personally oversee the implementation of this matter because, prior to taking up my present post, I was the Director of the London Office of the Arab League, which is charged with supervising the Arab boycott against Israel. I have a comprehensive list of British companies and on the Israeli connections of some of them. I presented the condition that companies interested in working with us should not have similar ties with Israel. [Asked how he intended to implement the boycott, al-Mudaris said] *There is no need for certificates of origin. We attach documents to any product exported from Britain to any part of the world. Such a document suffices because it identifies each company.* This will be implemented from October 4 [1976] [emphasis added].

British nervousness became acute, both because of the mounting attack by the Arab boycott offices and because of the signal and continuing failure of the British government to take a really firm anti-boycott stance. In January 1977, Benjamin Edgington (Sidcup) Ltd., a British company which manufactures tents, tarpaulins, flags and canvas goods, refused to fill even a small order of two tents for Israel because, as its letter put it, "each year we regularly supply in contract quantities heavy tentage of the type you briefly describe to Arab Defence Forces, and owing to the present ruling we are precluded from exporting such productions to your country." During the same month, Britain's Tetley Tea company announced it was pulling out of Israel—for "purely business considerations." By July,

[[136]]

mounting compliance led to the introduction of Britain's first anti-boycott bill. (More on this in Chapter X.)

ACROSS THE ENGLISH CHANNEL, the Arabs have occasionally encountered firmness. West Germany's booming economy ensures that it is no soft target for the boycotters. When Arab oil embargo and oil restrictions were imposed at the time of the 1973 war, the Arabs did not rate West Germany a "friendly" country. Saudi Arabia's Sheik Yamani suggested it could achieve this status by supplying arms and technology to his country; in January 1974 he added a demand for political support in the Middle East dispute. West Germany said it would offer all possible nonmilitary industrial assistance, but would continue to trade with Israel. As German-Arab trade continued on a normal basis thereafter, it appears the Arabs accepted the firm German stand.

They did, however, decide to "make an example" of a major West German firm and picked on Volkswagen, which, together with Lonrho, had licensed Israeli use of the Wankel rotary engine. In March 1973 they gave the company ninety days in which to end its arrangements with Israel. It was either to break its contract, get rid of the Wankel patent or divest itself of the NSU (Neckarsulm) company, from which it had inherited the engine. All this was "senseless," a leading West German paper pointed out, as VW's exports to the Arab world amounted to no more than two days' production at its Wolfsburg plant, or about 10,000 cars."" Furthermore, these threats ran counter to Arab interest in investing in West German industry; Kuwait, to give just one example, had bought shares in Daimler-Benz.[23]

The pressure on VW continued through 1976, with the boycott offices every six months issuing new warnings to VW to end its licensing arrangement with Israel, but the Arabs never did manage, throughout those three years, to find the courage to ban the automobile giant. And this was because the West German government, although not prepared to legislate against the boycott, was intervening on VW's behalf.

[[137]]

The official position regarding the boycott is much the same as it is in Britain. Bonn's Economics Ministry said West German firms must make their own decisions as to how they will react to boycott pressures, although the government was prepared to help behind the scenes, and much more firmly than their French and British counterparts.[24] As for the West German business community, it did not mince words in condemning the boycott. In March 1976 the Hamburg Chamber of Commerce called it "a particularly grotesque strain of discrimination against freedom of trade" and all West German chambers of commerce have ever since 1965 refused to validate negative certificates of origin. It came as no surprise, therefore, that the Association of German Chambers of Commerce and Industry was reported in August 1976 as being "clearly unhappy" about the formation of an Arabian-German Chamber under the auspices of the Arab League. London's *Times* said the Germans feared "that the new body could be used to put Israel at a disadvantage and in an extreme case could be used to promote a boycott of trade between West Germany and Israel."[25] West Germany has been running neck-and-neck with Britain as Israel's second most important trading partner (after the United States), and although it is reported that 200 West German firms are blacklisted by the Arabs, Bonn's Economics Ministry claims it has no record of any breach of contract in an export agreement resulting from the continuing refusal of chambers of commerce to validate negative certificates of origin.[26]

France presents a very different picture. Business and even government in France have freely complied with boycott demands. Banks and insurance companies have routinely required boycott-tainted negative certificates of origin before processing export documents or extending credit.

Yet, although the French government sides with the Arabs and has refused to help firms and banks which come under boycott threat, there appear to be more French than German firms on the Arab boycott blacklists. According to reasonably reliable reports, the French names on the lists total over 300.* One reason may be that France has a 700,000-strong Jewish community, with considerable commercial interests, while West Germany has only about 30,000 Jews.

The Arab Trade Boycott produced a test case for France in 1959. Renault, the state-owned automobile manufacturer, was blacklisted because it had entered into a contract with Kaiser-Frazer of Israel, to assemble 2,400 units in Israel over an eighteen-month period. After 800 had been assembled, Renault in August 1959 surrendered to Arab pressure and reneged on the rest of the agreement. At the same time, it announced it would build a much larger plant in Egypt, to produce 17,000 cars a year. This surrender brought rough justice. U.S. sales of Renaults dropped 25 percent, partly because the American Jewish community stopped buying them, and the company never regained its earlier position in the U.S. market. Then, ironically, the Egyptian contract went to Italy's Fiat instead of to Renault. Finally, when Renault in 1963 tried to resume operations in Israel, its offer was turned down. Surrender to the boycott had proved an economic disaster for the firm.

In contrast, the Marcel Dassault aircraft manufacturing company, blacklisted for supplying Mirage jets to Israel, continues to sell airplanes to Libya, Kuwait, Saudi Arabia, Abu Dhabi and Egypt.[28] All these are evidently prepared to ignore boycott regulations against arms help to Israel if they want a product badly enough.

A sensation was caused in France in 1962, when the Arab boycotters tried to compel two French oil companies to rid themselves of their chairman. He was, in both cases, war hero

---

* According to Dr. L. S. Leshnik, director of the ADL's European Affairs Department, 250 French companies are blacklisted by Lebanon alone; the authoritative *Frankfurter Allgemeine Zeitung* in 1975 gave the number as 323, and our own private sources in France indicate that 336 French firms are known to be blacklisted.[27]

and former Defense Minister General Pierre Koenig, who had incurred the Arab's displeasure by joining the France-Israel Friendship Association. That attempt at strong-arming was sternly rebuffed. More cooperative is a semi-governmental company, COFACE, which insures French exports, but won't guarantee exports to the Arab world if the companies involved also deal with Israel.[29] COFACE, and for that matter the French government, were thrown into confusion in 1977 by the passage of an anti-boycott law the government hadn't sponsored. (More on this in Chapter X.)

The government's attempts to woo the oil-rich Arabs, ever since the 1973 Yom Kippur War, led her in early 1977 into what the London *Times* described as almost a "foreign policy alliance" with Saudi Arabia. But these attempts haven't paid off.[30] France's Middle East trade declined.

Italy appears to have managed her trade with the Middle East better. She continues to be Israel's fourth largest trading partner, equal with Holland, and the Italians are reportedly adept at circumventing the demands of the boycotters through a variety of subterfuges. "Invoices," says an ADL report, "are frequently handled through dummy companies, goods are transported in vessels that do not call at Arab ports, and cans of food produced in Israel are distributed with neutral labels, mainly by ships' chandlers."[31] The Italian government, which officially avoids giving any guidance concerning the boycott, claims to be unaware that any Italian firm has been blacklisted by the Arabs. But the Arab boycott threat against Fiat, described earlier, had created enormous publicity, and the pressures are well known in Italian business circles. As to Fiat, early 1977 saw a radical change in its relations with Libya and with that country's ruler, Colonel Quaddafi, who had initiated the earlier action against the car manufacturer. In January 1977 the Libyan Arab Foreign Bank bought nearly 10 percent of Fiat, for several hundred million dollars of Libyan oil revenues. It was a good business deal for both parties, and the head of the Libyan bank, Abdulla A. Saudi, was even willing to wink at the fact that the Fiat board includes someone from Lazard Frères, that blacklisted "Jewish bank." *Fortune* magazine quoted Saudi as saying, "Profitability should be our guide."[32]

The Fiat deal was followed by others. Several more Italian companies won major contracts in the Arab world for various construction, energy and infrastructure projects, and London's *Financial Times* said on February 23, 1977, that Italy was making a major effort "to penetrate the new markets of the oil-producing countries of the Middle East." Boycott pressures within Italy, directed at Italian companies that trade with Israel while participating in this effort to penetrate the Arab world, are therefore almost certain to increase.

Both Holland and Denmark are "hero nations" to the Jewish people and, predictably, have produced no notable boycott cases. Royal Dutch Airlines (KLM) has always resisted Arab pressure for it to stop advertising tours to Israel, and the Dutch government has banned the listing of religious affiliations in municipal certificates, which had been sought by persons applying for jobs in Arab countries to prove they were not Jewish. Dutch officialdom refuses to notarize negative certificates of origin. This laudable brand of Dutch courage was matched in Denmark, and produced the results firmness usually does. The F. L. Smith company, which provided the only publicized Danish boycott case in recent years, was called upon by Iraq in 1975 to sign a clause in a contract stating it had no commercial dealings with Israel. The company refused to do so. Iraq gave in, and the $100 million deal, involving machinery for cement factories, went ahead satisfactorily.

In Sweden, seventy-nine companies are on just the Saudi Arabian blacklist. Pripps is blacklisted because it produces Coca-Cola for Sweden, and Saab, the automobile manufacturer, is blacklisted because it sells trucks to Israel. Anti-boycott legislation is a possibility in Sweden, thanks to the victory of the Liberals in 1976. The new Deputy Premier, Per Ahlmark, said he would study U.S. laws against the boycott before calling for passage of Swedish counterparts.[33]

A stir was caused when the Belgian government assured Saudi Arabia that no Jewish journalists would accompany King Baudouin on his visit to that country in November 1975.[34]

Portugal was threatened with an oil embargo after the 1973 war, for having allowed use of the Azores as a fueling stop for U.S. aircraft on their way to Israel. Firms in countries like Spain and Turkey have generally given in to the boycott, shunning all publicity. Post-Franco Spain is in fact wooing the Arabs, and being bought up by them as well. A great deal of real estate has gone to oil-rich sheiks, and the Spanish Finance Ministry has been seeking credits of up to $3 billion from Saudi Arabia, Kuwait, Abu Dhabi, Qatar and Libya. Small countries like Malta and Cyprus have also been careful to conform to boycott regulations.

Communist countries could hardly be expected to offend the Arabs, but Romania provided the single exception. Ever since 1970, Romania has been subjected to a wide range of Arab boycott restrictions, having been held "guilty" of re-exporting goods imported from Israel. The state airline, Tarom, was blacklisted in August 1975, though within two weeks it had opened a new air link to Tripoli, in Libya.[35] In early 1976 Romania bowed to Arab pressure and suspended purchase of Iranian oil channeled through Israel's Eilat-Ashkelon pipeline.[36] The boycott office hailed Romania's decision to switch to Arab oil, calling it a move "to consolidate Romania's relations with the Arab states." But Foreign Trade Minister Nicolae Nicolae denied his country was surrendering.

"If we were," he said on a visit to Israel, "I would not be here to sign a new trade agreement with you." Romanian-Israeli trade was worth $50 million in 1975. The question was whether Romania could get away with increasing trade with Israel while buying Arab oil shipped through the Suez Canal.[37]

India has not been a major target for the boycotters, but the Indians ran into trouble in August 1975, when they refused to issue visas to Israeli delegates-elect to the International Textile Conference scheduled to take place in Bombay in November. Prompt action was taken by the British senior vice-president of the International Federation of Cotton and Allied Textile Industries, which has its headquarters in Zurich, Switzerland. Tom Normanton, a British Member of Parliament, canceled the conference when the Indian government refused to change its mind. He had established beyond doubt that the Arab states had demanded the exclusion of the Israelis, and he considered such behavior unjustifiable.

About 150 Japanese companies are boycotted, among them Matsushita Electrical, the country's biggest electronics firm, in its case because of links with RCA, itself blacklisted by the Arabs.[38] But the classic story concerns JAL, Japan Air Lines. In the winter of 1967, Israeli-Japanese negotiations began over a proposed mutual air agreement between JAL and Israel's national carrier, El Al. But the Japanese failed to attend meetings which had been arranged and avoided answering correspondence. By 1969 it had become clear that Japan Air Lines was boycotting Israel. A year later its vice-president, Nobuo Matsamura, admitted that there was no intention of opening a service to Israel, giving as his reason that there was a shortage of planes and pilots for existing routes.[39] Protests by the Israeli government and U.S. Jewish organizations were politely but opaquely fobbed off. JAL used every possible argument—that it was contemplating a decision, correspondence had gone astray, it had to consult with the Japanese government, unspecified "economic reasons" for postponement of a decision had arisen. An unofficial boycott of JAL by members of B'nai B'rith produced no result.

Finally, a note on Canada—an inevitable target for the boycotters because of her connections with the United States. A figure of 100–200 Canadian blacklisted firms would not be wide of the mark.[40] In May 1975, the Canadian Minister of Trade and Industry, Alastair Gillespie, admitted that public money (upwards of $2 million) was being used to underwrite deals with Arab countries by Canadian firms which had knuckled under to the boycott.[41] The Canadian Council of Churches revealed that Saudi Arabia and Libya were demanding baptismal certificates for visiting Canadians; it called on member-churches to stop issuing these.[42] Other charges followed. Minister for External Affairs Allan MacEachen was accused in 1976 of avoiding the boycott question when he signed an economic cooperation pact with Saudi Arabia.[43] In addition, the government failed to back one firm, Logix Enterprises of Montreal, which refused to fill in the Kuwaiti boycott questionnaire—a refusal the Kuwaitis accepted, backing down. And an independent report published in January 1977 charged the government, its agencies and officials, with "acquiescing" in the boycott and "facilitating" its application, at the same time as Canada's Prime Minister Pierre Trudeau and External Affairs Minister Donald Jamieson were calling the boycott "repugnant" and "unacceptable."

Some anti-boycott action had been taken, however. In August 1976 the government stopped certifying documents enabling Canadians to travel in Saudi Arabia by proving them to be non-Jews. In October, Jamieson announced that companies complying with the boycott would face public exposure and lose government aid. But implementation of the new policy was slow, and Trudeau even said his government had gone as far as it could. Whether U.S. anti-boycott legislation will beef up these half-measures remains an open question.[44]

Refusal or hesitancy to act isn't confined to countries like Britain. Wherever one looks in Europe, Asia and the Third World, there is complaisance and concern, fear and a dim hopefulness that the problems caused by the economic war against the Jews will somehow vanish by and of themselves. The picture, outside the United States, Canada and France is mainly depressing, and one can only gain light relief from the absurdities of many aspects of this economic war. The fact that the works of Emile Zola are blacklisted by the Arabs because Zola's efforts helped free Captain Dreyfus, a Jew, from Devil's Island in the nineteenth century is one such irrelevance. Another occurred in 1975 when a Nicosia newspaper revealed that Cypriot refugee farmers had become targets of the Arab boycott. Arab governments, reported *Egon* on June 7, were considering banning all Cyprus's dairy products because they originated from the udders of Israeli cows. The Cyprus government had imported 187 cows from Israel and given them to refugee farmers; it planned to bring in 160 more, because the price was right. Not so the milk, however, nor the cheeses, as far as Arabs were concerned.[45]

CHAPTER VIII

The Imp
out of Hell

The *Times-Picayune* of New Orleans, Louisiana, on March 12, 1975, made the editorial comment that the boycott "seems clearly based on long-standing, indiscriminate anti-Semitism rather than present power politics. . . ." This fact has been overlooked by those who have not studied traditional, historic Arab attitudes towards the Jews, ignored by those who are beguiled by the notion that the Arabs, being "Semites" themselves, cannot be anti-Semitic in an anti-Jewish sense.

The Arabs of course deny any anti-Semitism on their part. Mohammed Mahgoub often claims the boycott "is not based on ethnic or religious considerations [and] does not discriminate on the basis of nationality or religion."[1] Foreign observers, however, aren't so sure. The *Wall Street Journal*, for example, on February 14, 1975, made the point that Arab blacklisting "appears less to be an attempt to undermine Israel than . . . to inject anti-Semitism into Western business practice." The Arabs always "had trouble distinguishing these two purposes."

The anti-Semitism which animates the boycott has ancient roots, although Arabs deny this too. President Quaddafi of Libya, for example, alleges that "reactions against the Jews were registered in Arab lands" only after 1948. One Arab spokesman after another has maintained that Jews lived in concord with Arabs until the "Zionist invasion" of the Middle

East began. They claim they are themselves "Semites" and cannot campaign against their own race. But the whole outside world recognizes anti-Semitism for what it is: an age-old discrimination against the Jews, partly racial, partly religious in origin. There has never been any such campaign against the Arabs; discrimination against them has been political, economic, colonial, coincidental.

True, Islamic persecution of the Jews has never been as deep-rooted or as virulent as Christian, but it has on occasion been quite as brutal. Moslems never regarded the Jews as guilty of deicide. Well before the Prophet Mohammed was carried on his way to Heaven on his white charger he put the Jews in their allotted place in the Moslem world, that of second-class citizens. That place requires explanation.

It begins with the Koran, Mohammed's book of divine revelation. As one scholar points out, because the Jews did not accept Islam "precisely at the moment when his critical situation required more than ever before the help of his allies in monotheistic belief," Mohammed felt betrayed by them. His disappointment is recognizable from this point on in the "revealed" verses of the Koran, proclaiming the "Divine Word":

> The Jews are the enemies of Allah, of the prophet and of the angels (2:97–98); they have always been disobedient (5:78); they exercise unrighteousness (5:61–79); they attempt to introduce corruption (5:64); they are enemies of the believers (5:82); they have twisted the word of Allah (2:59, 75–79, 211); they lie against Allah (4–50); they are damned by Allah because of their disobedience (2:88, 4:46, 52, 5:13, 60, 64, 78); they have killed the prophets of Allah (5:70); they will receive the punishment of hell-fire (59:3).[2]

Admittedly, the Jews were regarded as "people of the Book," believers in one God who are therefore to be granted "protection" by their Moslem conqueror, but protection as inferiors. They were "smitten with abasement and poverty," "met with wrath from God," "they were rebellious and had transgressed," and "hostile to the Muslims whose downfall they seek." They

[[147]]

are "falsifiers of Scripture" and, because they rejected the teaching of Mohammed, they aroused the anger of God, who "condemned them to humiliation and wretchedness."

Elsewhere in Arab writings the Jews are depicted as rebellious people who violate the "world order," as anti-socials, and even as doomed—"branded with the marks of wrath and malediction of the Lord."[3] In his *Introduction to the Science of History*, published in 1964, Abd al-Rahman ibn Khaldun claims that Jews are intrinsically evil; as a race, "corrupt and deceitful."[4]

Sheik Hassan Ma'moun, the rector of Al Azhar University, went further than this at Cairo's 1968 Fourth Conference of the Academy of Islamic Research. The "adherents" of Zionism today, he said, were "destined to dispersion by the Deity," and as for Jews, the Koran (II, 61) said, "humiliation and wretchedness were stamped upon them and they were visited with wroth from God."

That Cairo Conference produced a great body of anti-Jewish utterances, all meant as scholarly and definitive contributions to modern Islamic thought. A study of the Old Testament, presented by Kamal Ahmed Own, vice-principal of Tanta Institute, revealed that the "wickedness" of the Jews "is incurable unless they are subdued by force." He said:

> No good is expected from them. They are hostile to all human values in this life [and] their evil nature is not to be easily cured through temporary half-measures . . . evil, envy, hatred and cruelty are inherent in them . . . whenever they triumphed over an enemy, they were like wild beasts. They destroyed everything in their way whether it be human, or an animal, a plant, or an inanimate thing . . . The Jews' wicked nature never changes . . . Evil, wickedness, breach of vows and money worship are inherent qualities in them . . .
>
> One might ask why so many disasters and calamities befell those people in particular. The answer to this question is not difficult. Their wicked nature, which has always alienated them from mankind, lies at the bottom of this fact . . . Modern civilization has only increased their hypocrisy, their power, their wealth and their penetration

into the social life of nations from behind the scenes . . .
Zionists now repeat the barbaric actions and horrible crimes
of their ancestors in Palestine backed by imperialism, slay-
ing women and children and ripping up pregnant women . . .

A large number of Conference speakers spoke in similar
terms. Sheik Abd Allah al-Meshad characterized Jews as selfish,
envious usurers; Muhammed Azzah Darzawa concluded that "all
people want to get rid of the Jews by hook or by crook" and
the Jews "are thirsty for drinking more blood of the Muslims";
Professor Abdul Sattar al-Sayed, the Mufti of Tursos, Syria,
referred to Jews as "bringing about corruption, sowing the
seeds of enmity and hatred and breaking the bonds of brother-
hood between peoples . . . like germs of a malignant disease
where only one germ is sufficient to eliminate an entire nation
. . . a pest or a plague that is cursed like Satan . . ."[5]

This 1968 Conference was not expounding anything new. A
hadith (proclamation) of the eighth century stated, "A Jew will
not be found alone with a Muslim without plotting to kill him";
and a thirteenth-century Syrian writer, Abd al-Rahman al-
Jawbari, explained that "Jews were the agents of the Devil: It
is known that this group is the most cursed of all God's creation,
the most evil-natured, and the most deeply rooted in infidelity
and accursedness. They are the most evil-intentioned of mankind in their deeds, even though they are the most ostentatious
in humility and self-abasement."

Frantic vilification has continued down to the present. One
finds the Minister of Justice in the 1941 pro-Nazi Rashid Ali
government of Iraq claiming that Judaism is a threat to the
whole of mankind.[6] Thirty years later, King Faisal of Saudi
Arabia declared that the Jews would be reconsigned to the
humiliation and wretchedness reserved for them by the Koran.

President Anwar Sadat broadcast this same message over
Radio Cairo on April 25, 1972, the anniversary of the birth of
the Prophet Mohammed:

> Nobody can ever decide the fate of Jerusalem. We shall
> re-take it with the help of God out of the hands of those

of whom the Qu'ran [Koran] said, "It was written of them that they shall be demeaned and made wretched." . . . They are a nation of liars and traitors, contrivers of plots, a people born for deeds of treachery. . . . They shall return and be as the Qu'ran said of them, "condemned to humiliation and misery. . . ."

Some Moslem Arabs even accepted the "blood libel," which claimed that Jews slaughtered Christians—in particular Christian infants—in order to mix their blood with Passover bread. This myth originated in medieval Europe and was exported to the Arab world. The first alleged "case" in the Middle East was the Damascus blood libel of 1840, just two years after the first European consulates were established in Beirut and Jerusalem. In *Talmudic Human Sacrifices*, published in Cairo in 1890, Habib Faris called his book an "indictment, based upon clear-cut evidence that the Jewish people permit the shedding of blood as a religious duty enjoined in the Talmud."[7]

From then on, stories of ritual murder by Jews multiplied and have been "confirmed" by Arab writers of modern times. In 1936 Ibrahim al-Awra wrote that "mothers would caution their children not to go out alone late at night, lest the Jew . . . come and take their blood for the purpose of making matzot [unleavened bread] for Passover."[8] And this appeared in the newspaper *al-Mussawar* as recently as August 4, 1972:

> It happened that two years ago while I was in Paris on a visit, the police discovered five murdered children. Their blood had been drained, and it turned out that some Jews had murdered them in order to take their blood and mix it with the bread that they eat on this day [Passover]. This shows you what is the extent of their hatred and malice toward non-Jewish peoples.[9]

The speaker was King Faisal of Saudi Arabia.

Many Arab intellectuals and political leaders have accepted the malicious forgery of *The Protocols of the Elders of Zion*, that account of an alleged Jewish plot to destroy world civilization. Egypt's President Sadat quoted extensively from its pages in his book, *Quissat al-wahda al-Arabiya* (Cairo, 1957); his predecessor, President Nasser, gave a copy of the *Protocols* to an Indian journalist in 1958, and urged him to study it.

Ten years later, Nasser's brother, Shawqi Abd al-Nasir, published the extant, "popular" edition of the *Protocols*, and in the same year the former President of Iraq, Abdel Rahman Aref, publicly thanked an Arab historian for his published commentary on this document.[10] In 1974 we find King Faisal presenting copies of the *Protocols* to the visiting French Foreign Minister, Michel Jobert, with some of his officials noting that they were this medieval monarch's favorite reading.[11] Dr. Muhammad Nasr's *Zionism in International Affairs* (Cairo, 1957) cites Hitler's *Mein Kampf* as incontrovertible evidence of the authenticity of the *Protocols*.

The *Protocols* in fact have a bizarre history. In the 1860's a French satirist, Maurice Joly, wrote an imaginary conversation ("Dialogue aux Enfers") between Machiavelli and Montesquieu, aimed at French Emperor Napoleon III. A Jew, Dr. de Cyon, rewrote this satire at the beginning of this century, substituting Russia's progressive Finance Minister, Count de Witte, for the French emperor. A Russian official, Rachovsky, stole de Cyon's unpublished version and substituted the "Elders of Zion" for Count de Witte.

The Rachovsky document was then edited by an obscure monk, Brother Nilus, and by 1905 it had acquired sufficient "authenticity" to find its way into the possession of the Czar. Little was done with this forgery until 1918, when it began to be quoted in publications of all kinds. The British *Morning Post* devoted a long series of articles to "the Jewish plot" and the assistance of Henry Ford was enlisted in the United States. A British writer, Nesta Webster, wrote a book on the *Protocols*, fixing fatherhood of the nonexistent "plot" on an obscure Jacobin of the French Revolution, Gracchus Babeuf.

In 1921 the Constantinople correspondent of London's *Times* finally exposed the forgery and traced its roots back to Joly's satire of 1864. The true story of the *Protocols* is still not accepted by anti-Semites. It circulated throughout the 1930's, and in World War II, copies traveled in the knapsacks of the Waffen-SS. In 1967, and perhaps also in 1973, they were issued to Arab soldiers fighting Israel. In the 1970's, anti-Semites in the West were still quoting the *Protocols*—sometimes with a new twist. *Spearhead*, the organ of Britain's neo-Nazi National Front, argued that the *Protocols* may not be genuine, but that if they aren't, they might as well be, for what they contained was a truthful portrait of what "world Jewry" was up to. If it was fiction, these anti-Semites argued, it was inspired.

"NAZI ANTI-SEMITISM—theory, practice and policy—fitted the needs of the Arab nationalist movement [of the 1930's] like a glove," writes Dafna Allon, in *Arab Racialism* (Jerusalem, 1969). Arab youth clubs received support from Baldur von Schirach, leader of the Hitler Youth; Iraqi clubs sent delegates to the Nazi rallies at Nuremberg; and close ties with Hitler led to the Grand Mufti, Haj Amin al-Husseini, broadcasting over Radio Berlin during World War II, inciting Arabs to join the German forces wherever they met them. Nazi agents, propagandists and military officers found themselves welcomed throughout the Arab world. Nazis found refuge in Arab countries after the Allied victory and subsequently served the Egyptians, entered their army as officers and produced anti-Semitic propaganda for the Arab cause. One such, Johann von Leers, who adopted the name Omar Amin, was greeted by the Mufti in these words: "We thank you for venturing to take up the battle with the powers of darkness that have become incarnate in world Jewry."

A Hitler, even an Eichmann, cult has grown up in the Arab world. Tabbara's *The Jews in the Qu'ran* (Beirut, 1966) quotes Hitler extensively, and the Jordanian English-language daily, *Jerusalem Times*, published an "Open Letter to Eichmann" on April 24, 1961, congratulating him on the mass murder of Jews and promising that the surviving six million Jews of the world would be liquidated in their turn. In *The Danger of World Jewry to Islam and Christianity*, published in Cairo in 1964, Abdullah al-Tall called Eichmann "a martyr," and on June 9, 1960, the Lebanese newspaper *al-Anwar* produced a cartoon in which the Israeli leader David Ben-Gurion is shown in a shouting match with Eichmann. An extract from their conversation:

> BEN-GURION: You deserve the death penalty for killing six million Jews.
>
> EICHMANN: There are many who agree that I deserve it— for not finishing the job.

Some Arabs found overidentification with Nazi teaching embarrassing. They discovered a convenient alternative line of attack. Thus, Anis Sayegh, in *Palestine and Arab Nationalism* (Beirut, 1966) explains that "Zionism and Nazism stand on the same foundation and therefore they struggle with each other and interchange the most repulsive hostility . . . The Nazis slaughtered Jews and it was not the Jews who slaughtered the Nazis, but this was not because the Jews were good and the Nazis bad, but because the Nazis were stronger and more numerous. . . . If the proportions had been reversed, then the Zionists would have inflicted the same slaughter on the Nazis." A variant is that Jews were never the enemies of Nazi tyranny. Their struggle against Nazism was "merely" for survival.

ARAB DISCRIMINATION took clear shape as long ago as 717–720, when Caliph Omar II ordered that all non-Moslems, the *dhimmis* or the "protected," should wear distinctive dress. Thus Jewish women had to wear tinted shoes with bells on them. By the twelfth century, Jews were being ordered, in Christian as well as Moslem countries, to wear a yellow patch on their clothing; yellow is the color of shame, just as blue is the color of God and green of Mohammed.

The status of the *dhimmi* is explained by Antoine Fattal:

> The "dhimmi" is a second-class citizen. If he is tolerated, it is for reasons of a spiritual nature, since there is always the hope that he might be converted; or of a material nature, since he bears almost the whole tax burden. . . . He is marked out for social inequality and belongs to a despised

caste; unequal in regard to individual rights; unequal as regards taxes; unequal in the Law Courts as his evidence is not admitted by any Muslim tribunal, and for the same crime his punishment is greater than that imposed on Muslims.[12]

Louis Gardet points out that the *dhimmi* must "always behave as an inferior adopting a humble and contrite attitude. For example, on payment of the poll tax, the 'gadi,' on receiving the money, must make as if to give the *dhimmi* a light slap in the face so as to remind him of his place."[13]

Distinctive clothing, heavy taxation and simulated slaps were only a small part of the burdens of the Jews of the Arab world during the last twelve hundred years. Their homes were looted and they were swindled in the marketplace, a favorite trick being to pay them half, or less, of the agreed price. Jews could have recourse to the law, but their word could not be accepted against that of a Moslem. Members of Jewish communities were expelled from their homes or forbidden to leave them even for an hour's journey. In some parts of the Arab world, they could not own horses, only donkeys; in others, they were forced to dismount if they met an Arab.

The ghetto was an invention of the Moslem world. An early instance was the creation of a Jewish ghetto, or *mellah*, in the Bab-Zuwalya quarter of Cairo in the eleventh century. The walled-in *mellah* came later. The first was in Fez, in the fourteenth century, and within a hundred years this became the pattern for the whole of Morocco, with *mellahs* in Marakesh, Meknes, Tetuan, Rabat, Mogador, Sate.

Discrimination was supplemented by rigorous persecution. After Mohammed destroyed the Jewish tribes of the Hedjaz in 624–28, bitter persecution of the Jews occurred in almost every century. In 1033 more than six thousand Jews were massacred in Fez, in 1066 another five thousand were killed in the Spanish town of Granada, then in Moslem hands. Ruthless persecution became the rule in most of North Africa in the twelfth century. The "golden age" of the Jews of the Arab world was a myth, as has been explained by Professor Bernard Lewis:

The myth was invented by Jews in nineteenth-century Europe as a reproach to Christians and taken up by Muslims in our own time as a reproach to Jews. . . . European travellers to the East in the age of liberalism and emancipation are almost unanimous in deploring the degraded and precarious position of Jews in Muslim countries, and the dangers and humiliations to which they were subject. Jewish scholars, acquainted with the history of Islam and with the current situation in Islamic lands, can have no illusions on this score.[14]

Nor did matters improve in the nineteenth century. There were massacres of Jews in Algeria in 1805 and in Iraq in the first thirty years of the century. Thousands of Iraqi Jews fled to Persia and India. The Damascus "blood libel" of 1840 was duplicated four years later in Alexandria. From then on this became the pretext for periodic pogroms of the Jews. In 1864 there was a bestial attack on the Jews of the Tunisian island of Djerba, today a tourist paradise. According to one contemporary account, all the women and girls there were raped, and their menfolk obscenely tortured in their presence.

In 1869 there were further riots and murders of Jews in Tunisia; in 1875 it was the turn of the Jews of Morocco, with 43 slain in the streets of Taza and another 20 in Demnat. Fresh blood libels in Damascus and Alexandria brought mob violence in Syria and Egypt. In Libya, the Jews of Zliten became a special target for persecution. Their synagogues were looted and burned, and mobs rampaged through the Jewish quarter. In 1880 an old, pious and utterly harmless Jew of Entifa in Morocco was first crucified and then beaten to death, simply because he had taken in a poor Moslem woman and given her work and lodging. In the 1890's the center of violence shifted back to Libya, then to Algeria, while the new century was ushered in at Casablanca with a particularly revolting assault on the Jewish community. At least 30 Moroccan Jews were murdered, and more than 200, including young boys and girls, were abducted, raped and then ransomed. Moslem violence against the Jews raged like a plague, moving from one area to another, striking suddenly, without warning.

In 1884 the enlightened Sultan of Morocco decreed that certain disabilities suffered by the Jews of Demnat should be annulled. Revealingly, there were a score of them; among them were forced labor without pay, and on Jewish holy days; forced labor in the collection of refuse and the carrying of excessive burdens on their backs; heavy labor by women, and surrender of their beasts of burden. Financial disabilities included forced sale of goods at half value or for deferred payment when the price had dropped; acceptance of debased or counterfeit coinage in payment, as well as levies on money changed; arbitrarily levied taxes and contributions, and forced billeting of "government guests" and other officials; surrender of hides and sheep's wool without payment, and surrender of tanned hides for untreated skins.

One rabbi's account of life in Yemen gives a graphic description of the sufferings of his people there. When a Jew met a Moslem on the street, he had to greet him first, as "Sidi" (Lord). Jews could not ride horses or camels, only donkeys, but these only outside towns, and they had to dismount if they met a Moslem. If stoned in the streets, Jews could not defend themselves, other than to ask a Moslem to intervene. They could not even wear nicely framed spectacles or decent clothing, for that would be vanity and an offense to Moslems less well arrayed. The Jews of Yemen, in fact, were not much better than slaves; they were, on occasion, literally sold into slavery.[15]

There has been no improvement in the last seventy-five years. Frequent pogroms broke out in Morocco, Tunis and Algeria prior to 1914. In the 1920's, Moslem anti-Semitism shifted to Palestine, where riots organized by the Grand Mufti were given a new Palestinian nationalist as well as a religious flavor. In 1933 and 1934 there were vicious attacks on the Jewish community in Iraq, where at least 20 were murdered, and in Algeria, where 25 were killed in Constantine.

The situation in Iraq, in particular, smoldered dangerously; the 1941 pogrom was widespread, with more than £3 million worth of damage being inflicted on the Jews of Baghdad. Bloodier and more brutal was the November 1945 Arab rising in Tripoli, where about 130 Jews were massacred. In Yemen a new and obscene blood libel took place in 1948; 6 Jews were accused of the ritual murder of 2 Arab girls. In May of that year, a mass exodus of Yemenite Jews began, the spontaneous response to centuries of repression and to the realization that there was now a State of Israel which would at long last give them refuge.

In 1947 there were three days of rioting in Aden (under the protection of the British flag); 106 out of 170 Jewish shops were destroyed, 4 synagogues burned to the ground, 222 Jewish homes destroyed and 82 Jews murdered.

In Syria, there were anti-Jewish riots and murders from 1945 onwards. Those of 1947 might be thought to pale into insignificance by comparison with the torturing and burning alive of the Jews of Libya two years earlier. But the tally, once again, was horrifying—at least 200 Jewish homes utterly destroyed; about 20 synagogues and 5 schools wrecked; a probable 100 Jews dead. One might suggest that the Egyptians were relatively "civilized" by comparison; the Balfour Day riots of November 2, 1945, resulted in 10 Jews killed and 350 injured. Again, shops, synagogues and homes were systematically wrecked, and sacred Torahs (Scrolls of the Law) burned in the streets.

ALL THIS, one has to remember, *happened before the State of Israel came into being* and before the bitter civil war in Palestine from late 1947 until May 1948, when the armies of outside Arab states invaded Israel. The UN partitioning of Palestine did not inaugurate a new era in Jewish-Arab relations; it capped twelve centuries of periodic Arab oppression and persecution of Jewish minorities.

What happened in 1947–48 was a culmination of past events and *not* the cause of the Jewish-Arab dispute that has raged ever since. Without a State of Israel, the Jews of Palestine and of the Arab world would have been no better off than before. With a State of Israel, Jews everywhere had a refuge and focus for their national and social aspirations.

[[157]]

Israel's victory in 1948 inevitably brought increased persecution of those Jews still remaining in Arab lands. In Egypt more than 2,000 were arrested on May 15, 1948, the day after the State of Israel was proclaimed. Two weeks later, a new law confiscated their property. On May 25 another law prohibited departure from the country without a special permit. On June 20, 34 Jews were killed and over 80 wounded in Cairo. From July 15 to 20, stage-managed riots caused another 250 Jewish casualties and the looting or destruction of more than 500 Jewish shops. In August and September, laws were passed forbidding Jews from practicing medicine or working on the Cairo stock exchange. On September 22 a further 19 Jews were killed and 62 wounded in fresh riots.

Hundreds of Jews were arrested and imprisoned without trial. A calmer atmosphere was restored only at the end of 1948. This lasted only until 1954, when Nasser came to power, and when emigration had reduced the Jewish community in Egypt by perhaps 30,000, to around 45,000. Nasser arrested dozens of Jews as "spies," hanged two of them early in 1955, and banned emigration altogether—though he then expelled over 20,000 between 1956 and 1957, after seizing their property.

When the 1967 war broke out, all Jewish males between the ages of sixteen and fifty were arrested. Hundreds were crowded into the prisons of Tura and Abu-Zaabal, and subjected to revolting cruelties; a "refinement" was enforced sodomy. Mass expulsions followed, actually "acts of mercy," carried out after foreign governments and international organizations intervened. (Spain, for example, generously provided Egyptian and Libyan Jews with Spanish passports.) By 1969 the Jewish community in Egypt had been reduced from nearly 80,000 to 2,000, and by 1972 there were only 450 left, their average age over sixty. According to their leader, Rabbi Duek, "no marriages are contracted and no children are born any more."[16] Today, a mere handful may survive, cut off from the outside world and dying in total obscurity.

What happened in Egypt was repeated, sometimes in modified form, in other Arab countries, for instance in Iraq. There,

Zionism was made a capital offense in 1947, when mass emigration of Jews began. This law was implemented in 1948, when many Jews were imprisoned and some hanged. That year, too, the Iraqi Jewish community was fined 250,000 dinars, their contribution to the war against Israel. The maintenance of contact with the Jews of Israel was made a punishable offense, leading to a fresh wave of arrests. In 1949 and 1950 there were organized anti-Jewish riots, and in the latter year all property of Jews leaving for Israel, including bank accounts, was seized.

In 1958, when the "community status" of the Jews of Iraq was abolished, all communal property, including schools, hospitals and old people's homes, was confiscated. Worse was to come. In 1967, Iraqi Jews were deprived of their citizenship and debarred from lucrative employment of virtually every kind. Property was confiscated wholesale, and there were mass arrests and imprisonments. Extracts from the diary of Max Sawdayee, who managed to escape to Iran with the help of Kurdish tribesmen, reveal the horrors.

He tells of indiscriminate arrests, the impossibility of making a living, and police terror against suspected Zionists. On January 27, 1969, he noted:

> . . . the most horrible thing in the square is the nine victims hanged, eight Jews and one Christian. All are labelled with large sheets of paper, stating their religion and the reasons why they are hanged . . . The sight of the nine, their heads twisted and drooping, their bodies dangling from the gallows and swinging high in the air, with all these vengeful mobs, excited, cheering, dancing, chanting, singing, cursing the dead, spitting and throwing stones . . . is humiliating . . . unforgettable. It shakes even one's faith in humanity.[17]

The reactions of the outside world to these hangings, which included another eleven victims shortly afterwards, were such that the following batch of eighteen victims were hanged secretly in 1970–72.

In the four years up to June 1973, a campaign of Iraqi terror included thousands of Christians and Kurdish Moslems as well as Jews among its tormented victims. That ended only when the Chief of the Security Police, General Nadhim Kzar, was himself executed for high treason. By then the once prosperous Jewish community in Iraq had been reduced from around 150,000 to less than 400; 129,000 sought refuge in Israel, and nearly 5,000 in Britain and the United States.

The anti-Jewish campaign in the Arab world has had sensational demographic results. According to one expert, Mordechai Ben-Porat of the Israel Labor Party, the number of Jews living in the Arab world has been reduced from the 850,000 of 1948 to about 40,000 today.[18] Many fled from some of the oldest continuous settlements in the world; there were flourishing Jewish communities in Iraq and Libya, a thousand and six hundred respectively, *before* the Arab conquest.

About 700,000 Jews from Arab lands found new homes in Israel. The only substantial Jewish community left in the Arab world is in Morocco, where a little more than 20,000 survive out of the 285,000 living there up to 1948. Treatment of Jews has been marginally better in countries like Morocco and Tunisia, and very definitely better in Lebanon up to the 1975–76 civil war there. Treatment has been worst in Syria, where about 4,500 Jews still live in fear and duress, forbidden to leave the country. In most other Arab countries the Jewish communities have been totally or virtually wiped out.

IF THERE HAD BEEN no other reason for Zionism, it would have had to be invented in order to bring the centuries-long oppression of the Jews of the Arab world to an end. The Arabs today try to camouflage their anti-Jewish campaign as a purely anti-Zionist operation. They call Zionism "colonialist," and a "world movement"; they portray Zionists as brilliantly organized and in control of both the media and international finance.[19] Their attack on Zionism aims at unconditional surrender, as Egypt's President Sadat made plain in 1971: "The Zionist conquest to which we are being subjected will not be terminated by the return of the occupied territories. This is a new Crusaders' war which will persist during our generation and through the coming one."[20]

The Imp out of Hell

The picture created in Arab minds is that of an immensely powerful, cunning and threatening Jewish enemy. A typical expression of this view came from Dr. Anis Mansour, a well-known Egyptian journalist and intellectual, in 1975:

> The Jews are guilty, for they . . . disturb international security and peace among nations. They are the ones who use steel and fire, and the world can only curse the Jews . . . the Jews never relent from inflicting punishment upon themselves and others. . . . They brought all possible types of suffering upon mankind by means of their publishing-houses, newspapers and film companies, and they repaid their enemies a thousandfold. Then they sold mankind a measure of tranquillity for money, and provided sex in exchange for honour and ethical and religious values. . . . They destroy the very society in which they have been given the privilege of living.[21]

Reference has already been made to connections between Arab anti-Semitism and Nazi Germany. The Nazi example even inspires Arab press cartoonists; Egypt's resemble those of *Der Stürmer*'s.

One cartoon, in *al-Gumhuriyya*, shows an Israeli Jew being struck down by lightning; he is a dwarfish, evil-looking, hook-nosed little man, frenzied and frightened. Almost the identical figure confronts the reader in the pages of *Akhbar-el-Yom*; this time, the gesticulating homunculus is about to be smashed by a rock hurled by the Arab leaders. The Egyptian weekly *Rose-el-Yussef* turns "Israel" into a veritable imp out of Hell, drowning with millstones round his neck.

The imp-out-of-Hell theme is repeated in *al-Gumhuriyya*. It shows "Israel" with horns and tail, again being smashed, this time by an immense Arab fist. Most typical of all is a cartoon from *Akhbar-el-Yom* which appeared during May 1967. It shows a towering Arab soldier armed with a Tommy gun, confronting the Israeli Prime Minister, Levi Eshkol, leaping in the air from fright, with great gouts of sweat starting out of his head. He is tiny and terrified and this, indeed, is how Arab propagandists like to show Israel. In other cartoons, Israel

[[161]]

is a germ in a bottle, an obscene skeleton, a sacrificial goat, a squashed bug, and a many-headed monster labeled with the Stars and Stripes and Union Jack.[22]

Why such cartoons? They appear not only in Egypt, but in Iraq, Syria and Lebanon as well. Syria's Minister of Education in 1968, Suleyman al-Khash, had these words of advice to the young, which are self-explanatory: "The hatred which we indoctrinate into the minds of our children from their birth is sacred."

A single illustration of that hatred is provided by an official Egyptian schoolbook for nine-year-olds. The Ministry of Education's injunction to Israel goes like this:

> O mother of Israel! Dry your tears, your children's blood which is being spilled in the desert will produce naught but thorn and wormwood. Wipe off your blood, o mother of Israel, have mercy and spare the desert your filthy blood. Remove your slain, for their flesh has caused the ravens bellyache and their stink causes rheum. Cry, o mother of Israel, and wail. Let every house be the Wailing Wall of the Jews . . .

Israel's Professor Moshe Ma'oz notes the results of this anti-Israel and anti-Jewish indoctrination among young Arabs. It can, he says, "be seen side by side with the anti-Zionist anger and hostility of the previous generation . . . the Arabs are gradually losing their earlier deep-rooted image of the Jew, an image which is ambivalent . . . there is an attitude of affinity, kinship and respect alongside a sense of rejection and contempt. In place of this dual-value image, there has gradually developed among the Arab people an extreme and absolutely negative stereotype of the Jew, deriving from a new Arab ideology which . . . has not only intensified the Arab-Israel conflict; it has also turned the Arab states into new and active centers for an international anti-Semitic revival."[23]

Israel provided a focus not only for Jewish national and social aspirations but for Arab hatred, for a formidable enemy has replaced an object of distrust and contempt. This has led to a note of hysteria and irrationality.

The "Zionists," says Libya's Quaddafi, for example, "want to dominate and enslave the world";[24] already they "dominate banks and financial matters all over the world";[25] they "own America's gold, the publishing houses, broadcasting and TV stations and the press";[26] they "try to rule over the lives of 100 million Arabs"; and, again according to Quaddafi, "plan to occupy holy Medina" and "the whole Arabian Peninsula."[27] In 1972, King Faisal of Saudi Arabia identified the enemies of Islam as "the Jews and the infidels who are the authors of all evil in the world"[28]—not the "Zionists" at all.

Just how seriously Arabs take their anti-Semitism was revealed by Henry Kissinger's biographers, Bernard and Marvin Kalb. During the first meeting between the American Secretary of State and the late King Faisal, in November 1973, the latter explained that the Jews had led the 1917 Russian revolution, then set up the expansionist State of Israel. Looking straight at Kissinger, a Jew, the King said that "all over the world [the Jews] were putting themselves into positions of authority . . . were trying to run the world, but that he would stop them with his oil weapon."[29]

Anti-Zionism has been a convenience to bigots, for it permits anti-Semites to pose as anti-Israeli, while denying any anti-Jewish bias. In much the same way, the Arab economic war against the Jews allows the "outside" world to pursue anti-Israeli and even anti-Jewish policies, while pleading that no anti-Semitism is intended, or that business considerations, remaining paramount, compel them to cooperate in this war against the Jews.

Anti-Zionism today has an atheistical standard-bearer, the Soviet Union. Russian anti-Semitism, both before and after the Bolshevik Revolution of 1917, is notoriously well-known. Lenin, in *Critical Notes on the National Question*, denounced anyone proclaiming Jewish national culture as "an enemy of the proletariat, a partisan of retrograde elements . . . an accomplice of the rabbis and the bourgeoisie." But when Israel was created, Stalin believed she might align herself with "revolutionary socialism" after having struggled against British colonialism, and as a result, the USSR became the second major power, after the United States, to recognize Israel in 1948.

In view of Soviet vituperation in recent years, it is instructive to recall the different tone then. In April 1948, for example, Andrei Gromyko, the Soviet representative at the UN, said Jewish suffering during World War II and the failure of others to protect them against fascist violence "explains the aspirations of the Jews for their own state. The denial of this right to the Jewish people cannot be justified." The following month, another Soviet spokesman, M. Tarassenko, told the Security Council, "Jewish immigration cannot constitute a threat to the security of the Arab states. It is insignificant in comparison with the population of the Arab countries. . . ." And on May 21, 1948, Gromyko expressed "surprise" before the Security Council "at the position adopted by the Arab states in the Palestine question," and particularly that these states sent their troops to "suppress the national liberation movement of Palestine." As for the Arab League, a Soviet writer, A. Genin, called it "no union of peoples, but of the reactionary ruling circles helping England," in his book, *The Palestinian Problem* (Moscow, 1948).

These early statements were not made out of love for Jews or Israel. Soviet leaders thought the Arab world would probably remain under Western domination; they saw Israel as a natural counterpoise to an Egypt and a Transjordan under British influence, and a Syria and Lebanon under French. Furthermore, while Arabs resisted Communism, Socialist Israel looked receptive. The left wing of the Israeli labor movement had links with the Soviet Union, and a local Communist party was in the making. All in all, there were reasons to hope Israel might become the first strongpoint of Soviet influence in the Middle East. That illusion did not last long. Within a few years the Soviet Union would be voting on the Arab side in the United Nations and denouncing Israel as an outpost of American imperialism.

In the UN since then, the Soviet Union has supported every

anti-Israeli resolution of the last twenty years, even using anti-Semitic diatribe in the process. An epic example was the statement in September 1971 of Soviet Ambassador Malik, when Israel's delegate had expressed concern about the plight of Soviet Jews. Malik's reply included the sentence, "That is not your business, Mr. Tekoah; *don't stick your long nose* into our Soviet garden!"

Soviet Russia's role in promoting formal condemnation of Zionism by the UN General Assembly in November 1975 is not generally appreciated. Although the initiative for the resolution ostensibly came from the Arab states, the Syrian ambassador to France was within a few days after the vote quietly doing the rounds of Western embassies in Paris, explaining that the planning and priming of this move actually had been *carried out by the Soviet Union.*

For the Russians, this condemnation of Zionism was even more gratifying than it was to the Arabs. The Soviets contend that only a proportion of Soviet Jews are Zionists—and these by definition are troublemakers, ingrates, enemies of their Soviet homeland. The hundreds of thousands of Soviet Jews seeking to leave the country could now be condemned as racists, justifying the harsh measures against them.

The point has been made that the increasing anti-Semitism of the Arab world has made it a "new and active center for an international anti-Semitic revival." This spread of bigotry might never have taken place, however, had it not been for Soviet and Third World espousal of "anti-Zionism," and for the economic war against the Jews.

CHAPTER IX

Pressure Meets
Principles

THE COMPANIES which comply and cooperate with the Arab Trade Boycott are legion. Thousands of boycott-tainted deals are involved, hundreds of firms have surrendered to the *diktats* of Damascus, and most of them claim no other course is open to them.

That this is not true has already been demonstrated by companies which openly trade with both the Arabs and with Israel, others which outfox the Arabs by disguising their Israel business, and by those which, while ostensibly blacklisted for trading with the Jewish state, find that the Arab countries are willing to wink an eye at their transgressions.

But there are other companies that have taken a strong stand, out of principle, against the Arab Trade Boycott, and which have staunchly refused all demands by the Arabs that they bypass Israel in order to cash in on the promised petro-dollar bonanza.

One such company is Ford, blacklisted in 1966 for selling partially completed vehicles to an Israeli assembly plant. Today its business with Israel is not especially big, by the standards of major automobile manufacturers. About 5,000 Fords are annually assembled from the Ford Motor Company's knock-down kits supplied to the Israel Automobile Company, and Ford's position has always been that, although it would like to get off the blacklist, it won't do so by capitulating to pressure. As Henry Ford II said in 1973, "We are more than willing to do business with any country, but we are unwilling to refrain from doing business with one country as a prerequisite to doing business with others."[1]

Ford, said *Fortune* in July 1975, "must have an uneasy sensation watching General Motors progress with plans for an assembly plant near Jiddah."[2] Being blacklisted hasn't in fact prevented Ford (or many other companies) from doing business in the Arab world. It has sold trucks to the Jordanian army,[3] and as one Israeli diplomat who fought the Arabs told us, "almost every Arab vehicle we captured during the 1973 war seemed to have been a Ford."[4]

On October 18, 1975, a Ford Motor Company delegation began negotiating with the Nasr Automotive Manufacturing Company of Cairo about manufacturing diesel engines, trucks and cars in a $60 million plant (the estimate for which soon was revised to $150 million). It would either build this plant or start work in the old Ford factory at Alexandria, which the Egyptians had seized when Ford was blacklisted.

Two days after the talks began, Boycott Commissioner-General Mahgoub arrived in Cairo to investigate what seemed to him like an Egyptian sellout of boycott principles. He announced that Ford had requested removal from the blacklist but hadn't yet provided documentary evidence that it had cut its ties with Israel.[5] That was a warning, of course, to Egypt, which knew the facts perfectly well and was negotiating with the full knowledge that Ford had repeatedly said it wouldn't abandon Israel to get Arab business.

Late in 1975 Egypt announced she would go ahead with the Ford deal, closing her eyes to the company's blacklisting, *if* Ford's investment in Egypt were "much bigger" than in Israel.[6] Since 1975 Egypt has on occasion repeated this new line, to the intense irritation of more doctrinaire boycotters like Mahgoub. There have been recent signs that Syria is following Egypt's quest for Western investment and trade, and if Syria joins Egypt in more frequent abandonment of the hard boycott line, then Arab self-interest may really begin to crack the wall of trade restrictions. Companies trading with Isreal may then be asked only to supply larger quantities of any given goods or services to an Arab state in order to qualify for entry into Arab markets, if not for removal from Mahgoub's official blacklists.

Car manufacturers like Ford have always been peculiarly vulnerable to Arab coercion, for unlike other manufacturers they cannot hide behind what *The Economist* calls "a smoke-screen of artificial names and intermediate wholesalers," by conducting their Israeli trade without letting the Arabs know.[7]

That, however, is one side of the coin; the other is the Arabs' need of their specific products. British Leyland, the biggest automobile manufacturing conglomerate in the United Kingdom, and a company in which the British government holds more than 95 percent of the shares, provides an example.

British Leyland used to have a minority holding in an Israeli factory which assembled its Triumphs; this went bankrupt in 1972, but that didn't end British Leyland's connection with Israel. It had a contract to keep supplying cars and spare parts to Israel, as well as completely knocked-down trucks for assembly there, and it continued to honor this agreement, if not with much enthusiasm. (Israel had reminded the company of its contractual obligations and threatened to sue if these were not met.)

British Leyland escaped blacklisting for many years, despite its ties with Israel, simply because the Arabs needed its Land Rovers. That vehicle (which Leyland pointedly did not sell to Israel) was the best for desert use since the days Rommel's Afrika Korps used Kübelwagens, a Porsche-designed modification of the civilian Volkswagen. Denying themselves Land Rovers would not have been in the Arab interest.

In 1970, however, the Arabs decided that Leyland's modest investment in Israel was unbearably offensive; so, while continuing to buy Land Rovers from the company's Rover-Triumph subsidiary, they blacklisted the parent corporation to deny it potentially high truck and bus sales throughout the Arab world.

They timed their move well. For one thing, Leyland became

increasingly interested in the early 1970's in the Arab market, where Toyota had begun selling its competitive "Land Cruisers." For another, it was at this time that the Triumph assembly operation in Israel was beginning to fail.

Moves to get British Leyland off the boycott blacklist began. In December 1972 the company was reported to have signed a £50 million deal to assemble 10,000 Land Rovers a year in Egypt. Lord Stokes, then chairman of British Leyland, called on the Egyptian Premier on December 8, and Reuters reported from Cairo that he had "produced two documents affirming that the company was no longer collaborating with Israel" and that business in Israel had been suspended, which was untrue.

All this created the impression that British Leyland was surrendering to the boycotters, and Lord Stokes did nothing to put the record straight. London newspapers speculated that Leyland would therefore be off the Arab blacklists very soon, but the Arabs kept Leyland, the British government, the British press and the British public in a state of continuing anticipation, suspense and disappointment, literally for several years—proof again that their cherished weapons are uncertainty, confusion and fear.

Every time the Central Office for the Boycott of Israel staged one of its six-monthly conferences with representatives of the national boycott offices, there was renewed speculation that British Leyland was finally about to be taken off the blacklist, but it wasn't until 1976 that this actually happened. Mohammed Mahgoub announced in Alexandria on April 1 of that year, "British Leyland and all its subsidiary companies are no longer on the list of the Arab Boycott Office. The lifting of the ban affects all ninety-seven companies owned or partly owned by British Leyland."[8] And, although four days later *The Times* reported that Leyland was "still waiting for official confirmation," it did finally appear that Leyland was off the list.

The Israeli embassy in London was delighted, of course; it announced that the affair proved that a company which resisted the boycott could continue to do business with Israel and still win orders in the Arab world.[9]

"Resistance," in the Leyland matter, was something of an overstatement. The company had in fact weaved and wavered for years over the boycott. Already in late 1974 it had made "several" applications to the Damascus boycott headquarters, for removal from Arab blacklists.[10] In December of that year Lord Stokes was reported as having produced "a memorandum confirming that operations with Israel had reached a 'complete standstill.' "[11] This was untrue: Leyland still sold cars and spare parts to Israel.[12]

The Israeli ambassador expressed his concern to the British Secretary of State for Industry, Anthony Wedgwood Benn; two weeks later Benn replied that Lord Stokes had given him "a firm assurance that [the company] intended to adhere to all agreements with Israel and would continue to supply vehicles and spares."[13]

This flatly contradicted Lord Stokes's December 9 assurance to the Arabs that operations in Israel had come to a "complete standstill"; sometime between the 17th, when the ambassador saw Benn, and the 31st, when Benn reported back, Stokes apparently changed his mind—even about the facts, never mind the company's intentions.

Leyland was in fact trying to pursue two policies. It would continue to sell Israel knockdown kits for trucks, as well as cars and spare parts, but its Land Rovers and newer Range Rovers would go to the Arab world and not to Israel.

A curious sidelight on this arrangement emerged in 1974. That summer, in Israel, the West German Federal Minister of Justice, Dr. Hans-Jochen Vogel, discussed making a present of a Land Rover to an Israeli wildlife preservation society. Vogel asked the German-Israeli Society in Bonn (*Deutsch-Israelische Gesellschaft*) to act as intermediary and to order the vehicle from Leyland in Britain. The Society's Dr. Reiner Bernstein received a reply from Rover-Triumph sales representative P. McHarg.

"It is with great regret," McHarg wrote on September 19, "that we must inform you that Rover vehicles are not marketed in the territory of Israel, as we do not have any agents in this particular territory to maintain supply of spares, servicing and warranty coverage." Bernstein wrote McHarg again, saying he wanted only *one* vehicle, and this time was informed: "Respectfully we reiterate that we do not supply vehicles for the territory of Israel and that it is this company's policy not to supply vehicles for exportation to the aforementioned."[14] That striking instance of capitulation to the boycott was brought to the attention of the British House of Commons. A member of Parliament, Greville Janner, called it "quite monstrous that any company in which the public holds a substantial share should be involved in the boycott."[15]

In late 1975 the British anti-boycott forces decided to challenge the company to make an unequivocal public statement of its intentions towards Israel and to end its double-talk. The maneuver was even more successful than expected.

It began right after Greville Janner received a letter from Alex Park, then Leyland's chief executive, which said: "I can assure you quite categorically that we do in fact supply the Israel market with vehicles and we do have an on-going distribution network there, both for cars and for commercial vehicles." Regarding Land Rovers, Park explained: "We have not consciously marketed the Land Rover in Israel at any time simply because the Willys Jeep which is assembled there had a virtual monopoly, and we have not considered it an economic proposition to set up parts and service facilities for what would be an absolute minimum volume of sales in such a situation."[16]

The first part of this statement was put to good use. The British Anti-Boycott Coordinating (ABC) Committee, set up in 1975 under the aegis of the Anglo-Israel Chamber of Commerce, commended Leyland for "setting an example to all British industry by taking a firm stand in the face of the Arab Trade Boycott. . . ." Leyland had "removed doubts caused deliberately by confusing statements issued by the Central Boycott Office in Damascus," and its "categorical denial that it was acceding to Arab threats was therefore most welcome."[17]

The ABC Committee was challenging Leyland to affirm it was taking an anti-boycott stand, or—to its embarrasssment—

publicly deny it was doing so. Leyland's response was ambivalent. The *Times* reported the next morning that the company "was clearly embarrassed" and had said "nothing Leyland was doing was contrary to the boycott rules. The company believed that the supply of vehicles did not in any way breach the boycott regulations."[18] To a *Birmingham Post* reporter, Leyland admitted, "When it suits them, Arab states forget that the Land Rover is a British Leyland product."[19]

These statements focused public attention on the salient fact which apprehensive businessmen so often forget: business *can* be done with Israel without breaching boycott rules, and the Arabs themselves ignore the boycott when it suits them. Leyland, for its part, had at least plucked up a little courage.

London's *Jewish Observer and Middle East Review* analyzed the lessons from all this in April 1976:

> The anti-boycott activists have long stated that the only way to react to the boycott was by standing firm and refusing to submit to the demands of the Arab League. In the case of Leyland, they combined a policy of urging Leyland to stand firm, with threats from Israel of legal action if the company broke any of its contracts. This combination had the desired effect of strengthening the company's backbone and now appears to have proved once again that if an Arab country feels that it is in its interest to invite a company to participate in its economy, boycott regulations can be made very pliable . . .
>
> The Leyland case proves three things: that persistence pays off in the end; that waverers can be helped to stay on the path of moral rectitude without sacrificing commercial gain; and that national self-interest is a greater force in the Arab world than Arab unity . . .[20]

The implied compliment to Leyland for returning to the path of moral rectitude was, however, somewhat premature, as quickly became clear. British Leyland used to be a member of the Executive of the Anglo-Israel Chamber of Commerce, but had quit the Chamber when it was trying to get off the Arab blacklist, because membership in a bi-national Chamber of

Commerce with Israel is a specific breach of boycott regulations and meant to be punishable by automatic blacklisting. In mid-1976, eighteen months later, the Chamber invited British Leyland to resume its membership, now that it had been taken off the blacklist without sacrificing its Israeli connection. British Leyland agreed, but hinted that it wanted no publicity. But when its intention to return to the fold was announced by Sir Marcus Sieff, the Chamber's chairman, at its annual luncheon in November, the press published the news. British Leyland panicked and withdrew its application to rejoin the Chamber.

This was infuriating to the Israelis, especially as the head of British Leyland International's overseas division had just joined the board of the newly formed Arab-British Chamber of Commerce (and Leyland President Lord Stokes was made chairman of the British Arabian Advisory Company, partly financed by Saudi Arabia). The company's partisan position, in entering one bi-national Chamber while cold-shouldering another, was sharply criticized and brought to the government's attention, but British Leyland did not mend its ways. In February 1977 the Israelis retaliated. Its Transport Ministry canceled an order for several hundred bus chassis from British Leyland, as a mark of displeasure over the company's shabby action.[21] Meanwhile, ironically, plans for a Land Rover plant in Egypt were shelved.

A MORE COURAGEOUS stance was taken in the United States. As the Leyland story drew to its confused close, T. A. Murphy, chairman of General Motors, issued a statement in New York in reply to questions raised by American Jews. "General Motors has received occasional requests from Arab countries that it agree not to participate in future dealings with Israel or with Israeli companies. General Motors has made no such agreements and would not make any such agreements."

This was no isolated act of defiance of the Arab League; indeed, one might take the 1,500 U.S. company names on the published Saudi Arabian blacklist as a kind of roll of honor, and there is at least one American Jewish group, in Baltimore, Maryland, which is doing just that, by urging Jews to buy the products and patronize the services of companies blacklisted by the Arabs.

Will Maslow of the American Jewish Congress initiated a nationwide drive to get shareholders to ask companies whether they were participating in the Arab boycott or not. By 1977 this had resulted in written pledges from a great many large American corporations that they would refuse to submit to the boycott. They included such names as American Brands, Bethlehem Steel, Caterpillar Tractor, Borden, Continental Can, Dow Chemical, Eastman Kodak, General Foods, General Motors, Goodyear Tire, Greyhound, Gulf Oil, Kennecott Copper, McDonnell Douglas, Pitney-Bowes, RCA, Reynolds Industries, Scott Paper, Simmons, Standard Oil of California, Tenneco, Texaco, Textron, U.S. Gypsum and Xerox.

The Hertz car rental company is another which defies the boycott. Although blacklisted by the Arabs, it does business with Egypt, while continuing to trade with Israel, and it has recently been approached by other Arab countries about opening branches there.[22] Avis, IBM, Republic Steel and the Bank of America have reaffirmed their refusal to bow to the boycott or to discriminate against Jews.[23] Raytheon Corporation is another company to take a firm line. Admittedly, it can "afford" to do so, since the Saudi Arabians are sufficiently interested in Raytheon's Hawk ground-to-air missiles not to protest that the company supplies the same missiles, through the Pentagon, to Israel. Raytheon personnel are in both Israel and Saudi Arabia, to service these missiles and, although Raytheon also sells other products to Israel, it still is not on the Arab blacklist.[24]

AT&T is another corporation which has made a firm declaration against the boycott. The $100 million loan it received from Saudi Arabia in 1975 would not, it said, "compromise AT&T's commitment to recruit and promote the most qualified candidates into its jobs, including Jewish men and women." Executive Vice-President Charles L. Brown told the American Jewish Congress that he fully understood the concern caused by the Saudi Arabian loan. He added, "We clearly will not be governed by any blacklist or other restriction that could require us to discriminate in any aspect of our business."[25]

TWO COMPANIES which accepted blacklisting rather than compromise their principles are Miles Laboratories and RCA. In 1962, Miles became one of the first major U.S. companies to start operations in Israel under its own name. Today it operates two subsidiaries in Israel, both in Haifa, and two joint ventures, one in Jerusalem and one in Rehovot. They employ 350 persons and in 1974 earned $11.66 million, $3 million of this from exports.

The big advantage of operating in Israel, says Miles, is the availability there of advanced scientific research facilities and highly trained researchers at a lower cost than in America. (There are reportedly more research scientists per square mile of territory in Israel than anywhere else in the world, and more scientific literature is produced in Israel than in all South America and Africa combined.)

Miles, understandably, was blacklisted. In 1966 it was told it could get off that list if it ended all its operations in Israel. Instead, the company not only accepted blacklisting, but expanded its investment in Israel and made a well-earned profit by doing so. It pointedly reasserted its intention to continue investing in Israel two days after the outbreak of the 1973 war and plans a new $5 million venture on Haifa Bay.

George W. Orr, Jr., president of this non-Jewish firm, has become an enthusiast about Israel. "By their deeds ye shall know them," he was once quoted as saying. "Of all the places I visit, there is no question that the most exciting one, the one that has the most profound impact on me, is Israel. It has to be true that one of the great, incredible happenings in all the history of mankind is that a people could sustain a goal, a purpose—generation after generation—and achieve that goal by taking this abused land and transforming it literally into a land of milk and honey."[26]

RCA is yet another company which firmly resists the boycott. It was blacklisted by the Arabs in 1966 for granting a license to an Israeli record company to use the RCA label. Granting such licenses is prohibited by the boycott rules, although their application in this case makes nonsense of the claim that the boycott is "defensive" and meant only to prevent Israel's military and economic build-up.

As a result of blacklisting, RCA lost about $9 million in Arab world sales. It has also been routinely cut out of contracts by those companies surrendering to the boycotters' demands, and according to Sol Stern in the *New Republic,* is "automatically excluded" even "when the U.S. government channels business into Saudi Arabia."

Stern points out that RCA "could have maneuvered its way off the [boycott] list," but has "consistently refused to deal, though they too have been contacted by 'agents' offering to intercede with the boycott office—for a fee." He quotes RCA's International Vice-President, Eugene P. Seculow, as saying: "Our position has been very simple. We believe in free trade and we are attempting to do business everywhere in the world where it is not against U.S. laws. But we won't comply in any way with the boycott or try to negotiate our way off the list." Seculow called the boycott "capricious and insidious"—as indeed it is.[27]

There have been some instances of resistance to the boycott in the United Kingdom. A small company, Vetro-Plastics, came under fire for importing towelettes from an Israeli firm, Minipac of Tel Aviv, and was placed on the Arab blacklist; it went on trading with Israel, however. Vono, another British company, applied for registration of a trademark in Saudi Arabia, and was required to declare that it was neither owned by Jews nor Jewish-controlled. It refused to make such a declaration and in this case, as in so many others where resistance is encountered, the Arabs backed down. Saudi Arabia granted Vono its trademark registration.

A particularly eloquent rebuttal was given to the Arabs some years ago by Dr. E. Ring, head of the Swiss Ring hotel chain. Under threat from Damascus, he wrote directly to

Mahgoub: "Our worldwide organization can live without hotels in the Arab states. . . . We here in Basle, a Swiss city on the very frontier of Germany, were able to observe between 1933 and 1945 the cruel and lunatic manner in which the Jewish population was persecuted and tormented. . . . While fully appreciative of the Arab problems which derive from the Palestine question, and for which we certainly have a sympathetic understanding, we, as citizens of a traditionally neutral country, nevertheless feel we should point out that the course you have chosen of threatening people with boycott is an act of injustice which can only be detrimental to the esteem in which the Arab states are held."[28]

Such resolute courage has, however, been exceptional, especially in recent years, once the mad scramble for petrodollars combined with avarice and fear, causing cowardly companies and timid governments to surrender to Arab pressure. In 1975 it seemed that American colleges and universities would also be drawn into the net of the boycott, because Arab nations began offering them fairly large amounts of money, ostensibly to establish or expand departments of Arabic studies, or promote educational exchanges between American and Arab institutions. Such investments were worrisome because of the anti-Jewish discriminatory clauses either actually involved in the deals, hinted at or apprehensively anticipated. In that year, the American Jewish Committee felt impelled to write to campus presidents throughout the United States, asking (successfully for the most part) for declarations that they would not sell out their principles for petrodollars.

The concern shown was understandable, for some American universities had not waited for the Arabs to approach them; they went out to solicit Arab money, and the Association of Colleges and Universities invited Saudi Arabia to finance a $5.5 million teacher-training program. By and large, if the initiative came from the American side, bona fide projects resulted; if from the Arab states, other considerations often prevailed. Harvard was among several U.S. universities that rejected Arab proposals because of their discriminatory clauses. American universities that were invited to send scholars, scientists and technicians to such Arab states as Saudi Arabia would, after all, have had to exclude all Jewish professors and staff-members from their delegations.

The negotiations between Saudi Arabia and the Massachusetts Institute of Technology are instructive. MIT was discussing a $2 million contract to help the Saudis plan their water requirements for the next twenty years, and the Saudi side was represented by the Saline Water Conversion Corporation, whose chairman is Prince Mohammed Ibn Faisal, son of the late King Faisal.

MIT was to train Saudi technicians and graduate students on its campus in Cambridge, Massachusetts, but MIT President Dr. Jerome Wiesner stipulated that anyone required for the project should get a Saudi Arabian visa, regardless of that person's religious affiliation. Furthermore, Saudi Arabia should not deny a visa to any member of the work staff or academic personnel whom MIT wished to send out.

This unusual stipulation was actually accepted by the Saudi Arabian negotiators, but was then suddenly rejected by Prince Faisal, who broke off all negotiations with MIT. The tone of MIT's demand angered the Prince, who regarded the letter as offensive, although Dr. Wiesner denied having "written a threatening letter to the Prince or anyone else."[29] A private contract was later arranged between Saudi Arabia and some of the MIT staff members, acting on their own.

Also in 1975, the universities of Illinois, Minnesota, Indiana, Wisconsin and Michigan State, which had formed themselves into a Midwest Universities Consortium for International Activities (MUCIA), negotiated a fee of $72,400 plus travel and other expenses from Saudi Arabia, to send a team of ten professors to evaluate and advise the University of Riyadh. MUCIA submitted the names of thirty professors, and the Saudis picked the ten non-Jews on the list. When the dean of Michigan State (a Jew) applied for a visa to visit the Riyadh project as a MUCIA officer, he was refused entry. Michigan State promptly withdrew from the project. Learning that two

Jewish Wisconsin University professors were among those the Arabs rejected, Wisconsin also withdrew. Then the Midwest Consortium met and decided unanimously to abandon the entire project unless "an understanding can be reached" with the Saudis, to prevent any racial, religious, ethnic or sex discrimination. David Johnson, dean of international studies at Wisconsin, said, "We are not really dependent on an infusion of Arabian funds. Even if we were, this organization is not going to prostitute itself for oil money." And almost one hundred other American colleges and universities gave the same answer when the American Jewish Committee asked them to affirm that they would not discriminate against Jews as a *quid pro quo* for training and technical contracts with the Arabs.

FOR RESOLUTE RESISTANCE to the boycott, Hilton Hotels earns the Red Badge of Courage. In 1961, when Hilton was completing arrangements to build a hotel in Tel Aviv, it received the following letter from the Secretary of the American-Arab Association for Commerce and Industry, in New York:

> Perhaps you are not aware of the full details regarding the activities of the Boycott Committee and hence, as a member company of this Association, it is our duty to bring the facts as they were told to me to your attention.
>
> Should Hilton Hotels persist in going ahead with its contract in Israel, it will mean the loss of your holdings in Cairo and the end of any plans you might have for Tunis, Baghdad, Jerusalem or anywhere else in all Arab countries.
>
> It is important for me to put you on notice that the Arab visitors, including the Saudi royal family, Egyptian businessmen and the general flow of persons from the Arab world that have frequented your major hotels in New York City and elsewhere throughout the country, will unfortunately come to an end. And it may well adversely effect the ability of American companies from continuing to bring important business to your well-known establishments.
>
> I did what could be done to delay any action that the Boycott Committee will take. They have promised that no action to invoke the Boycott will be taken prior to the end

of January 1962, and I am writing to Col. Aidi to remind him of this. This will give you and the members of your Board of Directors an opportunity to review the decisions which have been made and to redress this serious situation.

As a friend to the Hilton Hotels and a long time political observer as well as the Counsel of this Association, I should personally add my own voice by asking you to consider whether your plan to enter into an economic relationship in Israel could possibly be worth the grave loss that you will be committing yourself to throughout the Arab World and in the United States . . .[30]

Here was not only the threat of a loss of business with the Arab world, but the ominous threat: ". . . It may well adversely affect the ability of American companies from continuing to bring important business to your well-known establishments"— showing that the organizers of the boycott were prepared to instruct American businessmen with whom the Arabs deal which hotels they may frequent at home and abroad.

Conrad Hilton's reply was polite yet masterly. He wrote:

Many thanks for your letter. It is thoughtful of you to have postponed the action of the Boycott Committee relative to Hilton Hotels Corporation.

What the Committee proposes is absolutely counter to the principles we live by and which we hold most dear. I speak about the principles of Americanism as set out by our founding fathers and of the principles for which America has stood since its founding. I also speak of the principles under which the Hilton Hotels Corporation goes about the world, establishing hotels so that people of all nations can gather in peace. We believe that through world travel we may be helping in the goal that all Americans seek— world peace.

As Americans we consider Arabs and Jews our friends and hope that ultimately we can all live in peace with one another. There was no threat from Israel when we opened our hotel in Cairo. Our Corporation finds it shocking that the Committee should invoke the threat of boycott condemnation in the case of our contract with the people of Israel.

Does the Committee also propose to boycott the United States government because it maintains diplomatic relations with Israel?[31]

Hilton had read the Arabs a lesson; this was the upshot:

The Tel Aviv Hilton was built and has been successfully operating ever since.

A new Israeli Hilton was built in Jerusalem, and is also successfully operating.

The Nile Hilton, in Cairo, was *not* seized by the Egyptians; they thought better of it and the hotel remains in Hilton's hands. Since then, other Hilton hotels have been built throughout the Arab world.

This Arab threat proved empty—presumably because it had been sternly rebuffed and because the Arabs wanted Hilton hotels in their countries. One might add a piquant postscript: the September 1974 Arab Summit Conference, held in Rabat, took place in the Hilton hotel of that city.

CHAPTER X

Foot-dragging and Stonewalling

WHEN JEWISH HOSTAGES at Uganda's Entebbe Airport were singled out for mass murder in mid-1976, the world's reaction was frighteningly similar to what it had been forty years earlier: men of good will the world over expressed horror and dismay, but did nothing. The parallel with 1936, however, ended there. Forty years earlier, German Jews pleaded in vain for assistance, and there was no Jewish state to succor them; in 1976, Israel acted heroically, but the point that it had needed Israel to save the Jews should not be missed or forgotten.

It has also needed Jews to lead the fight against the boycott, although later, as its implications for world trade became more widely recognized, non-Jews stepped in to help.

In the United States, the fight against discrimination against American Jews by foreign powers has a history over one hundred years long. In 1851, President Millard Fillmore acted against the Swiss Confederation, which was discriminating against American Jews, and in 1881, 1895 and 1911, the United States defended American Jews living in or visiting Russia, against the anti-Semitic policies of the Czarist regimes. In 1911 President William Howard Taft even abrogated a seventy-nine-year-old treaty with Russia because of just this discrimination, but even at that time, it had required a strong campaign by Jewish organizations in America to induce the U.S. government to act.

The lesson that Jews needed to lead any effort at countering anti-Semitism had been well learned by the time the Jewish state was established in 1948.

The fight against discrimination was resumed in the early 1950's because of Saudi Arabian refusal to allow American Jewish soldiers to serve at the U.S. base at Dhahran and U.S. connivance in that discriminatory agreement. During this period too, the American Jewish Congress was fighting its battle with ARAMCO because it refused to hire American Jews. Efforts against the boycott in general, and against the blockade of Israel, were also undertaken in the 1950's, but these were the years when the boycott itself was seen as a "paper tiger," even by many Jews. By the sixties, however, the boycotters were pressing their campaign against American firms trading with Israel more energetically and there was an increasing need for legislation to thwart them. In late 1964 an effort was made in Congress to amend the Export Administration Act of 1949. Almost thirty Senators and eleven Representatives sponsored an amendment to "oppose restrictive trade practices or boycotts fostered or imposed by foreign countries against any countries friendly with the United States," but the Administration rigidly opposed it. I. L. Kenen, one of the men behind it, recalls the atmosphere:

> Everyone deeply "deplored" the Arab boycott. No one had a kind word for it. But it was claimed the legislation would weaken U.S. efforts to enlist other governments in our programs of "economic denial" against Communist China, Cuba, North Vietnam and South Korea. It would challenge the Arab states to intensify their boycott; it would not end the boycott; on the contrary, failure to cooperate would hurt American business interests.[1]

Administration opposition had the effect of emasculating the amendment, but in 1965 a version of it was actually passed which declared U.S. opposition to the boycott. It required all recipients of boycott questionnaires or demands to report these to the U.S. Department of Commerce, or be subject to a fine.

Ten years later, Kenen notes, it was possible to build upon that amended Act.*

The year of the "big banking scandal," 1975, saw increasing demand for more effective anti-boycott action. The *New York Times* noted in April that "public pressures for a more vigorous backlash have mounted" and it quoted General Chaim Herzog, then the newly appointed Israeli Ambassador to the United Nations, as complaining of inactivity on this front. Herzog called for "an international Jewish economic organization to spearhead a world counterattack against the boycott and those who submit to it." The paper reported that Jews outside Israel had asked that country to supply the leadership, and also the names of companies and banks which were complying with the boycott. And it quoted Shmuel Tamir, a member of the Israel Knesset, as saying that American Jewish leaders had told him they planned "a vigorous counteraction." Even the use of a counter-boycott was not ruled out. Government officials in Israel, said the *New York Times*, "did not oppose a counter-boycott but were circumspect about offering advice in such matters to foreign citizens."[2]

Two months later Israel appointed Avraham Agmon, former director general of its Finance Ministry, to head a new unit concerned with "economic warfare." Its staff and budget were approved by September, and it was given its brief: to coordinate action against the boycott throughout the world with Jewish organizations and individuals spearheading the efforts in their own countries.[3]

Even before September, leaders of Jewish organizations, academics and various authorities and experts in the area of oil, petrodollars and economics, gathered from several nations to meet at Oxford University, England, in mid-July. There they exchanged ideas for three days, formulating the broad strategy of the anti-boycott effort; there they also took the significant

---

* Kenen, now retired, then headed AIPAC, the American Israel Public Affairs Committee, in Washington, D.C., and played a key role in every anti-boycott initiative undertaken during twenty years.

step of deciding *against* a Jewish counter-boycott of any kind. They took the position that Israel and the Jews were utterly opposed to boycotts, and in favor of free and unfettered trade with all, including the Arabs.

Later that year, a coordinated anti-boycott campaign was launched in the United States by a wide spectrum of Jewish organizations, the most active of which were the Anti-Defamation League of B'nai B'rith, the American Jewish Committee and the American Jewish Congress.* Britain's ABC Committee, already established, got down to business and launched a public relations campaign in September 1975. In France plans were discussed which led to the establishment of a similar group there, the Movement for Freedom in Commerce, formed in Paris on June 24, 1976. By September of that year Agmon stepped down, and his energetic young assistant, Dan Halperin, took over the leadership of the Israeli anti-boycott office.

Extensive U.S. Congressional hearings on the boycott throughout 1975 made clear that existing legal and legislative safeguards were inadequate. The Export Administration Act was indeed something on which to build, but was not an effective counter to boycott pressures in the United States. It did not declare the boycott *per se* to be illegal, nor compliance with it. Companies reporting to the Commerce Department weren't even required until October 1975 to tell the department in confidence what action they had taken with regard to the demands they received.

The publicity resulting from the hearings, notably those which exposed the way the U.S. Army's Corps of Engineers cooperated with Saudi Arabia's anti Jewish policies, did, how ever, force the Administration of President Gerald R. Ford into action. On November 20, 1975, the President announced

---

* Others active in the United States include the American Israel Public Affairs Committee, the National Jewish Community Relations Advisory Council, the Conference of Presidents of Major American Jewish Organizations and the Research Project on Energy and Economic Policy.

what he called a "comprehensive package" of directives aimed at preventing "any discrimination against Americans on the basis of race, color, religion, national origin or sex that might arise from foreign boycott practices." His Administration would "not countenance the translation of any foreign prejudice into domestic discrimination against American citizens."

This "package" included these new rules:

• Federal agencies making overseas assignments were forbidden to take into account any exclusionary policies of a host country based on race, color, religion, national origin or sex. No one could be excluded at any stage in the selection process because of these factors, nor could government job descriptions specify that a host country had an exclusionary entrance policy.

• The State Department was to be informed whenever a visa was rejected because of such exclusionary policies, and was to take diplomatic action on behalf of the individuals concerned.

• The Department of Labor was ordered to instruct companies working for the government to refrain from any job discrimination connected with work in or for a foreign state, and to inform the State Department of any visa rejections they had received. Diplomatic action would then be invoked on behalf of the persons concerned.

• The White House would support legislation prohibiting businesses from coercing anyone to discriminate against Americans or U.S. firms on the basis of race, color, religion, national origin or sex. It would also support legislation prohibiting financial institutions from discriminating against any credit applicant on these grounds, in any aspect of a credit transaction.

• The Commerce Department was ordered to prohibit exporters and "related service organizations" (i.e., banks, insurers, freight forwarders, shipping companies, etc.) from answering or complying with any boycott requests which could cause discrimination against U.S. citizens or firms on the basis of race, religion, national origin, and the rest. Furthermore, service organizations which received any boycott-related requests would now also have to report these to the Commerce Department, just as exporters were already required to do.

• The President further cited a Justice Department ruling that a U.S. firm refusing to deal with another American firm in order to comply with the boycott might be in violation of anti-trust laws.

A number of Executive Branch directives followed, all somewhat broader in their scope. They did not restrict themselves to the discriminatory aspects of the boycott, as the White House had done, but also aimed to stop or reduce U.S. government involvement in boycott-related actions.

The Commerce Department, for example, announced on December 1, 1975, that it would no longer disseminate foreign trade opportunities or tenders if these contained boycott provisions, or were even based on documents which contained them. It would also destroy any such commercial documents it had in its files, and any it might receive. U.S. embassies would similarly cease supplying such documents, and the State Department added that it would not certify papers which furthered or supported boycotts directed against countries friendly to the United States. Finally, the Federal Reserve Board warned banks that even "passive participation" in the boycott might put them in "direct violation" of anti-trust laws.

What was revealed by the revised Commerce and State rulings was, of course, that both departments had for years been acting as willing agents of the boycott offices, collecting and disseminating trade opportunities and tenders which demanded boycott compliance. While this was now halted, the Administration's "comprehensive package" was by no means the energetic anti-boycott program it was meant to seem. In the main, it dealt with the anti-Jewish discriminatory aspects of the boycott, but avoided countering the secondary or tertiary boycotts per se. Indeed, the package served to obscure the fact that the Ford Administration was actively opposing every attempt that was being made to pass really effective anti-boycott laws. As was apparent from the Bechtel case, the Administration sought refuge in anti-trust laws in dealing with the tertiary boycott, fearing that direct anti-boycott legislation would anger the Arabs.

[[187]]

That the Administration had no intention of striking directly at the boycott became even more clear a couple of months later. Commerce Under Secretary James A. Baker 3rd, speaking with the support of the U.S. Secretary of Commerce, told an audience in February 1976 that a businessman "should be free to make a choice between two countries when certain commercial relations with one may result in retaliation by the other. He, after all, is the best judge of the requirements of his business."

The *New York Times* said the speech showed that the Ford Administration was "waffling" on the issue and "virtually inviting business firms to flout stated principles of national policy in their present pursuit of Arab oil money."[4] It asked where this left "all the ringing policy declarations—and laws—against the boycott?" and said the Administration was rejecting "what should be a fundamental matter of principle to seek refuge in legal pettifogging."[5] Baker responded in a letter to the *Times* charges, but studiously avoided going any further than to say that the Administration opposed *discriminatory* boycott requests. He also tried to distinguish between such requests, which the Administration opposed, and those which "relate solely to the economic boycott of Israel by Arab states." The Commerce Department, he said, would make sure the line between "permissible economic conduct" and "discriminatory activity" was not breached.[6] But this argument seemed illogical to the anti-boycott forces. If it was official, stated government policy to oppose foreign boycotts aimed at countries friendly to the United States, how, then, could participation in the boycott of Israel be "permissible economic conduct"?

THE BATTLE between Congress and the Administration began over those tens of thousands of boycott reports in the files of the Commerce Department. That they were loaded with "dynamite" was suspected everywhere. Fifty thousand business deals between U.S. companies and Arab states had been reported to the department since 1970; in three quarters of these, the companies involved had declined to say whether they had complied with the boycott demands, suggesting they had done so.[7]

Commerce Secretary Rogers C. B. Morton refused to surrender these papers to the House subcommittee which was holding hearings on the subject. Resistance continued for some time, and grew in ferocity. Morton claimed to fear a (presumably Jewish) counter-boycott would result, if the names of companies which had bowed to Arab pressure became known. He was apparently under heavy pressure himself, from his "business constituency," which was probably frightened of a bad press.

Morton's resistance, even to a subpoena, finally crumbled after Representative John E. Moss, the subcommittee's chairman, cited him for contempt of Congress. The two men came to an accommodation; Morton would turn over the files and Moss would treat them confidentially. Shortly afterwards, Morton was replaced by Elliot L. Richardson, and the new Secretary of Commerce conceded a point or two to the anti-boycott forces. He would prohibit companies trading with the Arabs from answering questions about whether they were involved in pro-Israel activities, such as the United Jewish Appeal, and he would also make public the names of companies the department was charging with violation of the reporting requirement.[8]

Once the department's files had been opened to inspection, the full extent of boycott compliance became glaringly evident. Commerce had earlier claimed only about $10 million was involved in boycott-related deals, but other estimates for 1974 and 1975 alone had been $800 million,[9] and that figure rose to $4.5 billion after inspection was allowed. As for the frequency of compliance, the opened files showed that exporters had complied with boycott demands in 94 percent of 11,000 transactions reported during just the six months of March–September 1976.* A study of the October figure showed 87 percent compliance, and this was matched by the results of the American Jewish Congress's successful stockholders' project, in which companies were being directly asked to state whether they complied with

---

* A year earlier, compliance took place in 56 percent of 7,000 transactions, showing that it rose along with the level of business activity.

the boycott or not. "There is hardly a company in *Fortune*'s '500'," wrote the organization's executive director, Naomi Levine, in the January 1977 issue of *Congress Monthly*, "that is not involved in some way with the Arab boycott."

Also in the autumn of 1976, the Moss Subcommittee concluded from its study of 30,000 subpoenaed documents that the Commerce Department had deliberately misled Congress about the extent of compliance and had even encouraged companies to comply, often "by looking the other way."[10] Moreover, Commerce had advised companies they needn't supply information about the boycott, and had encouraged them "to find loopholes" in the law. Prior to 1975, when the department itself advised exporters to file reports on boycott demands, it had added that filing was not mandatory and compliance with the boycott not illegal.[11] These charges were all true, Secretary Richardson admitted, but as they related "almost entirely to past conditions that no longer exist in the department," they were largely "of historical interest."[12]

Just as Commerce had not budged until it was cited with contempt of Congress, so the White House didn't budge until similarly challenged.

This occurred on October 6, 1976, during the second of the three television debates between Gerald Ford and Jimmy Carter during the presidential campaign. Cornered into making an anti-boycott declaration, Ford pulled down all the walls which successive Secretaries of Commerce had so earnestly built around those company boycott reports. He ordered them released for public inspection as they were filed with Commerce, on a daily basis, although 50,000 previous reports were not disclosed. The first week's batch disclosed 335 boycott transactions and Commerce charges against twelve companies for failing to report boycott requests.

Predictably, a kind of panic reaction set in. *Newsweek* stated that frightened businessmen were telling the Commerce Department that they'd prefer risking fines of $1,000 each for failing to report boycott compliance, rather than have their companies' names made public. One California executive was quoted as saying, "We're goddamned scared of having our name linked with this boycott in any way."[13] *Newsweek* explained why: "What really seems to concern the business community isn't so much the new disclosure policy itself, but the growing anti-boycott sentiment it reflects."[14]

This sentiment was reflected during 1975 and 1976 by the fact that some two dozen bills dealing with the boycott were introduced in the Houses of Congress, and eight different Capitol Hill subcommittees held hearings on the matter. Yet, throughout this period, the Administration still "dragged its feet and stonewalled" every attempt to pass an effective law, as one anti-boycott leader put it. Administration spokesmen were joined by American oil-company representatives and others in what the ADL called "a desperate propaganda campaign" to defeat the anti-boycott laws being considered in 1976. The opponents argued that such laws would cause the United States to suffer political and economic reprisals, oil shortages, a recession and massive unemployment, and would turn it into "a second-rate economic power," as a Mobil Oil advertisement put it. The Commerce Department's Charles W. Hostler told Congress that except in the matter of religious discrimination, "American firms should not be restricted in their freedom to make economic decisions based on their own business interests." This was rebutted by the ADL's Seymour Graubard, who told a House committee it was absurd to argue that firms retained their "freedom to make economic decisions" when the Arab Trade Boycott in fact forces them to boycott Israel or to shun certain American companies.

The Treasury's most vociferous opponent of anti-boycott laws, Gerald L. Parsky, argued that "a peace settlement is the best way to bring a definitive end to the Arab boycott" and that anti-boycott laws would "cripple the United States effort" to negotiate such a settlement. Once more, Graubard rapped out a telling reply. He reminded the House committee before which he was testifying that almost exactly the same argument had been trotted out by Administration spokesmen in 1969; six years had gone by, there had been no peace settlement, and the argument was beginning to appear shopworn. (The argument was even older than Graubard said, for it had been offered twenty years earlier.)

Pressure on Congress to pass some kind of a federal anti-boycott bill was now emerging from an unexpected quarter—the individual states of the Union. By the end of 1976, state anti-boycott laws had been passed in New York, Illinois, Ohio, Maryland, Massachusetts and California, and the last-named was the toughest of all. Other states had either introduced anti-boycott bills or were actively considering them, and the pressure on the U.S. Congress to pass a law which would pre-empt all these was mounting. State governments feared that tough state laws could drive businesses away into states which had no anti-boycott laws on their books; a federal law would give none of them a place to hide, and make all states equally vulnerable, or safe.

Congress ultimately settled on two amendments to the Export Administration Act (due to expire September 30, 1976); these would make compliance with the boycott illegal and provide penalties of varying severity. The Senate's Stevenson-Williams amendment carried penalties of $20,000 and one year's imprisonment, prohibited all religious and other discrimination, required public disclosure of all secondary boycott requests and actions, and prohibited the tertiary boycott outright.* A House version, the Bingham-Rosenthal amendment, was even tougher. It carried penalties of up to $50,000 and jail terms of up to five years, and would have prohibited compliance with the boycott "on any grounds and in any way." Both bills were passed overwhelmingly by both Houses and were next to be sent to a conference committee, which was to produce a compromise bill which the President could sign into law.

Ford didn't want such a law, but he also didn't want to

---

* To clarify these distinctions again: the secondary boycott imposes Arab anti-Israeli demands upon companies in "third countries" (such as the United States); the tertiary boycott is involved when, for example, one U.S. company refuses to do business with another U.S. company which either is blacklisted by the Arabs or in violation of boycott rules.

veto an anti-boycott bill during his election campaign. As it turned out, he didn't have to. A filibuster was in progress when the House bill was sent over to the Senate, and a filibuster can only be interrupted if there is unanimous consent of the Senate. And that consent was needed if the bill was to be properly received and a conference committee appointed. One man, Senator John Tower of Texas, withheld his consent. He denied afterwards that he was running interference for the White House, but was not widely believed.

The White House also protested it wasn't behind Tower's unusual parliamentary maneuver, and a couple of days before Congress adjourned, offered a compromise bill of its own. This proved to be an emasculated version of the weaker of the two bills. This eleventh-hour Administration maneuver was rejected by those behind the stronger laws. For one thing, the two-page White House proposal had been labeled a "bootleg" copy, and no one knew for certain whether it was genuine and had the President's approval; the Administration officials who were offering it couldn't or wouldn't say. For another, this weakened bill would have proved divisive. The White House knew the Congressional conferees couldn't accept some aspects of it, and that would have shifted the onus for killing the legislation onto the Congress, where it most certainly didn't belong.*

Like the two anti-boycott bills, the Export Administration Act died, on September 30, 1976. Its provisions were extended

---

* A somewhat sinister note was struck by the ADL's charge that President Ford and some of his top officials were at that very time in conference with Arab emissaries, discussing how to defeat the anti-boycott bills. While Congress was meeting to discuss compromise legislation, Ford was taking part in "confidential and private" talks with representatives of Saudi Arabia and other oil-producing nations, in which "the problem of anti-boycott legislation was discussed," Arnold Forster says. Participating were Defense Secretary Rumsfeld, Treasury Secretary Simon, and Assistant Treasury Secretary Parsky.[15] And Simon had earlier played a questionable role, according to private information we have received. The Treasury Secretary's initiative in urging Saudi Arabia to modify its specifically anti-Jewish boycott questionnaires was successful precisely because he led the Saudis to believe that the Treasury would, in return, help fight the passage of anti-boycott legislation in the Congress.

the same day by President Ford, by means of Executive Order 11940, and he seized that opportunity to reduce its penalties.

Disgusted legislators sought their compromise bill anyway. Staff members met unofficially and quickly agreed on a bill which included the House's secondary boycott prohibition, and this formed the basis of the anti-boycott bills introduced into the 95th Congress the following year.

One piece of federal anti-boycott legislation did become law in 1976, and that was Senator Abraham Ribicoff's amendment to the Tax Reform Bill. While it didn't outlaw compliance with the boycott, it made it expensive. Tax benefits meant to encourage U.S. companies to operate abroad would be denied to those which complied with the boycott, although the penalties were limited.* Yet even this new law was soon to be undermined by the Ford Administration. On November 4, the Treasury Department issued "proposed guidelines" on the new Tax Reform Act. These advised companies as to how they could participate in the boycott and still continue to take the tax benefits. Senator Ribicoff wrote an outraged letter to Treasury Secretary Simon on December 7, charging his department with deliberately misinterpreting the new law and "encouraging circumvention" of it.

THE NEW CARTER ADMINISTRATION in 1977 raised the hopes of the anti-boycott forces. For one thing, Jimmy Carter had frequently denounced the boycott and said he would support laws which prohibited compliance. A letter he sent to Senator Henry Jackson during the election campaign was typical of several such statements. He wrote:

> Right now the Congress has an opportunity to enact the first new legislation in ten years dealing with the Arab-sponsored boycott of the State of Israel. We ought to resist all attempts by foreign governments to impose racial or

---

* The law doesn't affect boycott compliance by U.S. manufacturers or shippers that have no overseas investments or subsidiaries. For those that do, it applies penalties only to that portion of a company's income that is derived from transactions involving boycott compliance.

religious discrimination on American citizens as the price of doing business.

Moreover, in my judgment, legislation should be passed to make compliance with any secondary boycott of Israel illegal. I regret that the Ford Administration continues to oppose such legislation which seeks only to bring America's commercial practices into harmony with America's humane principles.

A public opinion poll by the Louis Harris organization showed that there was broad agreement in America with Carter's anti-boycott stance. Published in the *Chicago Tribune* on January 31, 1977, it showed that a sizable majority favored anti-boycott laws as well as penalties on companies which comply with the boycott.* But the forces that opposed legislation against the boycott were massing and making their voices heard as the new Congress began its deliberations in 1977. Their arguments were much the same as they had been the previous year, centering on the possibility of "Arab retaliation." Reviewing the mood in mid-December 1976, Arnold Forster warned that they had already "succeeded in undermining the conviction . . . that an effective anti-boycott law is necessary and would be good." He predicted a "gang-up" against such a law, and this did indeed seem to be developing.

One of the first in the lists was a rather counter-productive proponent of Arab interests, but a real one nevertheless. Former U.S. Vice-President Spiro Agnew, whose consulting firm, Pathlite Inc., promoted contacts between American business and the oil-rich states,[16] wrote in his newsletter, *Education for Democracy*, that anti-boycott laws "would erect an insurmountable wall between us and our staunch friends in the non-Communist Arab world." He warned that "millions of American jobs would be lost" as the Arabs switched their business elsewhere, that "our

---

* A 71-to-6 percent majority disapproved of the refusal of Arab oil-producing countries to buy products from or do business with U.S. companies that deal with Israel. A 44-to-27 percent majority favored tax penalties on U.S. companies that complied with the boycott, and 42-to-29 percent favored fines or imprisonment on any company that complied.

trade deficit would balloon, weakening the dollar and unleashing a wave of inflation." Passage of an anti-boycott bill would mean America would "commit hara-kiri to satisfy the small but powerful Zionist lobby in the U.S."[17]

A month later, the chairman of ARAMCO, Frank Jungers, joined the battle by giving a rare interview to *Events,* an Arab-financed English-language news magazine published in London.[18] He repeated the warning that business "will shift . . . from the U.S. to Western Europe or Japan or elsewhere."

"As an American citizen and as a businessman, I find that I must condemn any laws that are opposed to American interests," he said. "Quite frankly, I do not find any justification for these laws—the Arab boycott is a political measure similar in all respects to the American boycott of Cuba, North Korea and China. Furthermore, the Arab boycott is nothing new. It is more than 25 years old. Why, then, raise it at this time?" He said "Zionist elements" were trying to force America "into becoming part of" the Arab-Israeli dispute, and said, "I'll do my best to ensure that American legislators realize that anti-boycott laws will not end the Arab-Israeli dispute but will intensify it . . ."

This argument might have been written for Jungers by the agents of the boycott office, for it is identical with those they have always advanced. It is also no better. For the American boycotts mentioned are in fact very different from the one Congress was considering. No secondary or tertiary boycott had been launched by the United States; America never demanded that the British stop smoking Havana cigars, or that U.S. firms should cease dealing with foreign companies and countries which carried on trade with Communist China or North Korea. Furthermore, it was the Arab boycotters rather than the "Zionists" who were forcing America into "becoming part of" the Arab-Israeli dispute, and by imposing the boycott of Israel onto the United States and American firms.

ARAMCO of course has always had a vested interest in doing the Arabs' bidding, but in late 1976 and early 1977 others joined in to oppose the anti-boycott laws, some for related reasons, some out of genuine fear. The National Association of Manufacturers (NAM), the U.S. Chamber of Commerce, and the Emergency Committee for American Trade (ECAT) all assigned staffs to draft and coordinate policy with regard to anti-boycott legislation. Arab-American groups such as Full Employment in America Through Trade (FEATT), an offshoot of the National Association of Arab Americans (NAAA), became active, as did the American Mideast Trade Association of Austin, Texas, and the American Arab Chamber of Commerce, of Houston. Arab League lobbyists were busy in Washington, and they were joined by trade association and company officials in fighting the proposed laws.[19]

Scaremongering was endemic. The president of the Petroleum Equipment Suppliers Association warned that his industry would lose hundreds of thousands of jobs and more than one billion dollars in wages if anti-boycott bills were passed, and the Associated General Contractors said U.S. Middle East business would go to Western Europe, Korea and Japan. FEATT claimed that an anti-boycott law would cause the loss of $30–$50 billion, and 800,000 to 1,000,000 jobs, over a five-year period; a $30 billion loss (but this time *annually*) was then projected by the Agricultural Trade Council, which forecast the loss of one million jobs in just the first year of the bills' enactment, while the NAAA claimed that "intellectual terrorism" on behalf of a "certain minority" of American voters had kept "the truth about the Arab position from reaching the public." Two more oil companies entered the lists. Mobil Oil, which in 1976 had published newspaper advertisements against anti-boycott laws, was again active, so much so that it was charged by the American Jewish Congress with having spent "hundreds of thousands of dollars—perhaps millions—in company funds to attack anti-boycott legislation." Exxon Corporation joined by flooding Congress with letters urging members to vote against the anti-boycott bills being introduced into the 95th Congress.[20]

These consisted of four, two each in the Senate and the House. The anti-boycott forces favored the tougher and more comprehensive of them, the Senate's Williams-Proxmire Bill and its identical House counterpart, the Bingham-Rosenthal

Bill. These stated that U.S. policy was opposed to foreign boycotts directed against friendly countries, and it encouraged
(and in specified cases, required) U.S. companies to refuse
action in support of such boycotts, even if such action only
meant furnishing information.

It prohibited the secondary boycott by making it illegal for
a company to refrain from doing business with Israel in con-
formity with a boycott agreement, requirement or request. It
outlawed the tertiary boycott in that it forbade a company to
refrain from dealing with a blacklisted non-Israeli firm. It prohibited the furnishing of information on business relationships
with Israel or with non-Israeli blacklisted companies, or on the
religion or national origin of any American citizen. It forbade
discrimination in employment based on the race, religion and
national origin of any American citizen. It forbade negative
certificates of origin. It required both the reporting and public
disclosure of boycott requests and compliance intentions. And
it carried penalties for first-time violators of $25,000, and for
subsequent violators of $50,000.[21]

Both the new Commerce Secretary, Juanita Kreps, and
Treasury Secretary-designate Blumenthal had already declared
their support for anti-boycott legislation, and the latter added he
would immediately "review" those Treasury "guidelines" which
had subverted the anti-boycott provisions of the Tax Reform
Act. But when the new Secretary of State, Cyrus Vance, testified
at the beginning of March 1977, he tried to oppose all bills then
being considered, stating that the Carter Administration opposed
boycotts in principle and would propose alternative legislation
of its own. For a time, he sounded like Ford Administration
spokesmen, arguing that really tough anti-boycott laws would
hinder U.S. peace initiatives in the Middle East, hamper his
attempts to keep the price of oil down and discourage Arab
investments in the United States.[22]

Vance, said the Washington correspondent of London's
Guardian, was treading a "zig-zag path," trying not to alienate
Americans who opposed the boycott while also telling the Arabs
"that the United States had stood up to the anti-boycott hawks

in Congress and secured withdrawal of the legislation."[23] It was too late for that, however, as Vance discovered the very next day while testifying before a House panel. Congress, he was told, insisted on passing its own bills, and would allow only modifications to them by the Administration. Vance asked that companies be given a grace period of unspecified length, to fulfill existing commitments and transactions; and he opposed applying the provisions of a U.S. anti-boycott law to the foreign subsidiaries of U.S. corporations.[24] He also warned Congress that the United States "ought to stick to its own business" and not try to enlist other countries against the Arab boycott, for "that would cause trouble."[25] But the Carter Administration recognized the new and determined mood of Congress, as had an important segment of the U.S. business community. The chief executives of those 170 major American corporations represented on the "Business Roundtable" met with the Anti-Defamation League of B'nai B'rith during March and April to work out a "Joint Statement of Principles" over pending anti-boycott laws. The negotiations weren't easy and seemed for a time to be foundering, but eventually a compromise was reached between ADL National Chairman Burton M. Joseph and his team, and Business Roundtable Chairman Irving S. Shapiro (also chairman of Du Pont) in which the American Jewish Committee and the American Jewish Congress could concur. London's *Economist* noted these developments on March 19. "American business has done a smart about-turn on the Arab trade boycott of Israel," it said, and asked, "Why the change of heart?"

There had certainly been a *volte face*: even Exxon, that erstwhile opponent of all anti-boycott laws, had joined the Roundtable talks. Businessmen, said the *Economist*, realized that President Carter had been serious when he earlier called the boycott an "absolute disgrace" and that he intended, far more than his Secretary of State, to pass an effective anti-boycott law. Industry had realized the way the wind was blowing, and trimmed its sails accordingly.

By May, Carter could commend the Business Roundtable

and the three Jewish national organizations for having agreed on "legislative language" for an anti-boycott bill which he would "strongly recommend." That bill passed House and Senate by votes of 346 to 43 and 90 to 1, respectively; in June the House passed the "compromise bill" by a vote of 306 to 41, and it was this which Carter signed into law on June 22, 1977.

The fight for an effective law against economic coercion of the sort the Arab boycott represented had been a long one in the United States, and it was appropriate that Carter made much of the signing ceremony. It was unusually elaborate, staged in the White House's Rose Garden, and those attending were Roundtable and Jewish organizational leaders, legislators who had been at the forefront of the battle throughout, and an impressive array of Administration figures, including Vice-President Mondale, Secretary of State Vance, and National Security Adviser Brzezinski. Senators Harrison A. Williams, Jr., and Adlai Stevenson were there, Representatives Benjamin S. Rosenthal, Jonathan Bingham, Stephen J. Solarz, and others.

Carter recalled that he had described boycotts and discrimination against American businessmen on religious and ethnic grounds as "a profound moral issue which we should not shirk." His concern about foreign boycotts, he said, "stemmed from our special relationship with Israel, as well as from the economic, military and security needs of both our countries. But the issue also goes to the very heart of free trade among all nations."

The new law, he added, "does not threaten or question the sovereign right of any nation to regulate its own commerce with other countries." By that he referred to one element of the compromise worked out between the Roundtable and the ADL: the B'nai B'rith delegation had accepted language recognizing the "right" of Arab states to impose their "primary boycott" on Israel.

A White House press release said "the legislation will prohibit most forms of compliance with unsanctioned foreign boycotts without unnecessarily jeopardizing U.S. political and commercial interests in the Middle East." (Indeed, Carter had emphasized that, in his view, the new law's "enforcement will help lessen tensions in the Middle East and hopefully lead to permanent peace in that troubled region.")

The law which Carter promised he would enforce was an extension (until September 30, 1979) of the Export Administration Act (1969), amending it to include a "Prohibition on compliance with foreign boycotts." Its provisions prohibit Americans from:

• refusing to do business with blacklisted firms and boycotted friendly countries;

• discriminating against U.S. persons on grounds of race, religion, sex, or national origin;

• furnishing information about another person's race, religion, sex, or national origin;

• furnishing information about business dealings with boycotted countries or blacklisted persons.

It goes further still. It prohibits any person to discriminate against any firm because of the race, religion, sex or national origin of any of its owners, officers, directors or employees; it prohibits furnishing information about whether any person has contributed to (or is otherwise involved in) the activities of any charitable or fraternal organization, such as for example the United Jewish Appeal.

It prohibits attesting by means of negative certificates of origin that goods do not contain materials or components of Israeli origin, though this prohibition only becomes effective one year after the date of the law. It also prohibits the implementation of any letter of credit which contains any boycott condition or requirement.

The previous requirement for filing reports with the U.S. Department of Commerce is continued under the new Act, including a statement whether the person filing has complied or intends to comply with the boycott requests covered in the reports. Such reports will continue to be treated as "public documents," open for inspection. And the Act contains a "preemptive clause," under which the federal law effectively supersedes any state anti-boycott law.

Whoever "knowingly violates" the Act is subject to a

criminal penalty of not more than a $25,000 fine, or imprisonment of not more than one year, or both. In addition, the Commerce Department may impose a "civil penalty" of not more than $10,000 for other violations (after an administrative hearing). The Act guards against evasion by means of a clause which forbids any transaction or activity undertaken to evade the Act.

The new law, however, contains exceptions to its prohibitions, and it may be regarded as a certainty that Jewish national organizations in the United States and others, including members of Congress, who favor tougher action will be pressing for the elimination or modification of some or all of these. Under the new law, an American firm:

• may agree to comply with Arab requirements forbidding the importation of Israeli goods or services into Arab lands (thus again recognizing the Arabs' right to impose a "primary boycott" on Israel);

• may agree to comply with Arab requirements forbidding the shipment or transshipment of Arab exports to Israel;

• may issue "positive" certificates of origin attesting that goods sold were of exclusive U.S. origin;

• may allow an Arab customer to make a "unilateral and specific selection" of any carrier, insurer or supplier of services to be performed in Arab lands, or of specific goods identifiable by source;*

• may not become involved in Arab immigration or passport requirements (which might ban Jews), but an individual might do so for his own visa.

Finally, an American firm or individual, resident in an Arab land, may agree to comply with the laws of that country with respect to his activities there, and specifically agree to abide by laws governing imports into that country.

---

* Thus, an Arab customer can specify that trucks he has ordered be equipped with a specific brand of tires, provided the truck company is in no way involved in the selection. But an American firm may not agree to a general demand by an Arab customer that no blacklisted subcontractor be chosen.

The term "United States person," which is used in the Act to define what may and may not be done, assumes more than legalistic importance. The law broadly defines the term as including any U.S. resident or national, any American domestic concern *and any of its foreign subsidiaries or affiliates controlled by it,* and it also includes *any domestic (American) branch of a foreign business concern.* The international implications of this will be studied by corporate lawyers the world over.[26]

THROUGHOUT BOTH 1976 and 1977, the progress of U.S. anti-boycott legislation was being closely watched from abroad. On September 2, 1976, Mohammed Mahgoub warned the Ford Administration that the Arab states would take retaliatory action if an effective law was passed, and that "such sanctions" could only hurt American companies, as they would be met "by strong measures on our part."[27] The Arabs, he said, were prepared to be both "tough" and "uncompromising."[28] The same line came from Kuwait, whose Finance Minister, Abdul Rahman al-Atiqi, said, "Damn American law! We will boycott and we will continue our boycott, and we will never import anything from the United States!"[29]

Mahgoub's 1976 threat included the remark that U.S. anti-boycott laws would "not prevent the boycott office from implementing its regulations." This was reminiscent of the earlier statement from the Arab League's London spokesman, that negative certificates of origin weren't needed, as "positive vetting" would do nicely. There were even reports that the Central Boycott Office in Damascus was preparing to establish a computerized data bank, which would store information about companies with whom Arabs *were* permitted to trade, and on which all Arab nations and companies could freely draw.[30] The day of the negative certificate did, indeed, seem to be almost over in early 1977, at least in the United States. A number of Arab countries said they would stop requiring them of U.S. exporters,* al-

---

* "Soft-line" Arab countries, like Mauritania, Morocco, Algeria, Tunisia, Egypt, Sudan and Somalia, either never demanded negative certificates of origin or, as in the case of Egypt, had ceased doing so as a general practice.

though this was accompanied by a Saudi Arabian threat that they could be reimposed if tough anti-boycott laws were passed. Whether the Arab boycott will work effectively without such certificates remains to be seen. Arab protestations that they weren't needed sounded hollow; these certificates had been a major boycott instrument throughout all the preceding years.

WITH PASSAGE of the new American law imminent, Arab pressure intensified. In an exclusive interview with David Holden of London's *Sunday Times*, Crown Prince Fahd, Saudi Arabia's First Deputy Prime Minister, warned that his country's oil-price levels couldn't be guaranteed in the face of such American moves. The Arab states, he said, "are fully committed to the principles of boycott and will not give them up until the [Arab-Israeli] conflict is solved completely." An American anti-boycott law would only harm American companies, he said, and then added that Saudi Arabia's credibility in the Arab world would not survive "meek acceptance of American anti-boycott legislation."[31] Likewise in Kuwait, an official told Reuters that U.S. firms would be the losers, and that Kuwait "will not exempt any company, from whatever country, from the boycott regulations."[32] And in mid-May 1977 the Arab chambers of commerce and industry, meeting in Damascus, described the then-pending U.S. law as a "further example of imperialist interference with the exercise of the sovereignty of independent states." They recommended banning all dealings with any foreign firms which refused to cooperate with the Arab boycott.[33]

By coincidence, the U.S. anti-boycott law was being readied for signature just as the Arab League held another of its periodic boycott conferences. Convening the meeting in Alexandria on June 8, 1977, Commissioner-General Mohammed Mahgoub said it would take a "decisive stand" against the new law. His 110-point agenda led off with moves "to confront the Israeli anti-boycott drive," in the United States "as well as Zionist efforts to have similar laws passed in Britain and Canada." New rules and regulations would be formulated to meet the threat, he said, and these "will put an end to all these attempts."[34] He regarded them as part of "a campaign of hysterical laws and bills . . . which Israel and world Zionism are trying not only to enforce on the U.S. but also in some countries of western Europe."[35]

Mahgoub continued lashing out throughout the conference. Just ten days before Carter would sign the anti-boycott bill into law, Mahgoub said the Arabs would buy whatever they needed from Europe and Japan "should U.S. companies adhere to the legislation." He even claimed that European and Japanese firms "are informing the Arab boycott organization about Israeli dealings with American companies in order to get them blacklisted." They are, he said, "naturally interested in getting the Americans blacklisted in order to inherit the vast markets of the Arab world."[36] The conference then announced an embargo on raw-material supplies to any American firm which refused to observe boycott regulations; nor would the Arabs countenance any claim by an American company that it is subject to the laws of the United States.[37] The boycott office could not in any circumstances "allow foreign laws to interfere and disrupt its work."[38]

The threat regarding raw materials was puzzling. London's *Times* said that boycott officials "would not say how the ban on raw materials would be implemented or if it included oil." Libya and Iraq, it reported, demanded that oil should be included in the embargo, but Egypt reportedly opposed.[39] But oil is not imported from the Arab world by U.S. companies (other than oil companies); oil supplies that an American manufacturer needs are supplied domestically; nor does the Arab world export other essential raw materials which an American company could not purchase elsewhere.

As the Alexandria conference drew to a close on June 20, it was apparent that Mahgoub and the regional boycott commissioners were facing "what could be a trial of nerves," as London's *Financial Times* put it.[40] Even their deliberations concerning individual companies showed they were rattled.

American companies removed from the blacklists would, they said, in future be kept secret; the Arabs wanted companies complying with boycott regulations to be "protected from pressure."[41] That statement seemed to encourage U.S. firms to violate the laws of their country, and to protect them not against "pressure," but against legally mandated penalties.

The conference removed 10 companies from the blacklist, cleared 47 others after they had allegedly complied with an Arab ultimatum to mend their ways, gave 8 companies new ultimatums, shelved the cases of 11 others pending further information, and blacklisted 13.[42]

General Motors, Westinghouse Electric and General Electric were among those which had "cleared themselves of suspicion that they intended to invest in Israel," Mahgoub said, and were free to trade with Israel. "So long as they do not have plants in Israel that use Israeli labor and thus help the economy, it is fine," he said.[43]

That seemed more bluster. Asked if they had given Mahgoub's office any proof of compliance with anti-boycott rules, the three firms denied it. G.E. does business with both Israel and the Arabs, G.M. sold cars to Israel, and Westinghouse was bidding to supply an Israeli power plant with nuclear equipment.[44]

The names of newly blacklisted companies were not released, in order, said *The Times*, "to keep the companies guessing and to give the Arabs maximum leverage in future negotiations with those concerns."[45]*

The boycott conference produced at least one lighter touch, on which the press was quick to pounce. London's *Financial Times* reported it on June 22 as follows:

> Good news for President Sadat's conscience. Among the firms removed this week from the blacklist of the Arab Boycott of Israel Office is Ted Lapidus, the Paris designer, who for many years has supplied the Egyptian leader's natty

---

* Some names, however, were leaked by "sources at the conference." Among American firms were Honeywell, Delmont (and its British branch, Delmont International), Tropar Trophy Manufacturing, Garloc, and Goodman and Sons. Also blacked were Ideal Tour of Finland; Hitachi Shipbuilding and Engineering Co. of Japan; Minmetal SRL, a pipeline company in Italy; La Commerciale of Burundi; and a Turkish firm called Rubi Koll Stu Isak Ve Leon Rubinstaynex Ze Orgt.[46]

clothes, not least the eye-catching Parisian ties for which he is noted.[47]

The Arabs could not carry out all their dire threats against American companies. In the words of major U.S. Jewish organizations giving testimony before Congress early in 1977, "experience bears out that Arab boycotting countries will buy the best available product for the cheapest possible price in the shortest delivery time offered [and that] they are, first and foremost, businessmen [who] will trade with any nation on the face of the earth, except perhaps Israel itself." American industry's "know-how, technical genius and product superiority are the controlling criteria and, since the beginning, have been the major factors in Arab trade with the United States."[48]

However much, therefore, some Arab League spokesmen continued to threaten retaliatory action, Arab nations retain a strong interest in the goods, services, know-how and facilities only the United States and Europe can supply in massive quantities. Recognizing that, both Egypt and Syria were already in 1975 proving "flexible" on the boycott, allowing even blacklisted companies into their markets under certain conditions. The pro-Arab *Middle East Economic Digest*, reporting the 38th Central Boycott Office meeting in Cairo in mid-1975, said the "new and flexible approach" meant companies might be taken off the blacklist if they invested twice or perhaps three times as much in an Arab state as they had invested in Israel.[49] In spring 1976 another sign of a climb-down appeared in the *Jordan Times*, which quoted Saudi Arabia's Minister of Industry and Electricity, Dr. Ghazi al-Gosaibi, as hinting that the Saudis would no longer strictly enforce their policy of excluding Jews. "Any American citizen sent in fulfillment of contractual obligations will be welcome," he said. "There is," he added, "no substitute for the real McCoy." As for that, the test will come when the first McCoy named Ginsberg applies for a visa.

The Saudi Minister also admitted Saudi Arabia couldn't easily boycott the United States. "Certainly it would be disruptive to our five-year development plan to switch to other suppliers," he said. "It would hurt us." Saudi Arabia, he said, preferred to do business with the United States, because "American technology is superior, Saudi Arabia has had long experience with Americans through ARAMCO, and we like Americans." And while he wouldn't go so far as to remove all threats entirely ("No country is indispensable, not even the greatest," he said), he laid down the policy that if a company "is willing to do in the Arab world exactly what it does in Israel, it can be removed from the Arab boycott list."[50] A variation came from Beirut's Arab Press Service on April 26, 1976, which stated that certain companies might continue to invest in Israel, provided they place investments in one Arab project worth at least "double their total placements in Israel." This, APS said, was to allow "big world combines" to channel "know-how and investments into the Arab world," but won't "lessen the effectiveness of the economic war against Israel." In fact, the new flexibility would "prove much more effective a weapon against Israel than the straight boycott measures hitherto known" because it would allow the Arab nations to grow faster than Israel, reduce "world opposition to the boycott policy," and "neutralise Israel's counter-measures." Eventually, it "would isolate Israel from the Middle East economic area" and encourage a new and potentially powerful Afro-Arab strategy. APS said that African and Arab foreign ministers, meeting at Dakar early in 1976, had agreed to "coordinate" Arab blacklists with the "anti-apartheid" blacklists of member countries of the Organization of African Unity. This, it claimed, would allow the Arab boycott to "evolve" into "an international 'Boycott-Apartheid' move to be readily adhered to by the entire Third World."[51]

SUCCESSFUL COORDINATION of Arab and African blacklists could presage an all-out Third World economic campaign against the Western world, however unlikely such unified action looks. For Arab oil policies have disappointed, even alienated, some African states. Noting, for example, that 90 percent of OPEC aid went to Moslem countries, African diplomats were saying in 1975, "Arab petrodollar politics is aiming at buying colonies in Black Africa," and "Arabs tie their willingness to help Black Africans to willingness to line up solidly against Israel."[52]

An example of why this "oil weapon" was causing dismay in the Third World countries in 1975 is provided by Tanzania. The increased oil price added at least $10 million to her import bill, and her foreign exchange reserves were halved in just three years. Gasoline consumption had to be cut by 20 percent, and hope of the country achieving its development program targets abandoned.

What goes for Tanzania applies to other African states, and to countries like Brazil, which needs to import three-quarters of her oil requirements. The cost to Brazil in 1974 was $2.8 billion—the equivalent of more than half of its total exports. The subsequent 10 percent rise in OPEC's price added another $400 million to Brazil's annual import bill. These measures were forcing that country and others to restrict imports—not only of oil, but of essential raw materials and capital goods, inevitably slowing down the rate of growth. In Brazil, a growth rate of less than 5 percent a year means stagnation, increased unemployment and political instability.*

PASSAGE OF U.S. anti-boycott legislation will inevitably shift the battlefront to Europe. Secretary of State Vance has warned against trying to embroil other countries in the fight against the

---

* Political instability is in fact another product of expanding Arab influence, especially in developing countries in Africa. Although they were initially able to unite within OPEC, the Arabs have set a bad example of quarrelsomeness: Morocco and Algeria have been squabbling over ownership of the former Spanish Sahara, without regard to the welfare of its inhabitants; Egypt and Libya have had vitriolic battles of words which have nearly developed into something more serious; Somalia has a territorial claim against Kenya, and the Moslem General Idi Amin has threatened to invade Tanzania. Colonel Quaddafi of Libya has actually seized and occupied, apparently on a permanent footing, a large slice of the territory of neighboring Chad, and has tried to over-throw the government of the Sudan. Nigeria has become a country of military coups, in which a Moslem interest and involvement has become apparent. The Lebanese civil war is the most tragic recent example of Arabs destroying Arabs.

Arab Trade Boycott of Israel, but he will be under much pressure to do just that, whether he fears it will alienate the Arabs or not. For the U.S. business and financial communities, eager to prevent any drift of Arab business away from the United States and into countries which do not have anti-boycott laws, will find it is in their best interest to get just such laws passed throughout the industrialized world. Just as a federal U.S. law against the boycott was meant to preempt state anti-boycott laws, international action would in a sense be preempting the national laws of the United States.

Coordinated international action ought ideally to be attempted with the nine-nation European Economic Community, as only its combined strength can challenge the Arab boycotters as effectively as the United States has done. Arab states are as interested in the EEC's products, services and know-how as they are in America's. Britain, the newest EEC member, is, however, one of the weakest, and could try to resist such concerted action —or, for that matter, seek refuge in it. We have described the United Kingdom as a "willing victim" of Arab blackmail, and its dependence on Arab trade—partly real, partly imagined—has made its government unwilling to sponsor any anti-boycott legislation, even during the premiership of Sir Harold Wilson, a devoted friend of Israel. Nor has the British government offered to aid companies being threatened by the Arabs, as the West German government has done. It did not even give help to Britain's biggest bank, Barclays, when it was blacklisted late in 1976. As for government statements on the subject, these have been consistently flabby and ineffective.

Back in 1969 the Board (later Department) of Trade took the relatively firm line that the government opposed the secondary boycott and refused "to have any official dealings" with any boycott office. While that sounded good, and was repeated for some years, no action of any kind was ever once suggested. The only concrete government statement appeared in a two-page "Hints to Businessmen," which was intended as advice to firms threatened by the boycott. Prior to the 1973 war this seemed to encourage trade with Israel and resistance to the boycott, but it was soon watered down by the significant addition of a qualifying phrase. This was first given in the House of Commons on December 20, 1974, by government spokesman Eric Deakins. The government, he said, deplored "all trade boycotts other than those internationally supported and sanctioned by the United Nations," but he then added, "How firms should act in any particular case is a matter for the commercial judgment of the firm concerned." That formulation became the standard British government position on the matter, repeated endlessly despite the contradiction it involves. For if the government rejects boycotts, British firms ought to rely on this rejection, and on government support to uphold it, instead of their own "commercial judgment."

The charge of weakness was leveled even more strongly against the British government in the matter of negative certificates of origin. British chambers of commerce refuse to certify these, so the Arabs demanded they be authenticated by the Foreign and Commonwealth Office (FCO). The Foreign Office routinely gave in to this demand, lamely claiming it only certifies the *signature* of notaries public, and was not concerned with the actual content of the documents *it* signs.

A 1975 "White Paper" was equally unsatisfactory. This introduced a mysterious new exemption to proposed race relations laws, which permitted discrimination "for fulfillment of training and trade obligations to overseas countries"; as one civil rights leader put it, this was "presumably designed to exclude Jewish people from missions to Arab countries."[53] The then Home Secretary, Roy Jenkins, denied this, but the law remained vague and could be interpreted differently. Exclusion of Jews from trade delegations was, in any case, already occurring, and what was needed was a promise of firm government action to stop this, and not bland assurances.

But government action remained nil throughout 1976, even after a powerful attack on the boycott in the House of Commons by Eric Moonman, M.P., supported by Tim Sainsbury and Greville Janner. The government instructions afterwards remained as they had been: companies were left unprotected against boycott pressures, and were encouraged to surrender if compliance was in their "commercial interest."

Vigorous U.S. anti-boycott activity during the first months of the Carter Administration at best offered encouragement. Britain's new Foreign Secretary, David Owen, told the House of Commons in early 1977 that he wanted to make it "categorically clear" that he opposed the Arab Trade Boycott, and would have discussions with the Carter Administration on the measures the United States was taking. But soon he too was offering the House of Commons the same lame excuse which the Foreign and Commonwealth Office had always given over its authentication of signatures on boycott documents.[54] In mid-July 1977 Malcolm Rifkind and Greville Janner took the FCO to task in the Commons, charged that as many as 6,000 such documents a year were involved, and reminded Parliament that the U.S. State Department refused to provide a similar service for the Arabs. The FCO's Frank Judd responded with a restatement of the British Government's boycott position, adding comments about the new American laws:

> . . . we oppose and deplore all trade boycotts which do not have international support and authority . . . Nonetheless, the boycott is a fact of life which has been with us now for nearly 30 years and with which British exporters must deal. How companies act in specific cases must be a matter for their commercial judgment . . . The Government's role it seems to me is—while making clear its abhorrence of the boycott—and I underline that word—to do nothing that would further increase the difficulties of British firms dealing with the Middle East. Our aim as a Government is and must be to expand British exports throughout the world. The boycott is an obstacle, a highly objectionable obstacle, but one which we must help companies to surmount.
>
> We wish it were possible for British exporters to trade entirely freely with all countries of the Middle East and we hope that negotiations for a lasting and just peace in the area will bring it about. But until that hoped-for goal is achieved, the Government's efforts must be directed to ensuring that British firms can conduct their trade with the

[[212]]

minimum of hindrance . . . We shall naturally study the practical effects of the recent United States measures, in due course, with close attention. But to be realistic about it, they do not necessarily provide a model for us. It is important to bear in mind that the United States is far less dependent on exports than our own [country] . . .[55]

The British government has been "stonewalling" anti-boycott legislation just as the Ford Administration did—more so on the economic grounds mentioned by Judd. Additionally, the pro-Arab lobby is infinitely more powerful in Britain than in the United States,* British society (including the FCO) inevitably contains many "Arabists," Britain has historic ties with (and guilt-feelings about) the Arab world, and Britain's assimilated Jews are often reluctant to draw attention to themselves by making demands on the government. There is some residual anti-Semitism as well. But most operative, without doubt, is Britain's unwillingness to take a moral stand even on a boycott the government said it "abhorred," because of the desperate need to promote exports to the oil-rich Arab world.

By mid-1977, however, anti-boycott forces in Britain were beginning to mobilize. In May an All-Party Parliamentary Committee to Combat Foreign Boycotts was formed;† that same month, three major Jewish organizations (Board of Deputies of British Jews, Zionist Federation and B'nai B'rith) presented the Prime Minister and Parliament with a "Joint Memorandum"

---

* An example: in mid-July 1977 Foreign Secretary Owen opened London's new Arab-British Centre in the company of Mahmoud Riad, secretary-general of the Arab League. The Centre, Riad said, would play "an exceedingly important role" in promoting "a wholesome image" of the Arabs. It is in fact the Arab League's propaganda center in Britain, housing a battery of pro-Arab groups, prime among them CAABU (Council for the Advancement of Arab-British Understanding).[56]

† Under the chairmanship of a former Labour Minister, Arthur Bottomley, M.P., it included the Duke of Devonshire and Lord Byers in the House of Lords; in the House of Commons, its members were Greville Janner and Norman Lamont (joint honorary secretaries), Labour and Conservative M.P.'s respectively, as well as the Rt. Hon. Hugh Fraser (Conservative), and members of the Ulster Unionist and Scottish and Welsh Nationalist parties.

outlining what needed to be done to combat the Arab Trade Boycott's effects in Britain; finally, on July 12, Lord Byers introduced Britain's first anti-boycott bill in the House of Lords. The fact that this "private member's bill" (i.e., one unsponsored by the government) was being introduced by the leader of the Liberal Party in the Lords was noted; the Labour government, led by James Callaghan, was then surviving only because of a "Lib-Lab pact," which assured Callaghan the support of Liberal votes in Parliament.

The *Economist* noted that Byers' Foreign Boycott Bill had been introduced while a visiting delegation of American congressmen were meeting with European parliamentarians in London. "America wants Europe to follow its lead in legislating against foreign (read ' Arab League) trade boycotts," it stated. This message, it said, "has been rammed home" by the congressional delegation in its London talks.[57]

The Byers Bill should be given "government time" in October 1977, when Parliament reconvenes after its summer recess, the *Economist* said, but it "may have a rough passage in Parliament." It closely resembles U.S. anti-boycott legislation and imposes fines (even imprisonment) on those violating its provisions. Even if the government refuses to back the Bill, Byers would be happy if a parliamentary "select committee" is formed to examine the effects of the boycott in Britain, as this would oblige British company officials who are called to testify to explain their actions, and reveal the extent of Arab interference with normal business practice in the country.[58]

THE ANTI-BOYCOTT SCOREBOARD in mid-1977 marked up some major and some minor victories:

• In the United States, anti-boycott legislation was signed into law. It contained loopholes and other defects, but by and large seemed an effective way of protecting American businessmen against Arab threat and pressure.

• In Canada, government warnings that aid would be withheld from exporters who comply with the Arab boycott were having an effect. An anti-boycott law was still needed, along with more determined government vigilance and enforcement.

• In Britain, a bill to fight foreign boycotts was at long last introduced in Parliament.

• In Sweden, there was reason to hope that the Liberal Party, which in 1976 had urged anti-boycott legislation, might sponsor it now that its leader was Deputy Prime Minister.

• In France, an amendment to a race relations act, which could be used as an anti-boycott weapon, became law on June 7. It provided fines and jail terms for discriminatory trade practices on the grounds of race, religion and national origin. The *Jerusalem Post* noted that France had become "the first Western country to put an anti-boycott law on the statute books," fifteen days ahead of the United States, and that it was the work of parliamentarians, lawyers and business leaders in the Movement for Liberty of Commerce.* The Arab lobby had been caught napping, as, for that matter, had the the French Government which, being eager to woo the Arabs, had no interest in backing the law. Passage was assured because it was clear that no party or politician dared vote against a tightening of race-relations legislation and, because the Socialists backed the bill, even the Communists refrained from opposing it.

The new French law is in fact fairly comprehensive and prohibits any company or person (even government officials) from doing anything which would "under normal circumstances" create "more difficulty" in "any economic activity," either for persons or "legal entities" on ethnic, racial or religious grounds. Any group which has been active in combatting racism or discrimination for at least five years may initiate action under this law; and this would enable organizations fighting anti-Semitism to bring charges against individuals or firms discriminating against Jewish companies doing business with Israel. In fact, although pro-Arab forces at first sought to play down the im-

---

* The legislation was initiated in November 1976. Sponsors included the right wing political writer Raymond Aron, Socialist economist Jacques Attali, Gaullist former Justice Minister Jean Foyer, and Alfred Coste Floret, French prosecutor at the Nuremberg war-crimes trials.[59]

portance of the new French law, its efficacy in fighting the Arab Trade Boycott of Israel was specifically and clearly stated in the French National Assembly.[60]

The Arabs soon recognized the significance of the French law. Officials of the Franco-Arab Chamber of Commerce told London's Arab-backed newsmagazine *Events* that the situation was a "disaster."[61] Most worried appeared to be France's semi-governmental export credit agency, COFACE, a major enforcer of the Arab boycott by virtue of its consistent refusal to insure exporters who failed to comply with boycott rules. *Events* said COFACE had frozen "all insurance schemes with French companies in the Arab world" because it lacked clear instructions from the government regarding the new law and was therefore "interpreting this to mean that French companies cannot comply with Arab boycott of Israel regulations . . ."[62] French Foreign Trade Minister André Rossi, however, was quoted as promising he would "issue a directive providing for a 'flexible' interpretation of the law."[63]* That kind of flexibility will be watched carefully by France's anti-boycott forces.

In Israel, the anti-boycott scoreboard allowed for "cautious jubilation." America, wrote the *Jerusalem Post*, had "exceeded everyone's expectations"; so had the French, it said, and even the British were moving.[65] Dan Halperin, who heads the Israel Finance Ministry's authority against economic warfare, took "particular satisfaction" in the arguments used by President Carter to support the U.S. law: that the Arab boycott is basically un-American, and that it strikes at America's special relationship with Israel.[66]

But the economic war against the Jews has not ended. Its protagonists are massing a counterattack against any and all anti-boycott moves taken or planned. Their aims are various, nor

---

* An American counterpart to COFACE is AID (Agency for International Development), which finances exporters' credit lines. On March 23, 1977, it declared that it would "not finance any procurement in which boycott or other restrictive trade practices are applied."[64] Britain's counterpart is the ECGD (Export Credit Guarantee Department); this has not taken an anti-boycott stance.

can it be said that they all seek Israel's destruction through economic strangulation. In the Western world, some want only to facilitate trade with the oil-rich Arabs, or to placate the Arab states in the hope that this might promote peace in the Middle East. But in pursuing these ends, they align themselves solidly with those whose never-abandoned objective is to deny the Jewish state a permanent place on the map of the Middle East. For Israel, for Jews, and for those non-Jews who support Israel's right to a secure and peaceful existence, eternal vigilance remains the price of liberty.[67] And that includes liberty to trade freely with whom one will.

Epilogue

T HE FRENCH and the Americans had struck the Western world's first legislative counterblows in the economic war against the Jews. But, though "the first blow is half the battle,"[1] the war continued to rage. By mid-1977 it was possible to note the dangers ahead, as well as what needed to be done to counter them.

A patchy but vocal pro-Arab lobby was emerging in America, and it was becoming more aggressive as U.S. anti-boycott legislation worked its way through Congress. How effective this would prove to be would become apparent during 1977–1979. The amended Export Administration Act of 1969, which contained the new U.S. anti-boycott laws, had been extended only until 1979, and those forces urging compliance with the boycott clearly had two aims: to secure minimum enforcement of its anti-boycott provisions while these were on the books, and to make certain they remained dead once the current law had expired.

The U.S. pro-Arab forces appeared to be headquartered in Houston, Texas, which had "emerged as the center of U.S.-Arab trade relations." Also gaining momentum was a lobby, "drawn primarily from U.S. banking interests and exporting firms," which aimed "to counter pro-Israel and anti-boycott pressures on Congress and the administration," wrote the pro-Arab *Middle East Economic Digest* (MEED) in July 1977. A "war chest" for a publicity drive was being put together by a group calling itself the American Mid-East Association; its allies included the U.S.-based International Engineering & Construction Industry Council, and the American Middle East Trade Association (also in Houston).[2] They aimed to fight not only

[[218]]

those anti-boycott provisions of the Export Administration Act and the 1976 Tax Reform Act, but also unrelated tax measures which made it more difficult for American companies to operate in the Middle East. MEED noted that revised tax legislation was due in late 1977 or early 1978; the pro-Arab lobby would then have an opportunity to press for cancellation of those anti-boycott rules.

Mid-July 1977 also saw a group of San Francisco lawyers and businessmen take action against the new anti-boycott laws. They filed a $40 *billion* law suit in San Francisco federal court, contending the law was unconstitutional. According to another pro-Arab journal, *Events*, this court test was backed by major California corporations, as well as a San Francisco group called Concerned Black Americans in Support of Africa and the Middle East. The forty billion dollar figure was "warranted," *Events* claimed, because federal anti-boycott laws put that much U.S.-Middle East business in jeopardy.[3]

Figures such as these were being widely quoted in a transparent attempt at panicking public opinion. This propaganda line was already familiar, and had in May 1977 been concisely stated in an editorial in *Oil & Gas Journal*. This petroleum-industry publication, predictably taking a strong stand against anti-boycott laws, claimed they would do "great harm," place "U.S. industry in an impossible position," and even "boomerang" on the anti-boycott forces by prolonging the Arab Trade Boycott of Israel and hampering U.S. peace initiatives in the Middle East.[4]

Whether or not the Arabs would retaliate to any great extent remained to be seen. Anti-boycott groups predicted they wouldn't; those urging compliance with the boycott claimed to see only disaster ahead. But what had emerged from the Arab world in the wake of European and American anti-boycott initiatives had been mainly words, and these, under the circumstances, seemed remarkably restrained. Saudi Arabia's King Khaled, Egypt's President Sadat and Syria's President Assad threatened at their May 1977 tripartite summit in Riyadh to use the oil weapon "automatically" under certain circumstances, but the boycott didn't come up in this connection.* Egypt's Foreign Minister Ismail Fahmi warned in Cairo that "the world should not forget that the Arab oil weapon is no less significant than . . . the nuclear weapon," but he too was suggesting that it might be used only if a "just peace" were not reached.[5] Yet there *was* one hint that Arab oil might be used to coerce the Western world over the issue of the Arab Trade Boycott; this came from *Middle East Economic Survey*, an authoritative newsletter. Pointing out that Saudi Arabian oil policy "is determined in the light of a variety of political and economic factors," it warned that if "the Zionist lobby" in the United States was "powerful enough to frustrate" President Carter's plans in the Middle East, this in turn would "tend to erode Saudi Arabia's continued moderation on oil prices and, more importantly, oil production."[6]

Saudi Arabia alone had by mid-1977 spent about $27 billion in contracts with U.S. companies for supplies and services; in addition, it had about $30 billion invested in the United States.[7] These factors would tend to inhibit it from drastic retaliatory action, and despite all the warnings that America might lose as much as forty billion dollars worth of business because of its anti-boycott law, other Arab-world sources saw the matter differently. MEED, for example, cited American and Arab businessmen as predicting that the new law would "not seriously damage U.S.-Arab commercial relations," nor would it "have an immediate impact on U.S. trade with the Middle East."[8] Then, Mahgoub himself proposed an unexpected "concession." He said the boycott of Israel would continue until she withdrew from the West Bank, the Gaza Strip and Jerusalem, implying for the first time that the Boycott Commission might accept Israel within its 1967 boundaries.

It noted that Carter's signature did not signal immediate implementation of the anti-boycott law. That would not occur until the U.S. Department of Commerce had codified its pro-

---

* They would use it "if Israel did not withdraw from occupied Arab territories."

visions, which might not be until early 1978.⁹ How some of
the law's phraseology would be interpreted, and to what extent
Commerce would enforce the law's provisions, was being
watched closely.

An internal American Jewish Committee memorandum noted
some of the terms in question. The U.S. law contained possible
loopholes, notably the provision for "unilateral selection" of
carriers, insurers, suppliers, etc., by a boycotting country or
company in "the normal course of business." Another was the
freedom the law granted to "U.S. persons" in foreign countries
who were allowed to comply even with those local laws governing imports of products for that U.S. person's use. The terms
"in the normal course of business," "own use," and even "U.S.
persons" remain to be defined more precisely by the Commerce
Department; its rules would indicate just how tough America's
anti-boycott law would prove to be.¹⁰

Hyman ("Bookie") Bookbinder, the Washington representative of the American Jewish Committee, advised in December
1976 that an anti-boycott victory "on the legislative and
political front does not assure victory on the economic or
diplomatic front." He said the Arabs were unlikely to take
"the bulk of their business" out of the United States, but he
wondered what might happen if they placed only "a few"
billions elsewhere. "What would such a development do to
American public opinion?" he asked. Might it adversely affect
the American- Jewish community, or even Israel? One could not
be absolutely sure. Anti-boycott legislation had been needed,
despite this risk, because the chances were "reasonably good"
that the Arabs would "see the wisdom of relaxing their boycott practices," and because the law was "based on solid,
moral grounds." The American-Jewish community needed,
however, to be prepared for possible negative reactions, he
warned, and also to work with non-Jewish allies to explain
"the full meaning of its position to the American people."¹¹

Could a backlash, even an anti-Semitic one, then develop
in the event of Arab retaliation? The presence in the United
States of vocal pro-Arab groups, most of them busily attacking
"Zionists," seemed to suggest such a possibility. Nor was their

line of attack entirely economic. When *Events*, for example, reported the San Francisco law suit challenging the constitutionality of U.S. anti-boycott legislation, it quoted the two lawyers involved, Donald Warden and Roger C. Holmes, as complaining about the charge that the boycott involved anti-Jewish discrimination. "What about discrimination against Arabs and pro-Arab groups?" they reportedly said.[12]

That remark was similar to a line being used extensively in pro-Arab propaganda. It does not, of course, stand up, for there is in fact no discrimination against Arabs or pro-Arab groups, only legislative remedies against the discriminatory tactics imposed by the Arab Trade Boycott. No one, not even the Israelis, wanted to interfere with profitable trade with the Arab world; indeed, no one outside the Arab boycott offices is making such trade difficult. But to say that the line taken by pro-Arab lobbyists won't stand up is not to say that it could not be effective. Indeed, the millions of dollars that the Arabs have spent in recent years on advertising, public relations and propaganda have already had their effect. The Palestinians have manifestly replaced the Israelis as underdogs to be championed; the terrorist PLO has won a new image of respectability; the claim that Israel is intransigent is bruited about constantly and has come to be believed by many; the notion that Arab leaders are now more reasonable and inclined toward signing a peace agreement with Israel has currency, and the idea that a sinister "Jewish lobby" manipulates Washington even beguiles some persons, at least those who do not recognize in that charge the extreme anti-Semitic language of the Nazi era.

There are, then, dangers ahead, not only for Jews, but also for all opponents of racial and religious discrimination, anti-Semitism and the continuing effort to destroy the Jewish state. And these dangers, it should be noted, are the direct result of the economic war that we have been describing, a war not over yet.

The anti-Israeli forces have argued that an American anti-boycott law would put companies adhering to its provisions at a disadvantage with those that comply with the boycott, but this claim has been rebutted by Professor Irwin Cotler of McGill University, Montreal. Anti-boycott legislation in fact "restores the fair competitive situation that was hitherto considered normal," he said, "by forbidding *all* firms from complying." There is, he maintains, simply no substitute for anti-boycott legislation; what is needed is to place the Arab boycott "squarely outside the law." Only then would companies be able to say to the Arab boycotters that they are prevented from complying with the boycott's rules and regulations by the laws of their land. Business people need this kind of "shield" to protect them, and such shields should be internationalized.[13]

American laws were already having an international impact before the federal law was passed. As of January 1977, European branches of the Bank of America and other banks based in California scrupulously rejected all letters of credit containing boycott conditions in order to comply with the Californian anti-boycott law, which came into effect that month.[14] What was needed, however, were more national anti-boycott laws, at least in the industrialized countries of the Western world, or coordinated action by the nine-nation European Economic Community (EEC), the "Common Market."

The boycott in fact violates the principles of the Treaty of Rome, which governs the Common Market, and of GATT (General Agreement on Trade and Tariffs).* This has often been noted, even by the EEC. The EEC Commission reconfirmed its opposition to the boycotts on November 29, 1976, and stressed that in instances in which the nondiscrimination Articles 85 and 86 of the Treaty of Rome were violated, "the Commission is empowered to impose fines and to penalize the firms concerned."[16]

---

* The boycott even violates the United Nations Charter: Article 2 condemns "the threat or use of force" against any state, and this has been interpreted by the General Assembly to include "military, economic and any other form of coercion." In this connection, international jurists have pointed out that the Arabs took no account of international law when they used oil to blackmail and boycott for strictly political purposes. They have attempted to control the foreign policies and conduct of other countries through a manipulation of resources, without warning to the international community and without reference to the United Nations.[15]

The European Parliament's Committee on External Economic Relations had also stated its opposition to any boycott, from whatever quarter, against firms having business contacts with Israel. The president of the European Parliament noted that the EEC was "committed to pursuing a policy of non-discrimination, based on the principles of parallelism with all the Mediterranean countries. In November 1976 he told the Knesset that the Community, and especially its Parliament, "repeatedly and unequivocally declared its opposition to any form of boycott and discrimination." Such statements and assurances led Daniel Lack of the World Jewish Congress's Geneva office to conclude in June 1977 that "there can be little doubt that the EEC has firmly committed itself" to combating the Arab Trade Boycott, and that effective anti-boycott measures could "be introduced on a national, regional and international scale."[17]

But there are signs that the EEC in some ways is showing an increasing interest in wooing the Arabs. Early in 1977 the EEC refused to make the political declaration that the Arabs demanded at the Euro-Arab ministerial meeting then being held in Tunis; by May the position of "the Nine" had changed, and at their London meeting they committed themselves in support of a Palestinian homeland, presumably along lines proposed by the Arab states. The EEC was bowing to Arab pressures. According to the *Guardian*'s observer in Brussels, John Palmer, only the West Germans and the Dutch had tried to resist this "inevitable shift," and even they reportedly gave in after the election in Israel of what they regarded as a "right-wing extremist" government. "Europe, like the U.S.," wrote Palmer, "has come to accept the realities of Arab economic and political power" and was no longer seeing Israel "as an indispensable outpost of the Western world in the Middle East."* Israel noted

---

* The EEC has "association" agreements with Israel and most of the Mediterranean states, and ever since the oil embargo of 1973–1974 it has had relations with the Arab world as a whole, via an Euro-Arab dialogue, which led to an impressive increase in trade between the EEC and the Arab nations. The Arab world is today the EEC's largest customer, taking 13 percent of its exports (*vs.* the United States which takes 11 percent).[18]

this pro-Arab shift "with an air of dispirited resignation."[19]

In London, *The Times*'s expert on the Arab boycott, Malcolm Brown, observed the international scene in April 1977 and concluded that concerted action was needed because the British government's reluctance to act against the boycott "is unlikely to change without some strong outside encouragement." This would have to come from President Carter, who would soon "come under strong pressure from his own countrymen" to push "for some kind of common front with Europe on the issue . . . if only from motives of self-interest."[20]

The need for that kind of international action had already been recognized in September 1976; Representative John E. Moss's House subcommittee called for an alliance "with other industrialized nations for the purpose of establishing basic international business ethics and standards."[21] In early 1977, reports Arnold Forster, the ADL had discussed with the White House the possibility that the President might raise the issue of anti-boycott legislation with the EEC once the U.S. anti-boycott law had been passed.[22] And Yigal Allon, then Israel's Foreign Minister, said in May 1977 that he had raised the issue with every government he met. All were "hesitant to go it alone," he reported, underscoring the need for collective action.[23]

None of the EEC nations wanted to confront the Arabs directly, and in mid-1977 the French government was already trying to mollify the Arab world by declaring it would make use of a paragraph in the new French anti-boycott law that allowed it to block the legislation if it considered the new law not to be in the interest of the French community. But one conceivable means of obtaining concerted European action was provided by a declaration issued after the "Downing Street Summit" of European leaders in May 1977. This included a commitment to "expand opportunities for trade" and "to avoid approaches which restrict trade"; it stated further, "We consider that irregular practices and improper conduct should be eliminated from international trade, banking and commerce . . ."[24] While this was seen as a condemnation of commercial bribery and corporate payoffs, such language could be used to attack the boycott itself, for hardly anything today restricts trade as much as does the economic war the Arabs are waging, nor are there worse examples of irregular practices and improper conduct.

As *The Times*' Malcolm Brown noted, it is very much in the national interest of the United States to press for concerted international action. U.S. business and financial leaders remain anxious about the effects the American anti-boycott law may have on U.S.-Arab trade, and they will be reluctant to stand by idly while European countries that comply with the boycott capture Arab trade that normally would have gone to the United States.

A great deal could be done to fight the continuing Arab economic war against the Jews—and against the world business community. Some possibilities which need to be considered are the following:

• The United States could make it an offense for American companies to do business with foreign firms that comply with the boycott; further, it could refuse to deal with foreign firms that have a record of boycott-compliance.

• The U.S. government could indicate to friendly Western nations that it would regard it as an act of solidarity with the United States if they passed anti-boycott laws, and thereby demonstrated that they would not seek unfair competitive advantage over American industry as a result of America's action in defense of free trade.

• The U.S. government could make a major diplomatic effort to obtain a united European anti-boycott position, as well as a united Western position over Middle East peace.

• The U.S. government could press for an EEC anti-boycott declaration which goes far beyond the statements already issued by the EEC on this subject.

• The U.S. government might reconsider the granting of continuing economic aid to countries which, by countenancing the boycott, seem to be actively seeking unfair competitive advantage over the U.S.

• The U.S. government could prohibit American banks and other financial institutions from joining in international loans, etc., if other banks have been excluded from such deals because of boycott pressures or anti-Semitic discrimination.

• The U.S. government could encourage American banks to extend capital and other forms of cooperation to those foreign countries and companies that have taken a firm stand against the boycott.

In addition to governmental action, there is a case for wider civic participation in this fight. It is manifestly not in the interest of American workers for European (or Japanese) companies to siphon off Arab trade; American labor unions could therefore use their good offices to drive this lesson home to foreign companies that export to the United States.

• American longshoremen could decline to unload ships of foreign lines that comply with Arab boycott rules and regulations, as well as the products of foreign companies that have a record of boycott-compliance and other discriminatory practices.

• American labor unions could refuse to cooperate in the United States with foreign companies that in their home countries comply with the Arab boycott, thereby endangering U.S. jobs by seeking an unfair competitive advantage over American firms that are prohibited from boycott compliance.

• The labor union leadership in the United States could urge friendly free trade unions abroad to display solidarity with American—and Israeli—workers over this issue.

Similar action could be taken by such American business groups as chambers of commerce, who could press their foreign counterparts abroad to support anti-boycott laws in their countries. Furthermore, they could decline to cooperate with those foreign business organizations that refuse to take a firm stand against the boycott.

Public opinion could be mobilized far more than it is today. Lists of foreign companies that comply with the boycott could be widely publicized; American workers and consumers could, for example, be provided with periodic lists of imported products whose foreign manufacturers comply with the boycott and thereby endanger American jobs.

Compliance with the boycott could be made to hurt, even for firms in countries that have not yet taken action against trade discrimination and coercion of this kind. The pressure for concerted international action would inevitably mount. And if none of the major industrialized nations on which the Arab world depends countenances the boycott, the boycott will collapse. The victims of this international blackmail must unite. Almost thirty years' experience has shown that firm resistance to Arab pressure succeeds.

If such international resistance could be achieved, it would do much to bring about a world in which boycotts cannot exist. International action cannot be expected from the United Nations, already the tool of an anti-Israel/Soviet/Arab/Third World block, but the United States can lead a Western alliance against blackmail and extortion. It would not be in the long-term interests of the Arab states to fight an alliance of Western nations whose prosperity can give them the goods and services they need. Such an alliance would make a substantial contribution towards achieving a lasting peace in the Middle East.

Resistance to the boycott is a move towards such a peace, for the boycott has contributed to the psychological "block" in the Arab mind over a real and lasting settlement with Israel. As long as the Arabs (including such "moderates" as Sadat of Egypt and Assad of Syria) believe they can obliterate the State of Israel by first wrecking her economy by means of boycott and blockade, they will continue to rule out any true recognition and lasting acceptance of Israel. They will continue to hope that their economic war will bring them the success denied them by those four bloody and destructive Arab-Israeli wars, to which boycott and blockade made such a major and sinister contribution. With American material help, Israeli skill and valor triumphed in these four wars; with continued help from America and other Western friends, Israel will triumph in the economic war that seeks her strangulation still.

SOURCE NOTES

CHAPTER I

Scapegoats and Oil Spirals

1. James Parkes, *A History of the Jewish People*. London: Penguin, 1964, p. 182.
2. *Encyclopaedia Britannica*, 9th edition. London, published in installments, 1865–1889.
3. Winston Churchill, Speech in the British House of Commons (June 14, 1921).
4. Dan S. Chill, *The Arab Boycott of Israel: Economic Aggression and World Reaction*. New York: Praeger, 1976, p. 1, citing James H. Bahti, *The Arab Economic Boycott of Israel*. Washington, D.C.: The Brookings Institution, 1967, p. 1.
5. Chill, *op. cit.*, p. 1; also, Yuval Elizur, "The Arab Boycott," *Israel Magazine* (February 1972).
6. Stephen Aris, *The Jews in Business*. London: Penguin, 1973, p. 196.
7. John Bullock, reporting from Beirut in *Daily Telegraph*, London (August 8, 1972).
8. *Daily Telegraph*, London (June 23, 1974).
9. Interview in *Business Week* (January 1, 1975).
10. Interview in *Newsweek* (January 20, 1975).
11. *International Herald Tribune*, Paris (January 9, 1975).
12. Davidson Adamson, reporting from Algiers in *Daily Telegraph*, London (March 3, 1975).
13. *The Economist*, London (October 4, 1975).
14. *Foreign Affairs* (January 1976).
15. *The Times*, London (June 2, 1975).

[[229]]

16. Dick Wilson, in *Financial Times*, London (November 25, 1975).
17. J.O. Rouall, "A Note on Petrodollars." *Middle East Oil, Fact and Fiction*, American Professors for Peace in the Middle East, New York (January 1975).
18. *Ibid.*
19. *Ibid.*

CHAPTER II

Blackmail and Blacklists

1. Cited in "Do Economic Boycotts Ever Work?," by Adam Roberts, *New Society.* London (September 11, 1975), pp. 577–579. (Mr. Roberts is Lecturer in International Relations, London School of Economics).
2. *Ibid.*
3. *Ibid.*
4. Drawn from table included in Adam Roberts article, *op. cit.*
5. Remarks of Avraham Shavit, president, Israel Manufacturers Association, as given in American Jewish Committee press release (March 4, 1977).
6. Roberts, *op. cit.*
7. Paper dated April 1975, supplied by ADL.
8. *Ibid.*
9. Letter dated September 26, 1964, from Central Office for the Boycott of Israel, Damascus, taken from a photocopy of the letter, as provided by *What Is The Arab Boycott Against Israel?*, published by Federation of Bi-National Chambers of Commerce with and in Israel, Jerusalem (October 1975), Appendix E, pp. 12–13.
10. Saudi Arabian two-page form, headed "Authorization of Agent" (October 22, 1969).
11. Letter from Central Office for the Boycott of Israel, Damascus (September 27, 1971).

12. Letter from above source (March 21, 1971).
13. From *What Is The Arab Boycott of Israel?*, Appendix D, p. 11.
14. *General Principles for Boycott of Israel*, Damascus (June 1972), Articles 20 and 30.
15. *Ibid.*, Article 24.
16. *Ibid.*, Article 29.
17. Regulations for the Boycott of Israel, Saudi Arabia (undated).
18. *Ibid.*, Article 2.
19. *Ibid.*, Article 7.
20. *Ibid.*, Article 8/D/5.
21. Letter on "The Arab Boycott of Israel—Its Ground and Regulations" (January 3, 1967).
22. Elizur, *op. cit.*
23. *Jerusalem Post* (February 26, 1975).
24. Eric Silver, in *The Observer*, London (September 14, 1975).
25. Jack Foisie, in *International Herald Tribune*, Paris (August 25, 1975).
26. Malcolm Brown, in *The Times*, London (February 17, 1976).
27. Jack Anderson, in *Washington Post* (October 8, 1975).
28. Stella Shamoon, in *Daily Telegraph*, London (February 17, 1975).
29. David Norris, in *Sunday Telegraph*, London (February 28, 1976).
30. *Jewish Chronicle*, London (March 5, 1976).
31. *Sunday Telegraph*, London (April 25, 1976).
32. *Kuwait Official Gazette* (November 15, 1970).
33. Quoted by Meyer Eisenberg of ADL, at U.S. Senate hearings (July 22–23, 1975).
34. Earl Raab, "Candid Comments: Jews, Jobs and Arabs," *Bulletin*, San Francisco, California (March 7, 1975).
35. As quoted in William F. Buckley Jr., "Talking Back to Quaddafi," *New York Post* (January 8, 1974).
36. *Jewish Chronicle*, London (January 11, 1974).
37. Buckley, *op. cit.*
38. *Editor and Publisher* (February 15, 1975).
39. UPI dispatch from Cairo (March 1, 1975).
40. CBS News (March 3, 1975).

Source Notes

CHAPTER III

Images and Headhunting

1. Speech by Arnold Forster at Oxford Seminar, England (July 1975).
2. *Ibid.*; also, Elizur, *op. cit.*, and NJCRAC Israel Task Force Position Paper (November 7, 1975).
3. Wolf Blitzer, "Coca-Cola, Israel and the ADL," in *Jerusalem Post* (April 13, 1976).
4. *Ibid.*
5. Forster, *op. cit.*
6. *Ibid.*
7. Elizur, *op. cit.*
8. Forster, *op. cit.*
9. Elizur, *op. cit.*
10. Blitzer, *op. cit.*; also M. C. Blackman, in *New York Herald Tribune* (April 16, 1966).
11. Martin G. Berck, "Landing on the List," *Newsday* (March 1, 1976).
12. Youssef Ibrahim, "Boycott Blowup," *Mideast Markets* (February 2, 1976).
13. *News and Analysis Update*, published by National Zionist Affairs Department of Hadassah, New York (August 10, 1976); *Boycott Report No. 1*, Chicago Community Council of Jewish Organizations, Chicago, Illinois (1976); circular issued by Southern California Council for Soviet Jews, Los Angeles, California (1976).
14. *Near East Report, Boycott Supplement*, Washington, D.C. (May 1965), pp. B–9.
15. Daniel Kahn, *Newsday* (March 1, 1975).
16. Terence Prittie, various articles in *The Guardian*, London (1963–64).
17. Daphne Allon, *Arab Racialism* (Jerusalem, 1969).
18. Rabbi Jacob Hecht, "Focus," *Jewish Press* (date uncertain).
19. *Sentinel*, Chicago (September 11, 1976).
20. *Jewish Chronicle*, London (October 24, 1975).
21. *Daily Mail*, London (August 6, 1975).
22. Chill, *op. cit.*, p. 36; *Near East Report*, Washington, D.C.

(March 9, 1965); *Financial Times*, London (February 26, 1975); *The Guardian*, London (March 4, 1975).
23. *The Guardian*, London (March 15, 1975).
24. *Ibid.*
25. ADL Report, Atlanta, Georgia (February 27, 1975).
26. UPI dispatch from Cairo (June 12, 1977), as given in *Financial Times*, London (June 13, 1977).

CHAPTER IV

Buck-passing and Bigotry

1. *New York Post* (February 26, 1975); also, *New York Times* (same date).
2. *Philadelphia Inquirer* (February 27, 1975).
3. *JTA Daily News Bulletin* (February 27, 1975), and *Newsday* (February 27, 1975).
4. *Ibid.*
5. Naomi Levine, "Challenging Saudi Arabian Discrimination and American Involvement," *Congress Monthly* (January, 1977).
6. *Newsday* (February 27, 1975).
7. *Ibid.*
8. *New York Post* (April 9, 1975).
9. Transcript for record, House of Representatives Committee on Government Operations (April 9, 1975).
10. *New York Post* (April 10, 1975).
11. L. Peiretz, Interim ADL Report (May 9, 1975).
12. *Ibid.*
13. ADL press release (July 14, 1975).
14. Letter dated August 3, 1975.
15. Secretary of Defense Schlesinger, as quoted in NJCRAC Israel Task Force Position Paper (November 7, 1975).
16. Letter from Sidney Sober, Deputy Assistant Secretary, to Richard E. Hull, Assistant General Counsel for Domestic International Business, U.S. Department of Commerce (July 21, 1975).
17. NJCRAC Israel Task Force Position Paper (November 7, 1975).

18. *New York Post* (February 12, 1975).
19. Press release issued by American Jewish Committee (October 7, 1975); also, Religious News Service (October 10, 1975), and *Newsday* (July 23, 1975).
20. "Recent Boycott-Related Matters," issued by Ministry of Finance, Jerusalem (October 20, 1975).
21. Arnold Forster, *op. cit.*
22. *Progressive Architecture* (April 1975).
23. ADL internal memoranda, May/June 1975.
24. *Ibid.*
25. *Ibid.*
26. *Ibid.*
27. *Village Voice* (March 22, 1976).
28. *New York Times* (November 16, 1975); also, *Los Angeles Times* (November 18, 1975); *Christian Science Monitor* (November 28, 1975); ADL press releases (November 14, 17, 19, 25 and 28, 1975).
29. *New York Times* (November 16, 1975).
30. ADL press release (April 23, 1975).
31. *New York Post* (February 12, 1976); also *The Times*, London (September 13 and 15, 1975).
32. *New York Post* (February 12, 1976).
33. *Ibid.*
34. *Ibid.*
35. Forster, *op. cit.*; also, *National Observer* (week ending May 10, 1975); *Trenton Evening Times* (February 26, 1975).

CHAPTER V

Boardroom Compliance and Baksheesh

1. Copy of letter, as supplied by ADL.
2. ADL press release, *op. cit.*
3. ADL press release (March 4, 1975); also *Miami News* (March 6, 1975).
4. *New York Times* (March 4, 1975).
5. *New York Post* (March 4, 1975).

6. *Journal of Commerce,* New York (March 5, 1975).
7. *Near East Report, Boycott Supplement,* Washington, D.C. (May 1965).
8. *Journal of Commerce,* New York (March 13, 1975).
9. *Ibid* (March 20, 1975).
10. *New Orleans Statesman Item,* New Orleans, Louisiana (March 12, 1975).
11. *Journal of Commerce,* New York (March 27, 1975).
12. Hearings before the Subcommittee on International Finance of the Committee on Banking, Housing and Urban Affairs, U.S. Senate, 94th Congress, First Session (July 22 and 23, 1975).
13. *Washington Post* (January 26, 1975).
14. *Ibid.* (January 11, 1977).
15. *Financial Times,* London (January 11, 1977); also, American Jewish Congress *Boycott Report* (May 1977).
16. *New York Times* (January 14, 1976); also *Financial Times,* London (January 14, 1976).
17. *Miami Herald* (March 2, 1975).
18. *Jerusalem Post* (August 29, 1975); also, ADL press release (September 3, 1975).
19. *Jewish Observer and Middle East Review,* London (January 9, 1976).
20. Sol Stern, *New Republic* (March 27, 1976).
21. *The Times,* London (December 21, 1976); also *Sunday Times,* London (May 22, 1977).
22. Private source.
23. *Near East Report, Boycott Supplement,* Washington, D.C. (May 1965), p. B–10.
24. *Ibid.,* p. B–5.

CHAPTER VI

The Big Banking Scandal

1. Carl Gewirtz, "Arabs Begin Blacklisting Some Banks," *International Herald Tribune,* Paris (February 8, 1975).
2. Jack Maurice, "French Wary on Arab Ban of Jewish Banks," *Jerusalem Post* (February 12, 1975).

3. *Sunday Telegraph*, London (February 9, 1975).
4. *Evening Standard*, London (February 10, 1975).
5. *Ibid.*
6. Terry Robards, of New York Times News Service, in *St. Louis Post-Dispatch* (February 10, 1975).
7. *Ibid.*
8. Stella Shamoon, " 'Suicide' If City Made Stand on Arab Boycott," *Daily Telegraph*, London (February 10, 1975).
9. *Ibid.*
10. *Ibid.*
11. *Ibid.*
12. *Ibid.*
13. *The Times*, London (February 10, 1975).
14. *Evening Standard*, London (February 10, 1975).
15. *Ibid.*
16. *Wall Street Journal*, New York (February 10, 1975); also *Financial Times*, London (February 11, 1975) and *International Herald Tribune*, Paris (February 12, 1975).
17. Terry Robards, *New York Times* (February 11, 1975).
18. ———, *New York Times* (February 11, 1975).
19. Maurice, *op. cit.*
20. *Ibid.*
21. Carl Gewirtz, in *International Herald Tribune*, Paris (February 12, 1975), quoting Roger Azar, a Lebanese director of the Banque Arabe et Internationale d'Investissement, Paris.
22. Richard Johns, in *Financial Times*, London (February 13, 1975).
23. *Ibid.*
24. *Wall Street Journal*, New York (February 14, 1975).
25. James Buxton and Alain Cass, in *Financial Times*, London (February 17, 1975).
26. *The Times*, London (February 18, 1975).
27. *Ibid.*
28. *Ibid.*
29. Alexander Cockburn and James Ridgeway, in *The Village Voice* (February 24, 1975).
30. *Ibid.*
31. *Ibid.*
32. *American Examiner-Jewish Week* (March 1, 1975).
33. As quoted by Yigal Allon, Deputy Prime Minister and Minister for Foreign Affairs, Israel, *News from Israel* (March 15, 1975).

34. John Thackray, *Institutional Investor* (May 1975).
35. *The Guardian*, London (February 27, 1975); also, *Newsday* (February 27, 1975), and *JTA Daily News Bulletin* (February 28, 1975).
36. As quoted in *Long Island Daily Press* (February 26, 1976).
37. As reported by Robert Lenzner, in *Boston Globe* (March 2, 1975).
38. ADL internal memorandum (March 10, 1975).
39. *Journal of Commerce*, New York (March 14, 1975).
40. *Jerusalem Post* (March 14, 1975).
41. *Ibid.*
42. *Newsday* (March 18, 1975); also, *Pittsburgh Press* (March 19, 1975); *Washington Post* (March 19, 1975), and *St. Louis Globe-Democrat* (March 24, 1975).
43. *Ibid.*
44. *New York Post* (March 19, 1975).
45. ADL press release (March 11, 1976).
46. *Ibid.*
47. Letter to the Jewish Federation Council of Greater Los Angeles (May 20, 1975).
48. Forster, *op. cit.*
49. Testimony before Subcommittee on Human Rights, Standing Committee on Governmental Operations, The Assembly, State of New York (February 6, 1975).
50. Sol Stein, *New Republic* (March 27, 1976).
51. *The Times*, London (June 10, 1976).
52. American Jewish Congress press release (July 22, 1976); also, *Jewish Chronicle*, London (July 30, 1976).
53. American Jewish Committee press release (October 15, 1976).
54. *Jewish Observer and Middle East Review*, London (August 20, 1976).

CHAPTER VII

The Willing Victims

1. Ray Vicker, in *Wall Street Journal* (December 30, 1974).
2. Ian Markham-Smith, in *Sunday Telegraph*, London (May 30, 1976); also, Robert Langton in *Evening Standard*, London

(May 27, 1976); Paul Callan, in *Daily Mirror*, London (June 23, 1976), and Nicholas Bannister in *The Guardian*, London (June 23, 1976).

3. John Fairhall, in *The Guardian*, London (June 9, 1976); also, Andrew Fyall, in *Daily Express, London* (June 9, 1976); *Daily Mirror*, London (July 14, 1977), and *Daily Telegraph*, London (same date).

4. Peter T. Kilborn, in *International Herald Tribune*, Paris (June 18, 1976).

5. Lord Winterbottom, House of Lords (March 2, 1977).

6. *Building Magazine*, London (May 28 and June 11, 1976).

7. Private source (February 1976).

8. Advertisement from *Nottingham Evening Post* (September 5, 1976); other instance from *Middle East Construction*, London (March 1976).

9. *PRADS International Media List*, Section 1Z8, The London Correspondents of principal Middle Eastern News Media. No date available.

10. Kennedy & Donkin material, as supplied by ADL, New York, February 1976.

11. Most British papers (February 1977); also, *The Guardian*, London (June 18, 1977) and *Export Times*, London (June 1977).

12. Robert Margolin, *Jewish Chronicle*, London (July 11, 1975).

13. *Jewish Chronicle*, London (July 18, 1975); also, *The Times*, London (April 30, 1977).

14. Letter from The Board of Deputies of British Jews (May 14, 1976).

15. *Jewish Observer and Middle East Review*, London (August 6 and 13, 1971); also, *Financial Times*, London (August 9, 1971), and *Jewish Chronicle*, London (August 13, 1971).

16. *Jewish Observer*, London (August 13, 1971).

17. Malcolm Brown, in *The Times*, London (October 8, 1975).

18. *Ibid.*

19. Peter Rodgers, in *The Guardian*, London (September 2, 1975).

20. Private source.

21. *Daily Telegraph*, London (September 2, 1975).

22. *Deutsche Zeitung*, Düsseldorf (March 7, 1975).

23. Edwin C. Dale Jr., in *New York Times* (March 23, 1975).

24. Statements by Parliamentary Secretary of State Gruener to members of West German Bundestag, February 28, March 14

and September 4, 1975, as supplied by Embassy of Federal Republic of Germany, London, to Anglo-Israel Chamber of Commerce, London; letter dated March 25, 1976.

25. Business Diary, *The Times*, London (August 9, 1976).

26. Dr. Lawrence S. Leshnik, "The Arab Boycott of Israel in Europe," ADL report (May 1976).

27. *Ibid*; also, *Frankfurter Allgemeine Zeitung*, Frankfurt (April 19, 1975).

28. Statement by Israeli Minister of Commerce and Industry, Haim Bar-Lev, to *Yorkshire Post*, Leeds (November 17, 1975); also, Chill, *op. cit.*, p. 37.

29. Jack Maurice, in *Jerusalem Post* (June 23, 1976).

30. *The Times*, London (January 26, 1977).

31. Leshnik, *op. cit.*

32. *Financial Times*, London (March 18, 1977); also, *Fortune* (January 1977).

33. *Expressen*, Stockholm, June 14, 1976; also, American Jewish Congress *Boycott Report* (May 1977).

34. *International Herald Tribune*, Paris (November 2, 1975).

35. *Ibid.* (September 15, 1975).

36. *Al-Ahram*, Cairo (March 11, 1976), as cited in *The Times*, London (March 12, 1976); also, *Jewish Observer and Middle East Review*, London (March 19, 1976).

37. *Jerusalem Post* (March 12, 1976); also *Jewish Observer and Middle East Review*, London (March 19, 1976).

38. *Financial Times*, London (May 26, 1977); also, "Japan Air Lines and the Arab Boycott," ADL memo (December 1972).

39. *Ibid.*

40. *Toronto Post* (June 5, 1976); also, "The Arab Boycott in Canada," Report of the Commission on Economic Coercion and Discrimination, published in association with the Centre for Law and Public Policy, Montreal, Canada (January 11, 1977).

41. *Jewish Chronicle*, London (May 9, 1975).

42. *Toronto Star* (May 22, 1975).

43. *Toronto Post* (June 5, 1975).

44. JTA *Daily News Bulletin* (February 11, 1977); also, *Behind the Headlines*, Canadian Zionist Federation (January 28, 1977), citing "The Arab Boycott in Canada," *op. cit.*

45. *Egon*, Nicosia, Cyprus (June 7, 1976).

Source Notes

CHAPTER VIII

The Imp out of Hell

1. UPI dispatch from Cairo (March 1975).
2. Johan Bouman, *"Die arabische Welt angesichts Israel,"* *Emmuna*, VIII, 4:245–63 (1973).
3. G. E. von Grunebaum, *Medieval Islam* (Chicago: University of Chicago, 1962).
4. Hebrew edition (Jerusalem, 1964).
5. D. F. Green, ed., *Arab Theologians on Jews and Israel.* Extracts from the proceedings of the Fourth Conference of the Academy of Islamic Research, Cairo, 1968 (Geneva: Editions de l'Avenir, 1974).
6. Sylvia Haim, *Arabic Anti-Semitic Literature* (1956).
7. Habib Faris, *Talmudic Human Sacrifices* (Cairo, 1890).
8. *Tarikh Wilayat Sulayman Basha-al-Adil* (Sidon, 1936).
9. *Al-Musawwar*, Cairo (August 4, 1972).
10. Yehosophat Harkhabi, *Arab Attitudes to Israel* (London, 1972).
11. *Ha'aretz*, Tel Aviv (January 29, 1974).
12. Antoine Fattal, *Le Statut Légal des Musulmans en Pays d'Islam* (Beirut, 1958).
13. Louis Gardet, *La Cité musulmane: Vie sociale et politique* (Paris, 1954).
14. Bernard Lewis, "The Pro-Islamic Jews," in *Judaism*, Vol. 17, No. 4 (1968).
15. Simon Schwarzfuchs, in *L'Arche*, Paris (December 1973).
16. *Information*, Association of Jewish Refugees in Britain, Vol. XXX, No. 7 (July 1975).
17. From *Present Tense*, New York (August 1975).
18. Speech in Knesset (January 1, 1976).
19. See in this connection John Laffin, *The Arab Mind* (London, 1975); also, Anis Sayegh, *Palestine and Arab Nationalism* (Beirut, 1966).
20. Speech to the Egyptian National Council (June 2, 1971).
21. In *Ahir Sa'a*, Cairo (December 3, 1975).
22. *Al-Gumhuriyya*, Cairo (February 1 and April 1, 1965); *Akhber-el-Yom*, Cairo (September 18, 1965, and May 20, 1967).

23. *The Image of the Jew in Official Arab Literature*, Shazar Library (Jerusalem, 1976).
24. Tripoli Radio (December 4, 1972), as supplied in "Arab Anti-Semitism," *Patterns of Prejudice*, London (March April 1974).
25. Abd al-Quddous, ed., *Akhbar al-Yom*, Cairo (January 20, 1973).
26. Anis Mansour, Egyptian author, in *al-Akhbar*, Cairo (September 11, 1972), as supplied by *Patterns of Prejudice, op. cit.*
27. Tripoli Radio (March 6, 1973), as supplied by *Patterns of Prejudice, op. cit.*
28. Statement on an official visit to Nigeria, reported in *Le Temps du Niger*, Niamey (November 27, 1972), as supplied by *Patterns of Prejudice, op. cit.*
29. As given by Sol Stern in *New Republic, op. cit.*

CHAPTER IX

Pressure Meets Principles

1. Speech, May 29, 1973, before Israel Manufacturers Association, Tel Aviv Hilton, Tel Aviv, Israel, as supplied by Ministry of Finance, Jerusalem.
2. *Fortune* (July 1975).
3. *New Republic, op. cit.*
4. Private source.
5. *Wall Street Journal* (August 29, 1975).
6. AP dispatch from Cairo, in *Sun Times*, Chicago, Illinois (October 21, 1975).
7. *The Economist*, London (August 1, 1970).
8. *Financial Times*, London (April 1, 1976); also *Sunday Times*, London (May 22, 1977).
9. *Jewish Chronicle*, London (February 15, 1974).
10. *Daily Telegraph*, London (October 26, 1974).
11. *Ibid.* (December 9, 1974).
12. *The Guardian*, London (December 9, 1974).
13. Private source.
14. *Ibid.*

15. Letter to T. C. F. Prittie (July 1, 1975).
16. Private source.
17. ABC press release, London (December 3, 1975).
18. *The Times*, London (December 4, 1975).
19. *Birmingham Post* (December 4, 1975).
20. *Jewish Observer and Middle East Review*, London (April 9, 1975).
21. *Financial Times*, London (February 2, 1977).
22. Haim Bar-Lev, in *Yorkshire Post, op. cit.*
23. *Jewish Observer and Middle East Review*, London (May 23, 1975).
24. *Boston Globe* (March 2, 1975).
25. NJCRAC Israel Task Force Position Paper, New York (November 7, 1975).
26. *Journal & Constitution*, Atlanta, Georgia (July 13, 1975); also, *Newark Star-Ledger*, Newark, New Jersey (date uncertain but 1975).
27. *New Republic, op. cit.*
28. "Special Survey," *Near East Report*, Washington, D.C. (May 1965), p. B–13.
29. *Jewish Week and American Examiner*, New York (May 24, 1975).
30. As supplied by Ministry of Finance, Jerusalem.
31. *Ibid.*

CHAPTER X

Foot-dragging and Stonewalling

1. I. L. Kenen, excerpt from Chapter 9 of a draft manuscript of a book on U.S.-Israel relations, as supplied by the author.
2. *New York Times* (April 20, 1975).
3. *Financial Times*, London (July 11, 1975).
4. *New York Times* (March 12, 1976).
5. *Ibid.*

6. Letter to *New York Times* (March 30, 1976).
7. *Mideast Economic File*, Jerusalem (September 1976).
8. American Jewish Committee press release (May 3, 1976); also, ADL press release (April 27, 1976).
9. Data from Rep. Moss's House Subcommittee, as supplied June 1, 1976, by Research Project on Energy and Economic Policy, Washington, D.C.; also, *Facts*, ADL (November 1976).
10. *Financial Times*, London (September 8, 1976); also, *Post-Dispatch*, St. Louis, Missouri (October 10, 1976), and as reported September 9, 1976, by Research Project on Energy and Economic Policy, Washington, D.C.
11. David Binder, in *New York Times*, as reprinted in *International Herald Tribune*, Paris (September 9, 1976).
12. *Ibid.*
13. *Newsweek* (October 25, 1976).
14. *Ibid.*
15. ADL memorandum (December 14, 1976).
16. *JTA Daily News Bulletin* (December 14, 1976).
17. As reprinted in *Jerusalem Post* (December 13, 1976).
18. *Events*, London (January 14, 1977).
19. As supplied January 25, 1977, by Research Project on Energy and Economic Policy, Washington, D.C., quoting ADL.
20. *International Herald Tribune*, Paris (February 24, 1977); also American Jewish Congress press release (May 5, 1977); FEATT, Washington, D.C. (Vol. 1, Issue 1, December 1976); Agricultural Trade Council press release (n.d., but December 1976); *Oil Daily* (November 22, 1976).
21. As supplied January 25, 1977, by Research Project on Energy and Economic Policy, Washington, D.C.
22. *The Times*, London (March 1, 1977).
23. *The Guardian*, London (March 1, 1977).
24. *Washington Post* report, as reprinted in *International Herald Tribune*, Paris (March 1, 1977).
25. AP dispatch, as reprinted in *International Herald Tribune*, Paris (March 3, 1977).
26. ADL press release (June 22, 1977); also, most U.S. and U.K. press (June 23, 1977); *J.T.A. Daily News Bulletin*, London (June 24, 1977); *Near East Report*, Washington, D.C. (June 29, 1977); American Jewish Congress *Boycott Report* (June 1977).

27. *International Herald Tribune*, Paris (September 9, 1976).
28. *Financial Times*, London (November 9, 1976), quoting *Middle East Economic Survey*.
29. *Washington Post* (September 26, 1976).
30. *International Herald Tribune*, Paris (September 9, 1976); also, Nelson T. Joyner, Jr., *Arab Boycott/Anti-Boycott: The Effect on U.S. Business* (McLean, Virginia: Rockville Consulting Group Inc., 1976), pp. 108–109.
31. *Sunday Times*, London (April 4, 1977).
32. *Financial Times*, London (April 26, 1977).
33. *Middle East Economic Digest*, London (May 27, 1977).
34. *Yorkshire Post*, Leeds (June 8, 1976); also, *Daily Telegraph*, London (June 8, 1977); *The Times*, London (June 8, 1977); *Financial Times*, London (same date).
35. Richard Johns, in *Financial Times*, London (June 9, 1977).
36. AP dispatch, in *Jerusalem Post* (June 12, 1977).
37. *Financial Times*, London (June 17, 1977) and *Glasgow Herald*, Glasgow (June 18, 1977).
38. *Financial Times*, London (June 21, 1977).
39. *The Times*, London (June 21, 1977).
40. Michael Tingay, in *Financial Times*, London (June 21, 1977).
41. *Ibid.*
42. *Daily Telegraph*, London (June 21, 1977).
43. *Jerusalem Post* (June 21, 1977).
44. ADL press release (July 8, 1977).
45. *The Times*, London (June 21, 1977).
46. *Ibid.*
47. *Financial Times*, London (June 22, 1977).
48. American Jewish Congress *Boycott Report* (March 1977).
49. *Middle East Economic Digest* (August 22, 1975).
50. *Jordan Times* (April 14, 1976).
51. APS, Beirut (April 26, 1976).
52. Thomas A. Johnson, *International Herald Tribune*, Paris (November 25, 1975).
53. David Stephen, director of the Runnymede Trust, as quoted in *The Guardian*, London (September 12, 1975).
54. House of Commons, June 15, 1977.
55. House of Commons, July 4, 1977.
56. *The Times*, London (July 14, 1977).
57. *The Economist*, London (July 16, 1977).

58. *Ibid.*
59. *Jerusalem Post* (June 5, 1977).
60. Report by Daniel Lack, World Jewish Congress, Geneva (June 10, 1977), quoting *Le Monde*, Paris (June 4, 1977) and *Le Figaro*, Paris (June 3, 1977).
61. *Events*, London (July 15, 1977).
62. *Ibid.*
63. *Ibid.*
64. "A.I.D. Small Business Memo," issued by Department of State, Agency for International Development, Office of Small Business, Washington, D.C. (March 23, 1977).
65. *Jerusalem Post* (June 24, 1977).
66. *Ibid.*
67. Paraphrase of remarks by John Philpot Curran, in Speech on the Right of Election of Lord Mayor of Dublin (July 10, 1790). (Actually, "The condition upon which God hath given liberty to man is eternal vigilance . . .")

EPILOGUE

1. Oliver Goldsmith, *She Stoops to Conquer.*
2. *Middle East Economic Digest*, London (July 8, 1977).
3. *Events*, London (July 15, 1977).
4. *Oil & Gas Journal*, Tulsa, Oklahoma (May 23, 1977).
5. InterPress dispatch from Beirut, in *The Guardian*, London May 24, 1977); also, Cairo dispatch, in *Daily Telegraph*, London (same date).
6. *Middle East Economic Survey* (July 18, 1977), as quoted in *The Guardian*, London (July 19, 1977).
7. William Greider and J. P. Smith, in *International Herald Tribune*, Paris (July 12, 1977).
8. *Middle East Economic Digest*, op. cit.
9. *Ibid.*
10. American Jewish Committee memorandum (June 30, 1977).

11. Letter to W. H. Nelson (December 7, 1976).
12. *Events, op. cit.*
13. From interview with David Krivine, *Jerusalem Post* (April 26, 1977).
14. According to Ministry of Finance, Jerusalem, memorandum dated January 1977.
15. Jordan J. Paust and Albert P. Blaustein, "The Arab Oil Weapon —A Threat to International Peace," *Middle East Information Series*, New York: American Academic Association for Peace in the Middle East, Spring/Summer 1974, pp. 87–88; also, *New York Times* (February 22, 1974).
16. Written answer to M. Giraud, French Member of the European Parliament, as provided by Ministry of Finance, Jerusalem, in memorandum dated January 1977.
17. Lack memorandum, June 10, 1977.
18. Report of the Committee on External Relations of the European Parliament on the Cooperation Agreements between the EEC and the Mashreq countries (May 11, 1977), as cited in Lack, *op. cit.*
19. John Palmer, in *The Guardian*, London (July 1, 1977).
20. *The Times*, London (April 15, 1977).
21. *The Arab Boycott and American Business*, Report by the Subcommittee on Oversight and Investigations of the Committee on Interstate and Foreign Commerce, U.S. House of Representatives (September 1976).
22. Forster letter to Lewis R. Goodman (March 3, 1977).
23. *JTA Bulletin* (May 13, 1977).
24. *Financial Times*, London (May 9, 1977).

INDEX

Index

Index

Index

Mudaris, Abdul Karim al-, 135
Murphy, T. A., 173

Napoleon III, 151
Nasir, Sheik, 134
Nasir, Shawqi Abd al-, 151
Nasr, Dr. Muhammad, 151
Nasr Automotive Manufacturing
  Company, 167
Nasser, Gamal Abdel, 13, 14, 27,
  151, 158
Nathan's Famous, 53
National Association of Arab
  Americans (NAAA), 197
National Association of
  Manufacturers (NAM),
  196-97
National Association of
  Securities Dealers (NASD),
  119
National Broadcasting Company
  (NBC), 49-50
National Front (Great Britain),
  152
National Jewish Community
  Relations Advisory Council,
  185
National Peace (ship), 86
Nazi party, 9, 10, 68, 152-53,
  161
Near East Report, 43, 47, 56, 92,
  93, 98, 100, 101
Neff, John C., 84
negative certificates of origin,
  34-35, 141, 203
New Orleans *Times-Picayune,*
  146

New Republic, 94, 98-99, 115,
  176
New York City Human Rights
  Commission, 79
New York *Jewish Press,* 63
New York Post, 89, 116
New York State Supreme Court,
  76
New York Times, The, 88, 108,
  184, 188
Newman, Paul, 64
Newsday (publication), 57
Newsweek (magazine), 190, 191
Nicolae, Nicolae, 142
Nigeria, 209
Nilus, Brother, 151
Nixon, Richard, 115
Normanton, Tom, 143
North Korea, 196
North Vietnam, 183
Norton, Eleanor Holmes, 79
Norwich Union Insurance
  Company, 18, 60-63, 129
NSU (Neckarsulm) Company,
  137

Occidental Oil Company, 22
Ocean Drilling and Exploration
  Company, 22
oil: embargo of 1973-74, 19-20,
  137, 224; of Iran, 11, 19, 37,
  142; nationalization policy,
  23; political instability and,
  209; price rises, 19, 20, 24,
  104, 124, 209; tax to support
  "confrontation states," 5; as a
  weapon, 18-21, 27, 208-9,

Index

About the Authors

WALTER HENRY NELSON has worked as a special agent for U.S. Military Intelligence, as a news editor and as a free-lance writer contributing to such magazines as *Holiday*, the *Atlantic* and the *Saturday Evening Post*, among others. He is the author of *Small Wonder, The Berliners, The Soldier Kings, The Londoners, The Great Discount Delusion* and *Germany Rearmed*.

TERENCE C. F. PRITTIE is a leading British journalist, for many years a senior correspondent for *The Guardian*. His fourteen books include *Willy Brandt, Konrad Adenauer: A Study in Fortitude, Israel: Miracle in the Desert, Germans Against Hitler* and *Eshkol: The Man and the Nation*. He has written for *Atlantic Monthly, New Republic*, the *Wall Street Journal*, the *New York Times*, the Los Angeles *Times, Commentary, The Nation* and *Fortune*.